New Directions
for College Counselors

A Handbook for
Redesigning Professional Roles

Charles F. Warnath,

&

Associates

New Directions for College Counselors

Jossey-Bass Publishers
San Francisco • Washington • London • 1973

NEW DIRECTIONS FOR COLLEGE COUNSELORS
A Handbook for Redesigning Professional Roles
by Charles F. Warnath and Associates

Copyright © 1973 by: Jossey-Bass, Inc., Publishers
615 Montgomery Street
San Francisco, California 94111
&
Jossey-Bass Limited
3 Henrietta Street
London WC2E 8LU

Library of Congress Catalogue Card Number LC 73-7150

International Standard Book Number ISBN 0-87589-193-4

Manufactured in the United States of America

JACKET DESIGN BY WILLI BAUM

FIRST EDITION

Code 7348

26072

The Jossey-Bass Series
in Higher Education and Behavioral Science

Preface

New Directions for College Counselors is about higher education. Its focus is primarily college counseling services, but it confronts many of the issues currently central to postsecondary education. In fact, the major significance of the book is that it places helping services within the broad context of higher education. It views those services as part of the educational process within an institutional setting. Thus, the general problems of higher education become the specific problems of the service personnel and vice versa.

Higher education is in a period of rapid and profound change. The number of community colleges has multiplied within the past decade, and their enrollments continue to climb. Concurrently, a financial crisis confronts the four-year colleges as their enrollments level off or begin to decline. In the late sixties campuses throughout the country were in turmoil over such issues as the Vietnam war, race, free speech, and depersonalization. A surface calm has returned, but new students on campus have new goals and different needs from those of the typical undergraduate. Ethnic minorities, militant women, and older students are in evidence and ask for (or demand) programs and services that meet their particular needs.

As institutions and their student bodies have changed, a growing suspicion has emerged not only within the institutional administrations but also within the counseling centers that traditional counseling is effective only for a limited clientele. For the first time, counselors are forced to view their activities as an integral part of the institution for which they work. During the period of continuing growth in higher education which began in the early forties, counselors maintained an illusion of aloofness from the political affairs of the institution; however, as positions are lost, staff dispersed to other units in the institution, and pressure applied for the hiring of personnel in certain ethnic and sex categories, counselors are confronted by the reality of their embeddedness in the institutional structure.

Thus, the issues with which counselors must contend are those of higher education. The authors of *New Directions for College Counselors* were asked to write about the helping services in higher education as part of the institution: the impact of the institution on that service and the impact which counselors and student service personnel in general might make on the institution. The contents of this book were solicited mostly through invitations to some of the 200 counseling center directors who responded to a survey I conducted during 1972. Except for a few chapters written by authors of books or articles that I felt raised fundamental questions about the helping services in the institutional framework, this book is uniquely a practitioner's production—the helping services in the college as seen through the eyes of people actively engaged in their delivery.

Part One presents the framework within which the reader is encouraged to place the material of the book. These chapters question several of the basic assumptions which professional counselors have made about their detachment from institutional political entanglements, their unique effectiveness in serving as facilitators of student development because of their professional roles, and the implications of the model they have chosen for the delivery of their services. The authors take a critical look at professional counselors and service personnel in the context of their work settings.

Part Two discusses issues which I consider to be of special concern to the profession because they highlight the point of view introduced in Part One: the discrepancies between the professional counselor's view of his role from the restricted perspective of his counseling room and the view of the counselor's activities in the context of his position in the institution and the society. These special issues relate to the incongruities in the professional counselor's role, and the discussions suggest means by which the counselor might achieve consistency between his perceptions of his contributions to his clientele and his actual achievements on their behalf.

Although each of the counseling center case studies presented in the chapters in Part Three reflects in its own way on one or more of the issues discussed or alluded to in previous chapters, each is unique in that it places the issues in a specific college setting. Four chapters describe approaches to the involvement of counseling center staff outside the counseling room in order to make their resources available to the total campus community. The other two chapters describe the impact of institutional pressures on the counseling center as an operational unit of the college.

The two chapters of Part Four discuss student services in Canadian and English colleges. They indicate that student services do exist in colleges in Canada and England but, more significantly, that these services confront many of the same problems as those in the United States. The similarities as well as the differences in approach to student services in these countries place the problems facing counseling on the campuses of the United States in a new perspective.

In discussing the potential contributions of student services to education, *New Directions for College Counselors* reflects on the question of what constitutes higher education. In discussing the counselor's position within the institutional framework, it reveals the impact of bureaucracy on all parts of an institution. In discussing possible functions of service personnel, it points up the interactions and the conflicts which may facilitate or impede the contributions of any higher education enterprise in attempting to implement programs for students.

The authors have been candid and forthright. Many of them have revealed defeats and disappointments as well as successes. They say what they have to say in their own style, and, in some cases, their personal experiences lead them to conclusions or solutions which differ from those of the others. These are people heavily involved with students at all levels of higher education. They are service personnel who write, rather than academic writers who view students as abstractions, categories, or research subjects. What they have to say should have significance not only for professional counselors and other service personnel but also for faculty and administrators. If, in fact, higher education is to be made meaningful for the variety of students entering college in the seventies, those who are responsible for the operation of the colleges would be well advised to read what these professional service personnel have written.

Parts of the Prologue are based on an article I wrote for *The Personnel and Guidance Journal*. Parts of the chapter by Richard Thoreson and Charles Krauskopf are based on an article written by them for *The American Psychologist*.

Corvallis, Oregon   CHARLES F. WARNATH
September 1973

Contents

xiii

Contents

Contributors

JANE B. BERRY, *assistant dean, Division for Continuing Education, University of Missouri–Kansas City*

RICHARD A. BROWN, *counselor, Educational Opportunities Program, Oregon State University*

BURNS BALLANTYNE CROOKSTON, *professor of higher education, University of Connecticut*

SEYMOUR HALLECK, *professor of psychiatry, School of Medicine, University of North Carolina*

LENORE W. HARMON, *director, Department of Student Counseling, and professor, University of Wisconsin–Milwaukee*

DAVID A. HILLS, *director, Center for Psychological Services, and professor of psychology, Wake Forest University*

THOMAS K. HOCKING, *director, University Counseling Center, University of Wisconsin–Oshkosh*

xvii

HOWARD C. KRAMER, *director, Counseling Center,*
Cornell University

CHARLES J. KRAUSKOPF, *associate director, University*
Testing and Counseling Service, and professor of
psychology, University of Missouri–Columbia

CHARLES E. LARSEN, *director, Student Development and*
Counseling, South Dakota State University

SUMNER B. MORRIS, *director, Counseling Center,*
and lecturer in applied behavioral sciences,
University of California, Davis

AUDREY NEWSOME, *head, Appointments and Counseling*
Service, University of Keele

MASON L. NIBLACK, *director, University Centre,*
University of Calgary

DAVID W. PALMER, *director, Student Counseling Services,*
University of California, Los Angeles

HARRIETT A. ROSE, *director, Counseling Center, and*
professor of psychology, University of Kentucky

THEODORE SLOVIN, *Community Psychology Program,*
University of Massachusetts

J. ALFRED SOUTHWORTH, *director, Counseling Center,*
University of Massachusetts

JOSEPH STUBBINS, *professor of counseling, Los Angeles*
State University

RICHARD W. THORESON, *professor, Department of*
Counseling and Personnel Services, and director,
Graduate Program in Rehabilitation,
University of Missouri–Columbia

CHARLES F. WARNATH, *professor of psychology,*
and former director, Counseling Center,
Oregon State University

New Directions
for College Counselors

A Handbook for
Redesigning Professional Roles

Prologue

Whom Does the College Counselor Serve?

Charles F. Warnath

Unconditional positive regard is not enough. The scientist-practitioner model is impractical and the medical model gives status but limited effectiveness. The college counselor must change his service orientation or he will no longer have a place on campus. Some counseling centers are literally fighting for existence. Some have already lost their fight and been dismantled or their staff scattered to other departments.

It is ironic that while professional counselors are supposed to have a natural surplus of sensitivity and awareness which they employ in their efforts to assist their clients, they have displayed almost no recognition of the forces which have been unleashed around them. Tied to models of service delivery which have restricted their own world to the four walls of a counseling cubicle and absolved them from any responsibility for the institutional environment, they have been blind to the factors which have been influencing their

1

work. They have presumed to help clients cope with a radically different college environment, with little interest on their part in testing the realities of that environment and, while assuming a generally liberal stance about the need for the institution's altering its relationship to students, they have insisted on one absolute: their familiar service model. The student body might triple in size; the white faces on campus might become covered with hair and be joined by red, black, and brown faces; the proportion of women might increase significantly and modest knee-length skirts be replaced by hot pants and jeans; the smell of tear gas might become part of the campus atmosphere; but the professional counseling staff could be counted on to continue to closet itself with a trickle of students no matter how things changed outside.

Carrying a job title which has had no specific meaning to the community, counselors have clung to a set of activities and techniques which have grown increasingly ineffective for making any significant impact on that changing community. They have continued for the most part to sit in their cubicles waiting for students to come to them with problems which they, then, have encouraged the students to solve by applications of self-initiative, greater motivation, or acceptance of the status quo. Counselors rationalized their goals in terms of improving interpersonal relationships, achievement of maturity and self-acceptance, increased coping behavior, and the like; but they were working within a framework which required that clients accept their situation outside the counseling room as a given and, therefore, counselors were in the long run simply helping clients to adjust to things as they were. Nevertheless, what counselors were trained to do seemed reasonably appropriate for the narrow cultural range in the colleges a few years ago. At least no one raised any serious questions and counselors took comfort in the thought that their clients seemed pleased to have someone on campus who would give them undivided attention. Counselors took for granted that their desire to do good was sufficient justification for what they were doing. And they also took for granted that their counseling was uncontaminated by events outside the counseling room and that somehow they were detached from the organizational and personal pressures to which their clients and others on the campus were subject.

Events within the past few years have shaken this complacency. Professional counselors have suddenly been faced with demands that they account for their efforts, not in simple one-on-one, counselor-client terms but in terms of contributions to the instituion. They have found themselves ignored by some of the students, such as ethnic minorities and radicals who see their services as coopted by the establishment, and attacked by others, such as women's lib members who see counseling as a means of imposing traditional values on women clients. Concurrently, counseling centers have been caught in the general financial squeeze in higher education. In some schools, counseling positions have been eliminated and in others, centers have been dismantled, with senior staff distributed to teaching departments or other student services. In a survey of more than 200 counseling centers which I conducted in January 1972, results indicated that in the two-year period covered by the survey, the great majority of centers had had no staff additions, whereas in the remainder, the number of staff cutbacks were coming close to balancing out staff additions. Within the free-response section of the survey, it was apparent that the staff additions were to a large extent composed of subdoctoral specialists or minority group personnel. Professional counseling on the college campus appears to have peaked out. It has lost its momentum.

The process has been painful for a number of counseling center staffs. Ironically, however, the leaders in the profession who should be organizing efforts to evaluate the current situation are managing to avoid the critical issues involved. Most represent the larger counselor education operations in the country and have felt the situation as academic department heads whose losses have been absorbed through relatively minor reductions in clerical and ancillary staff and, perhaps, a few assistantships; they have not felt the current crisis as a life-or-death struggle, as the smaller service agencies have. The lack of relationship between the counselor education corporations with their captive clinics and the bulk of service centers with two or three doctoral-level staff—a gap described by Thoreson and Krauskopf in a later chapter—is highlighted by the general lack of response by counselor educators to the current crisis facing college counseling.

This should be a period of serious reassessment of professional counseling within institutional settings, but the professional organizations with their academic executive groups have generally tended to ignore issues raised by those involved in the delivery of services. Fifteen years ago, after my first two years as a counselor in a college counseling center, I wrote of the discrepancies I experienced between the model of the counselor as presented in the professional literature and the expectations of the counselor by his institutional employer (Warnath, 1956). Again, a few years ago, as a director of a university counseling center, I wrote of the unrealistic expectations which new counselors have been given of the counselor's role in a service agency during their graduate training (Warnath, 1969). The response was underwhelming. However, those previous articles were written during periods of affluence: the first when professional leadership was concerned with boarding the VA traineeship gravy train and the second while APA-approved programs appeared to have an unlimited growth potential. The cries of pain from those service agencies undergoing amputations today and the reports of new approaches to service being undertaken by other counseling centers may possibly force the counselor educators and academicians to pay attention.

What specifically does the profession need to pay attention to? In my judgment, we are facing a crisis because our professional myths, rather than supporting and strengthening the service roles of counselors within the changing college setting, now impede the adaptations necessary for professional counselors to make a significant contribution. A myth, by one definition, is a belief given uncritical acceptance by the members of a group especially in support of existing or traditional practices. During periods of little or no change, myths serve to give stability to a professional group and help establish its claims to particular areas of expertise and types of service delivery. They also tend to establish status hierarchies within a profession. If changes begin to occur at a rapid rate, however, the professional myths interfere with the adaptability of the profession to new conditions, since levels and types of training, types of service, relationships with clientele, and discriminations between status levels within the profession no longer apply. To change a professional orientation, therefore, requires more than asking simple questions about the new priorities the practitioner should establish in his responsibilities to the institution, his clients, his personal relationships, and so forth. In my judgment, there is no way to make meaningful adjustments in service priorities without first examining the myths on which the assumptions about the original service priorities were based. This book was designed to examine the mythology of professional counseling and to present alternatives. It might be helpful at this point to introduce several of the myths of professional counseling to which the authors will direct their discussions.

Myth of the Independent Practitioner

Counselors have been naive about the sociological and political factors which affect them in their work. Halleck (1971) has argued that society or the institution in which the counselor works defines the limits of his practice and uses him as a tool to accomplish specific social (or institutional) goals. The counselor's training has been mostly based on the private-practitioner model and has given him little awareness of the operation of bureaucracies. When he takes a position in a college counseling center, he has little understanding of his expected role in the bureaucratic structure. He assumes that he alone will determine the extent or limits of his activities. As President James Bond of Sacramento State University pointed out in his address to the annual conference of college counseling center directors (1972), this generally meant that, "We forgot what we knew about division of labor and the use and allocation of resources, and we started to do everything that everyone asked us to do without sorting out clearly where we could make the best kind of impact. We found in many instances, because of the very strong existential flavor of our operations, that what we had were not really counseling departments or counseling centers as such. We had a collection of discrete professionals who were busy doing their own thing, but no umbrella thrown over the whole thing, no concerns about goals, very little concern about the context in which we function. As a matter of fact, very few of us even wanted to bother with the context in which we functioned. We did not relate to the university. We did not concern ourselves about what was happening to the university."

The myth of the independent practitioner distorts the perspective of the counselor both toward the college and toward his student clientele. As Bond has pointed out above, the counselor has shown very little concern about the context in which he functions. He has not recognized that he would not have been hired unless the college administration felt that whatever he would do would fit into the goals, purposes, and image of the institution. During the years of rapid expansion in higher education, it was simply taken for granted that counselors were doing something constructive for the institution—if only a public relations activity, the social welfare unit of the bureaucracy which symbolizes the college's concern for students. The independent-practitioner model served the needs of both the counselor and the institution since it permitted the counselor to operate in a familiar and comfortable manner while providing college administrators with a defense against the charge that no one on campus seemed to want to help students with their problems. As conditions in higher education have changed and some counselors have moved out to offer different services, they have discovered the institution's true expectations for their service. They now find that their assumption of freedom to determine what to do and how to do it was an illusion. The private-practitioner model is applicable only insofar as it meets the needs of the institution.

Halleck (1971)` and Stubbins (1970)` point out that counseling and psychotherapy are integral parts of the political forces within an institution. As such, the criteria for the content and quality of the counselor's work will be determined ultimately by the institutional managers. From a practical standpoint, this means that the counselor's primary service role is to assist his clients back into productive activities within the institution. The managers of the college have not been prepared to have the counselor serve as a commentator on the system itself. For them, the structure is a given to which the students must adjust. Here, again, the myth of the private practitioner which locates problems within the client has reinforced institutional needs by diverting attention from the possibility that a student's problems might, indeed, be the result of poor functioning in the system. Counseling has contributed to the stability of the college by placing the locus of problems within the individual and by reducing frictions between individuals who come for counseling and others within the system. In working with students who present problems of poor grades, disruptive behavior, or inadequate choice of major, the counselor relieves the college administrators of examining the possible contributions of the system itself to these problems. Thus, the good which a counselor thinks he is doing for one student may, in the long run, as pointed out in Halleck's chapter, cause or permit added distress for many students.

Scientist-practitioner. A corollary of the myth of the independent practitioner is that of the scientist (researcher)-practitioner. Almost all graduate education programs in counseling hang an albatross of guilt around the necks of those graduates who go into service agency counseling, by presenting models of prestige based on research and writing. The message comes through clearly that to be a truly acceptable professional, the counselor should emulate his graduate professors, adopt academic priorities, and embark on research projects that will culminate in a publication list. Like good sons and daughters, the newly minted doctorates should reflect the respectability and rigor of their upbringing by engaging in academically acceptable production. Like it or not, the counselor's esteem in the eyes of his professional colleagues is welded to his ability to meet standards within an academic framework.

But the counselor in a college counseling center, with the exception of a minority tied to academic departments, is not judged by institutional managers on the basis of his academic production. He is judged by his ability to meet service standards. Research may be acceptable to a dean of students as a counselor idiosyncrasy as long as it does not appear to interfere with the counselor's time with clients or his meeting other institutional obligations. However, in some colleges, it is actually discouraged on the basis that it leads to poor public relations, either by giving the impression that counselors are not devoting full time to their primary service responsibilities or that they are using clients as guinea pigs. The counselor, then, may be placed in a double bind since he feels he cannot meet the standards of his profession unless he publishes, yet his dedication to his service obligations may be questioned if he does. Counselor educators have never understood that at some institutions, service personnel are assumed to be on 24-hour call. Meaningful research is not likely to be generated by someone who is forced to turn his primary commitments on or off to fit a service schedule.

The great majority of service personnel do *not* publish, not even to complain about the unrealistic standards imposed by their academically oriented colleagues who, to paraphrase an old chestnut, have "never made a full caseload." Those who do get in print and spawn progeny which they hope will add lustre to their reputations set the standards for the profession simply because theirs are the only ideas which gain widespread exposure and also because, in a profession based on the psychological analysis of conflict, the sons and daughters do not wish to risk being accused of attacking the parent figures of the profession, no matter how out-of-touch their elders may be with reality.

The attitudes of counselor educators toward research by service personnel is part of the practitioner mentality with which counselors are imbued at the doctoral level. Those in leadership positions who lament the fact that so few counselors carry on research after being trained for it during their graduate programs show a lack of awareness of the working conditions and service standards in the typical college counseling center. Our counselor educators have ill prepared their graduates for work in an institutional structure by their inability to comprehend the political and bureaucratic forces in such institutions, a point which Stubbins argues in Chapter One.

Medical model. Another corollary of the myth of the independent practitioner is the adoption of the medical model as the core of counselor practice. Several other authors in this book discuss the problems this model has caused for college counseling and I have dealt with it in another context (Warnath, 1971). Suffice it to say that with this model, counselors have accepted several basic values regardless of their theoretical orientation. First, the medical model implies an inherently superior-subordinate relationship. Counselor and client do not—and cannot—meet as two individuals. The client arrives at the counselor's office to meet a person *in an institutional role*. More often than not, the counselor reinforces the difference between them by introducing himself by his title while calling the client by his first name. The counselor arranges for the client to see him at a scheduled hour, not because this is necessarily best for meeting the client's needs, but because it best fits the organizational structure. The counselor will not ordinarily intervene on behalf of the client in any situation outside the counseling room, rationalizing that this would encourage client dependence—even though the client can in no way cope with the situation alone. Thus the medical model enables the counselor to avoid the pressing realities with which his client is faced and, incidentally, any possible clash with the institutional structure. The client may feel more alone while he is working with a professional counselor than if he had shared his problem with a concerned friend (Stubbins, 1971).

Second, as the physician treats his patient for the patient's physical ailment, the counselor working with a client within the framework of the medical model accepts the problem presented as the client's ailment. He assumes that the client can achieve personal salvation (good mental health, an appropriate decision, and so forth) by his own personal efforts regardless of the impact of the social and institutional forces directed toward him. Counseling is basically an American phenomenon in that it is part of the American mythology that despite external circumstances the individual can overcome any obstacles with adequate motivation and good advice. Counseling takes into account only those potential forces within the individual which might be directed outward toward the environment; it completely ignores the forces pressing in on the client.

Myth of the Detached Counselor

The college counselor is a human being with his own historical development. He lives in a community with a family and friends, works in an institution with colleagues and administrators. He has spent eighteen years or more as a student to qualify for the position he holds. In short, the counselor cannot free himself from personal and social pressures any more than his clients can. But he is encouraged to ignore these forces by the almost total emphasis throughout his graduate preparation and during in-service activities on his professional interactions. Although he uses himself as the major tool in offering assistance to others, his own needs, values, goals, and personal anxieties are generally as closed to examination by others as those of a bricklayer or plumber. If he is under obvious pressures from a disintegrating marriage or if he pounds on the desk of his director for more money to reflect his personal evaluation of his worth as a counselor, these incidents are assumed to have little if any impact on his work within his counseling office. Somehow, as he walks into his cubicle with a client, his frustrations with the growing alienation of his wife, his anger at the director for not recognizing his value, his disappointment in having a journal article rejected, and all his other psychological aches and pains are expected to drop away and he is transformed into a creature not unlike a computer whose programs for the world outside have been disconnected.

This model of the counselor stimulates the academic researcher in his efforts to create the computer-counselor. This is the logical extension of the counseling process to the point where its essence—perhaps its only significant uniqueness as Palmer discusses in his chapter—has been squeezed out: the humanness of the counselor. Now the profession is giving its kudos to those counselor educators who can best squeeze the most human interaction out of what is called "counseling". The increased efficiency of data and information transactions between machine and student cannot be denied and, with the tendency of all those in counseling to act as if that person called counselor somehow loses all his human ties when he enters the counseling room, it is probably inevitable that the technocrats would mistake myth for reality and attempt to replace the human counselor with a vending machine.

The counselor, however, does *not* lose his humanity when he enters the counseling room. This is a two-edged sword. The person of the counselor is the agent of client change, growth, and development; his technique or technical skill (the part of the counselor being machine duplicated) may improve the efficiency of data processing but the person of the counselor influences the person of the client for better or worse to make use of the information received. The machine can be far superior in dispensing correct and up-to-date information and even in forcing the client to learn certain decision-making steps, but the absence of the person removes the one in-gredient that most clients in these days of impersonality want and need—human contact, someone who seems to care.

The other edge of the sword is that the counselor's unwill-ingness to accept his place in his environment leads him to withhold part of himself and to play a detached role stripped of any per-sonal investment. The flat bored drone of the counselors on commer-cially produced training tapes, particularly those of the client-centered specialists, carries the message of controlled technique. It is impos-sible to determine whether the counselor is having a good day or a bad day, if his wife screamed him out of the house or gave him a cheery good-bye kiss, or even if he is enjoying his work. The counse-lor does not meet the client on equal terms, for despite being urged by counseling literature to be authentic and open, the counselor tends to put on his mask of professional impartiality as soon as he walks through the door of the counseling room.

The counselor's flat voice and scientific manner are the professional filters through which he strains his own emotions; however, embedded in the responses by which he encourages or ignores portions of the client's messages are the effects of his own past and current experiences. The counselor has his own needs for security and approval, for instance, which cannot be completely met by his clients, yet threaten his independence in working with clients in a completely impartial manner. He needs among other things to be sensitive to the values and expectations of his superiors for they, not the clients, control the institutional reward system on which his economic security and his sense of value in the community are based. The counselor cannot settle comfortably into a long-term relation-ship with clients, for example, if he is expected to maintain the average of two to three contacts of most counseling centers. Nor can he reject vocational clients if his director or dean of students per-ceive vocational problems as the core of counselor activity.

The idealism of the graduate school becomes watered down in the reality of doing a job and in the impersonality of being part of the bureaucratic structure. The anxieties produced by this conflict are often expressed through petty confrontations among staff mem-bers and angry overreactions to the perceived source of the counse-lor's internal struggle, the father figure of the director. These are the open and observable displays of the tensions of counselors in their work setting but we have little evidence of how the reaction to the discrepancies between ideals and reality are manifested within the counseling room. Case conferences tend to be restricted to analysis of the interactions within the counseling session and the external factors affecting the client's communications while discussion of the counselor's own communications are limited to appropriate terms of abstract theoretical considerations and the stimuli provided by the client. No one asks whether the counselor's seeming abruptness or his leading into test administration might be due to his feeling that he needs a termination or case turnover to meet what he perceives to be the organization's general standards for closed cases or client load.

Other possible influences on his service work are those originating in his family, friendship, and community connections. The counseling literature discusses the effects of these factors on clients and, more recently, have included the impact of significant changes in our society on people in general and young people in particular. Still, the literature omits one category—the counselor. As if he were a plumber or bricklayer, the counselor is assumed to function in a technically adequate manner no matter what inputs he gets from outside and despite the fact that he himself is the major instrument of his service. Even if the instrument is out of tune or broken, it is assumed that it will be in tune or repaired whenever the counselor enters the counseling room or offers some other service to students. Obviously this could not be the case. If, for instance, the counselor's wife is seeking acceptance in the community, particularly with the student services wives or the faculty wives; or if the family has begun to establish roots in the schools, a church or civic groups, the counselor may be reluctant to involve himself in high-risk activities which could be questioned by his superiors. Ironically, counseling theories generally encourage greater openness and candor than is accepted in society in order to assist the client to achieve greater self-esteem. Because of his tendency to ignore the forces which shape his own behavior both inside and outside the counseling room, the counselor may be less aware than his clients that he cannot live up to the procedures he presses on the client if he is to live within the structure of which he is a part. My experience has been that the members of a counseling center staff are extremely reluctant to share their feelings on a personal level with each other, preferring, like a work group of laymen, to project their frustrations outside the center in terms of being unappreciated by the state legislature, the state board, the president of the institution or the dean of students. It is my impression that this reluctance to adopt for themselves the same open manner that they urge on their clients is itself a source of anxiety.

Myth of Universal Empathy

No matter what their theoretical orientation, professional counselors have held one belief in common: that they were uniquely sensitive to and knowledgeable about the full range of human problems. On the college campus, the relative homogeneity of student bodies for years permitted counselors to maintain this myth. At least there were no direct challenges to this assumption.

With the enrollment of distinctly nontraditional students in the late 60s, counseling center staff became aware that few of these students were using their services. With the establishment of drug crash pads, ethnic minority programs, women's studies offices, abortion referral offices, and the like, most of which included counseling services of some sort, it became clear that the official counseling center was no longer perceived by many students as the place to go for counseling help. The spontaneous emergence of these specialized services underlines the fact that the counselor's belief that he was perceived as particularly empathic has been a myth.

Individual counselors have been able to maintain contact with one or another of these nontraditional student groups but the relationship has been due more to the counselor's personal characteristics or life style than to his formal status as professional counselor. These students are making clear one of the contentions stated by Palmer in Chapter Three—that professionalism does not in itself guarantee assurance, understanding, or sensitivity. Moreover, some of these groups are obviously antiestablishment and noninstitutional. By creating their own counseling services they point up their suspicion that they can not expect adequate assistance from members of an organization within the institutional structure. These students appear to be more aware than the counselors themselves of the discrepancies between the role of the professional counselor, with its emphasis on techniques, procedures, and style, and the position of the counselor within the bureaucratic structure which reduces his ability to empathize with students who are not willing to adjust to the traditional standards of the institution.

Two groups in particular have within the past few years directly challenged the competence of the traditional counselor to cope with their unique problems: the ethnic minorities and the liberated women. While demanding their own counseling services, they have been explicit in their charges that the role of the professional counselor on campus has been to define problems in traditional middle-class ways and, thus, to reinforce the status quo. As President Bond (1972) points out, ethnic minority students are confronted with problems of survival and don't have time to worry about identity concerns and psychologically defined neuroses—the types of problems which middle-class kids can afford to spend hours talking about and about which professional counselors encourage their clients to introspect. These students see their problems as immediate and concrete. Brown, in his chapter, discusses several issues related to the counseling of minority students and particularly emphasizes the barriers which the organization of the counseling center places between the counselor and the minority student.

Charges made by liberated women are related but different. Unlike ethnic minorities, women have been willing clients and, as Chessler (1972) has pointed out, a higher proportion have become patients and clients than might be predicted from their actual numbers in any population. Chessler also accuses counselors, psychiatrists, and others in the mental health professions of defining the woman who is different, creative, or defiant of the status quo as psychologically deviant and treating her as if she had an abnormality which required adjusting. The findings of Thomas and Stewart (1971) which revealed the biases of counselors (both male and female) against young women with nonfeminine career goals tend to support this charge. The inability of professional counselors to empathize with the new woman is the theme which Jane Berry has examined from several perspectives later in this book.

Each identifiable group that has conspicuously avoided using the formal counseling services has given notice that it does not accept those services as appropriate to meet its high-priority needs and that it does not trust the professional counselors to have the necessary understanding or sensitivity to deal effectively with those needs. Since these groups comprise a significant part of an increasingly heterogeneous student body, their rejection of the professional counselor's assumptions about his generalized empathy for all types of people raises serious questions about whether he can play a meaningful role on campus if he continues to deliver his traditional counseling service through the traditional counseling center delivery system.

Myths of Vocationalism and Testing Effectiveness

The core of counselor training has been educational-vocational decision-making. The counselor's courses have made him familiar with occupational information; a variety of theories of vocational development; the meaning of work in our society; the relationship of family, socioeconomic, educational, and other factors to vocational choice; and educational-vocational testing. He is an applied vocational psychologist. As such, he is not free from a strong value orientation based on goal directedness and clarity of vocational purpose. Maturity, at least for males, is evaluated on the basis of factors related to purposeful behavior toward a work goal. For the professional counselor, vocational success is *the* goal of the mature well-integrated male. Since the vocational theorists have never seriously concerned themselves with women's goals, the assumption has been that the maturity of women was not an issue as long as they were moving toward the traditional housewife role— with the allowance that they might, until they married and had children, work in some acceptable women's occupation such as nurse, librarian, or schoolteacher. A woman, however, might be judged as lacking maturity if she rejected this career pattern.

The issue of job satisfaction has entered prominently into the thinking of professional counselors and job satisfaction studies have been a regular part of the literature. Vocational theories have a distinctly upper-middle-class white male Protestant orientation: almost without exception they frame the ideal human as competing successfully through a series of well-planned academic and vocational preparation levels to reach a logical ultimate choice in a job through which the individual fulfills most of his needs and receives the major share of his satisfactions. There is considerable interest among the theorists in classifying, stratifying, compartmentalizing and, more recently, computerizing. While purporting to have as its major purpose the facilitation of a person's educational-vocational planning, its effect is to stabilize the economic system by offering hope that there are reasonable logical paths through the maze of occupational structure to the one best job that can make each individual happy and satisfied. In addition, college counselors have promised that they could identify hidden talents and aptitudes and thus salvage the potential failures in one department who might be successful or reveal possibilities for persons to aspire to a higher occupational level than they might ordinarily have considered.

In his vocational work, the counselor has been a protector of the work ethic as well as a contributor to the American dream and, in the process, has tended to reinforce traditional values and standards. On the assumption that the best predictors for the future are extrapolations from the past, and using instruments heavily loaded with experience factors, counselors have been more successful in confirming expectations than in uncovering talents unnoticed by the client himself, his teachers, and family. We have little evidence that counselors have played any significant part in discovering talents for higher education or professional occupations such as engineering, pharmacy, or science within ethnic minority groups or managerial talent among women. Quite the contrary. Many successful college students from minority groups complain that they have enrolled in college despite discouragements from their high school counselors. As mentioned earlier, women's groups have been explicit in their denunciation of counselors who tend to steer women toward acceptance of the traditional women's role of wife and mother.

Two other groups also raise serious questions about the vocational orientation of professional counselors: young people in the counterculture who reject traditional work values and the futurists such as Toffler (1970) who argue convincingly that the pace of change in our society is accelerating to the point where planning for more than a few years in the future is a meaningless exercise. It remains to be seen whether the counterculture is a temporary phenomenon since, as this is being written, college students seem again to be more concerned about finding a job than in finding themselves; however, it continues to cast a shadow over many of the basic assumptions of professional counselors about the need for satisfactions derived only from work. A suspicion remains that work may be of decreasing appeal to many, if not most, people except as it provides the financial resources to do other more satisfying things. This theme is also central to the futurists who point to the decreasing work week, the shortened work life, and the acceleration of work mobility for a growing number of people, which will lead to minimal personal investment in work.

In sum, the criticisms by ethnic minorities and women, the suspicions raised by counterculture youth that there may be acceptable alternatives to the work ethic for achieving personal satisfaction, and the projections of the futurists indicating the possible futility of long-range planning confront professional counseling with serious questions about its traditional assumptions and main focus. But an additional problem looms for the profession. Testing has been central to the counseling method and this technique is under attack from various quarters, particularly ethnic minorities and women who point out that tests discriminate against them because of their content and the normative groups used in their standardization. The arguments have been covered at length in a variety of books, articles, speeches, and popular magazines, and it would be redundant to report them here. One issue, however, which has not been given adequate coverage is that raised by Goldman (1972). Briefly, Goldman contends that tests have been developed mainly as selection devices where the specific job to be filled is known and criteria can be established to pick out those applicants with the highest probability of success for that job. The objectives of the counselor using tests is, of course, quite different. He is working with one client to help that client select from a variety of occupational possibilities. As Goldman points out, this reversal of purpose reduces the probability for meaningful results to the point where tests generally tell the client little more than he already knows about himself. It has been my personal experience that the longer a counselor works in a college center the more readily he will admit that testing doesn't add much to his work and his use of tests declines significantly. A confrontation with the dean of students can very well occur when the number of tests drops in a center, for the dean may view the reduction as a reduction of "vocational case load." But whether the dean of students understands or not, the point is that the use of tests in counseling has been a sad disappointment and has added little to counseling effectiveness.

The problem would seem to be easily solved by the professional counselor's simply admitting the bankruptcy of testing procedures but much too much of his professional role has been tied to testing and, as in the example above, outsiders tend to see tests as critical to his vocational guidance role. Like the rattles and drum of the medicine man, tests serve as part of the counselor's mystique. To eliminate testing in a counseling center would force the counselors to justify the one part of their procedures which now is simply taken for granted by the institutional managers. The dilemma for the counselor is that his continued use of instruments, which have relatively little value except to stimulate discussion with a client, is a deception he must live with. As with encouraging clients to be more open and authentic than he himself can be, he must cope with still another discrepancy between his professed honesty and the knowledge that his instruments are relatively ineffective for the task clients expect them to perform.

Looking Ahead

The college campus should be different because of the presence of professional counselors. The truth is, however, that the great majority of those in the college community have not even known that a counseling center existed. The model used by college counselors based on a number of myths borrowed from physicians and psychotherapists in private practice has given the college administrators a center to symbolize the bureaucracy cares while insuring that the counselors made no significant impact on the institution. Counselors have accepted this role because it was comfortable; they have always felt needed by *some* students; and no one questioned their service mythology. Now that set of beliefs, too, is being seriously challenged. Trained to look inward for the source of problems and still reinforced by a steady case load of the usual student clientele, some counseling center staff are still unaware of the threat to their professional existence.

Some centers have felt the effects of changes within higher education as evidenced by the chapters of Hocking and Hills. As increasing numbers of counselors move out on campus, they discover they are considered part of the structure of the bureaucracy. Some have received a favorable response to their efforts as noted in the chapters by Rose and by Southworth and Slovin. However, in other cases, they have encountered opposition (Morris' chapter) or been directed to engage more heavily in certain types of traditional services. Counselors are on the horns of a dilemma. If they attempt to adjust their services to more adequately meet the needs which students are expressing as suggested for college services by Mills (1971)', Oetting (1970)', and Warnath (1968, 1971) or for other types of institutions by Aubrey (1969)', Matheney (1971)', and Stewart and Warnath (1965)', they run the risk of being reminded by their institutional administrators in rather specific ways that they have been hired to serve the institution.

It is becoming increasingly clear that if professional counselors do not align themselves with students and attempt to respond directly to a wider range of student needs more than in the past, they will continue to lose credibility (noted in several chapters and, most specifically, that of Harmon)'. There are no easy solutions but it is becoming apparent that the integrity of the profession may be at stake. The present mythology of the profession, with its core in the private practitioner model, has, as Stubbins has written for this book, placed counselors in the position of supporting the status quo and, hence, alienated many of the very students who most need the assistance of a sympathetic adult in coping with the system. Obviously, no solutions to the counselor's dilemma can be found when counselors are not aware that a dilemma actually exists. Some professionals expectedly will prefer to retain the comfortable conservative model of individual practitioner with which they are familiar, and their institutional managers, for the reasons already stated, may be content to allow them to do so. These counselors will stop their ears to the bells tolling for counseling centers on other campuses until the winds of change blow strong enough on their own campuses to threaten their own private world. In line with the contention of Thoreson and Krauskopf, some counselor education programs can be expected to continue producing professionals who are already obsolete when they receive their degrees. These professors need strong feedback about the changing conditions confronting service personnel in higher education. I hope this book will serve to focus the attention of those professional counselors who have been so far unaffected by change and those counselor educators who have been ignoring change on some of the basic issues and problems which must be confronted if the profession is to survive in institutions of higher education.

I

Social Context of College Counseling

Joseph Stubbins

Some forty years after counseling services were initiated in colleges, the role of the counselor is often unknown or unappreciated by students and generally assigned some minor place in their thinking. Counseling still must justify its existence with administrators and faculty, has gained little of the security that comes from middle age, and has not made good on much of its early promise. In an early text, Williamson (1939, p. 124) wrote, "Counseling is that part of student personnel work in which a counselor marshals the resources

I am indebted to Ronald A. Roston of the University of California, Riverside, for his reactions to an original draft of this paper and for making available a number of studies of university counseling centers.

of an institution and of the community to assist a student to achieve the optimum of adjustment of which he is capable."

When practicing counselors—by which I mean those who have earned at least a master's degree and are offering psychological and vocational services, not those whose main responsibilities are remedial reading, study habits, speech and hearing problems, or that host of paraprofessionals who have in recent years been incorporated within counseling centers—are queried about the state of their profession, they rarely respond in terms of the adequacy or inadequacy of a counseling theory. Rather, they point to the context in which they function as facilitative or obstructive.

A survey of university and college counseling centers (Warnath, 1972) suggests widespread concern among directors about the institutional relations of their centers. This concern appears to stem primarily from fear of budgetary cuts and staff curtailment, and appears only incidentally related to embeddedness in and widespread dependence of counseling on institutional controls. The Warnath survey, as well as various policy statements of the University and College Counseling Center Directors, clearly points to an expanding interest in analyzing bureaucratic relations and their impact on student personnel services.

Traditional Views

The student personnel movement originally emphasized the need to humanize the educational environment (for example, Lloyd-Jones and Smith, 1938). In typical textbooks, counseling of the individual was covered in a couple of chapters. However, as professional psychologists gained a stronger foothold in student personnel work, they diverted attention toward individual treatment of students in a setting divorced from the main business of the college or university. This trend was not unnoticed. In a paper read at the American College Personnel Association (ACPA) at Boston in 1963, Black quoted a report of ACPA as follows: "For too long student personnel workers have neglected participation in policy development on their campuses and in so doing have assumed the role of technicians in higher education." Black accounted for this in part: "In trying to establish ourselves in the educational enterprise, which seldom welcomes anything new with open arms, we have often compromised our convictions in order to win acceptance."

We are now in a better position to assess the consequences of the influence of professional psychology on student personnel services. Today's college counselor is trained, and prefers to view himself, as a humanistic and scientific functionary in a rational bureaucracy. The counselor's humanism is based on his respect for individuality and self-actualization, and a general belief in the basically social nature of man and his perfectability. The counselor is scientific in that he employs a technology based on psychology. By the term *bureaucracy*, I do not imply the popular assumption of rigidity, conservatism, and inefficiency, but rather Weber's definition (1947) of a system of management consisting of hierarchical control, impersonal rules, and an emphasis on efficiency. While the early leaders of the student personnel movement recognized this industrial model as counterproductive for the individual students in higher education, they underestimated the rapidity of its growth, the fantastic specialization that it generated, and especially its immense power to compel compliance. True, college center directors affirm that college counselors serve as consultants to the administration, but in practice few counselors do. Thus, counselors behave as if they functioned in a college structure which was rational. This assumption frees them to go about their business of psychological and vocational counseling. Some students so counseled leave the process with more appropriate vocational goals, new perspectives, more prosocial behaviors, and more constructive modes of coping with life. College centers are now attempting to broaden their services through group counseling, outreach programs, special services for women and ethnic minority students, paraprofessional counseling, and making themselves available for faculty consultation. However, such achievements and experimental approaches have not immunized the college counseling center from serious criticism and budget cutting.

As generally practiced, psychological counseling is just about the last bulwark of radical individualism. Most college counselors assume that their duty is to work with what lies inside the client's head. The problems inside may be overwhelmed by what is outside, but that merely means the challenge is greater. The original aim of counseling to humanize the educational environment has been taken up by the students and a few counseling centers—but even this faction has occasionally been seduced by romantic individualism. Reich (1970), for instance, in spite of his radical criticism of American institutions, is squarely in the American tradition of ascribing near miraculous powers to the individual. It is not necessary to change American institutions by means of social and political action, Reich holds; these will be transformed as a consequence of each person's going his own way and doing his own thing. It is curious that such untrammeled individualism can coexist with radical environmentalism in the same person. Younger psychologists manifest it through their interest in community psychology and in preventive social approaches usually thought of as the province of sociology.

But while the counselor believes himself to be a humanistic functionary, the more aware college student views him quite differently. The student sees the counselor as socially embedded in his job with office hours from nine to four, as a product of his own personal social developmental history, and in a way, as hung up on a particular restricted way of relating to him. Whether the counselor takes his cues from Carl Rogers, Fritz Perls, Viktor Frankl, or some other system-builder, he still betrays his technological commitment to handling his client as an isolated ego. Generally the counselor takes his world of the individual, self-made ego for granted. It is a world that economics and political science have long since discarded—a perspective that ignores the fact that the student's world has already taught him that socioeconomic status, racial origin, and power are more determinative than aptitude or interests. The dyadic relationship of counseling ascribes a disproportionate strength to the student's ability to operate free of environmental constraints. Traditional counseling distorts reality since it assumes that the client as an isolated ego is more determinative than reality indicates.

"Throwness"

Counselors suffer an excessive amount of guilt concerning their success "batting average"—the same kind of guilt complex generated by the competitive aspects of our society. It was first widely brought to the American public attention by Horney (1937), later was expanded in the writings of Erich Fromm, who stressed that a man's worth was measured by his marketability, and most recently has become a major theme of social critics. Somehow, the counselor expects the student he serves to be a better functioning person by deriving more satisfaction from his situation—by improving his grades, his social skills, his study habits, or his sense of responsibility.

The counselor's vague sense that he has not quite met with success and that the student is leaving the college center not quite satisfied can be illuminated by Heidegger's concept (1962) of "throwness." Its most comprehensive connotation suggests that man is not quite master of his ship, that he was thrown into the ship, that its course was set for him, and that most of his activities on board are predetermined. In looking at the givens that determine the counselor's course, I do not deny that he is surrounded by an ambit of choice, but I do assert that his position or set prior to choice determines the range of options.

The counselor is inclined to define client self-realization in intrapsychic terms. During the years after World War II and the Cold War, the goal of most young people was to find a secure place in business and industry. Most recently, an increasing number of youth have been more concerned with a self-realization that will yield peace of mind and a cosmic sense of belonging that has been destroyed by urbanization (Roszak, 1969). College counseling tends to be in the mainstream of popular ideologies rather than ahead of them—altogether too eager to please, to accommodate, and to sell its wares on terms laid down by the institution to be in a position to project creatively new interpretations of the students' basic problems. The counselor is as much a product of popular ideologies as his clients. In this sense, he is thrown: he is already in a world of values and attitudes. While the counselor cannot jump out of his boots, I suggest that one of his tasks is to understand what is limiting his effectiveness with clients.

The givens a counselor must subject to critical examination are versions of self-realization, the constraints of his organizational ties, and the biases of his social class. And he must think through all of them while tied down to a job that nurtures his family and himself. To the extent that he remains bound by givens, the college counselor is essentially a technician serving his institution. If he can transcend them in his imagination, he has grasped his throwness and opened up possibilities of serving his clients that could not otherwise have occurred to him. Instead of the position into which he was thrust he has achieved some new perspectives and even a practical utopia. Previously, counselors were thrown into a world in which self-realization was a deepening of self-awareness in the transient experience of an encounter group. They were not thrown into a world in which self-realization is a sense of community, reciprocity, and caring.

Here and there, college counselors are coming to grips with the duality of self-realization. Various counseling centers are doing studies on the causes of attrition in the student body, fomenting a larger role for students on faculty committees, suggesting practical methods of involving students in meaningful academically related activities off-campus, and striving for a voice in the college councils where important decisions affecting student welfare are made. Such beginnings attest to the recognition that self-realization need not be viewed as the peak functioning of a finely tuned thing, but something that resonates with the social environment and draws its meaning and value from this intricate relationship. To justify the promotion of student activities such as those above, one need not postulate a need for altruism. It is sufficient to recognize the interdependence of all segments of the community of which the campus is a part.

Professional Socialization

The preparation for becoming a doctor of the ego begins in graduate school, where the student of counseling is most likely indoctrinated by professors sensitive to the opinions of their rigorous scientific colleagues. Counselor educators are suspect as social scientists and are usually in a defensive posture vis-à-vis other social scientists. Because of their dubious status, they tend to emphasize the technical aspects of training at the expense of the humanistic. Technicism derives its inspiration and guiding philosophy from science and the discovery of uniformities of behavior; it is concerned with the best means of achieving the goals of counseling with efficiency and control. Humanism is concerned with the ideals and goals of human potential, with the integrity of man, and with his relatedness to others (Blackman, 1963). Humanism is concerned with utopia.

The technical preoccupation of counselor educators has tended to give counseling an amoral cast. Experts in behavioral change can be hired by anyone who can pay the fee. The humanistic aspect of counselor graduate education is a haphazard business. Students learn that their profession has a code of ethics, that counseling is related to a larger enterprise of social welfare that has a long history in the Anglo-American countries, and so on; but rarely is the graduate student confronted with the practical obstacles that bedevil his practice in the real world. The curriculum scarcely comes to grips with the task of equipping the college counselor with inner strength to resist institutional encroachments, with the social skills needed to survive in an environment indifferent to his projects, and with the means to initiate institutional changes he feels are indicated. Scientific preoccupations at the expense of humanistic ones cause counselor educators to focus on that which falls within the purview of their techniques and to ignore other matters of human welfare. Thus, when counseling was defined as a one-to-one relationship between a willing client and a nondirective counselor, the client's failure to appear did not raise questions about the effectiveness of the counseling. He was simply regarded as unmotivated and unfeasible for counseling. To think of outreach programs to help him or to create a constituency for the counseling center did not fall within the scope of scientific training. These are acts of creation that spring from caring.

Technical psychological knowledge strains to match the natural sciences in terms of precision. Consequently the counselor's diagnostic skills are more fully developed than his treatment skills. Thus counselors have been largely unresourceful in dealing with racial minorities, social deviants, and others who are not respected by the majority culture. And psychological diagnosis is itself in a state of disarray, partly because of the challenge of phenomenology and its uncovering of the valuational bases of all diagnostic procedures (Giorgi, 1970).

The diagnostic function assigns disproportionate weight to the client's problems in terms of current traits, personal development, and local culture to the practical exclusion of the role of institutions in generating or maintaining them. As a psychometrist, the college counselor can readily determine the academic shortcomings of socially disadvantaged students. However, the process of remediation—whether in fact the counseling center should engage in remediation at all—lies outside the scientific role of the counselor. In those instances where counseling centers do engage in academic remediation, its participation has no doubt been determined at the administrative level.

I have brought into focus the diagnostic bias since it sets up the conditions that enable the counselor to be used as technician. Psychological findings do not speak for themselves. They are subject to interpretation from a particular framework, and this framework is inevitably a valuational one. However, if the counselor is not aware of the interpretative slant given his data, he may participate in the client's betrayal. This possibility is not limited to the "bad diagnosis" resulting from poor training. It inheres in the authority system of any institution that can employ a counselor and use his technical results without consulting him, especially when case records belong to the university and not to the individual counselors.

Counselor education has been slow to respond to the challenges of writers such as Louch (1969), Halleck (1971), Halmos (1966), Giorgi (1970), and Szasz (1961), who have exposed the myth of an objective social science. Another problem is that the graduate student's role model is not in fact that of practitioner. Years may have passed since the professor last counseled a student or carried out the social change-agent functions discussed in this chapter. Counseling students often suspect that much that is taught is not practiced generally, even by those counselor educators who assert that they are involved in practice. Generally, supervision of the practicum and field work is assigned to an advanced graduate student or to an instructor. Consequently, as Warnath (1971) points out, very few graduate students have ever seen their professors engaged in either the traditional or the new roles of the college counselor. The professor may be admired for his reputation as a writer or researcher, his position in a professional organization, his skill in grantmanship, his capacity to dramatize his lecture—but rarely because students have seen him in counseling action and can identify strongly with him on this score.

Thus the counseling psychologist or counselor-to-be as he moves through graduate training becomes aware that his teachers do not regard counseling as a valued function. Not surprisingly, soon after the newly graduated counselor lands his first job in a college counseling center, he is already looking to the day that he can move on to college teaching, administration, or another position with more status and money. Indeed counseling centers often attract the best qualified clinical and counseling psychologists by offering them academic rank or a dual appointment. A survey by Poole (1971) of counseling centers of the University of California and the California State University indicated that they overwhelmingly favored (95 percent and 89 percent, respectively) "the concept of counselors as parttime teaching faculty in academic departments."

If humanism exists in graduate education, students must look for it in the lifestyles of the counselor educators—their use of working and nonworking hours, the causes they espouse, and their definitions of success as demonstrated in their own lives. If graduate education is to provide the necessary humanistic base for those students who plan to enter service positions, counselor educators might modify their currently heavy emphasis on training scientific functionaries and strike a better balance between the ideals of science and service. They may lose some points with the hard-line scientists, but they would present more inspiring and functional models to their students.

Finally, counselor educators should acknowledge that they have not been very successful at anticipating social change and forseeing its implications for counseling practice. In coping with the problems of change, they have been inclined to make accommodations and to copy innovations tried elsewhere—even minor innovations. Counselor educators are ever so fearful of antagonizing potential employers of graduates. For example, departments of counselor education have not taken clear positions on the proper role of the counselor in the schools; nor have they been critical of counseling programs that misuse the talents of counselors. Basically, they have been providing functionaries with formal credentials for the local institutions to use and absorb as they see fit. Counselor education has provided little leadership in defining, researching, demonstrating, or publicizing ways in which the counselor can function more professionally. If evidence is needed for this rather dour assessment of counselor education, one need only look at its products.

Being on the Job

However informal the graduate student's humanistic indoctrination, it has left some impact. The literature of his profession and the general idiom of his professionalism have tended to define what he is about to enter as a calling (for example, American Personnel and Guidance Association, 1961). The extent of the college counselor's freedom and autonomy varies according to his academic rank and whether he has the lesser status of staff. Other factors such as the professional status associated with academic degrees, earned professional recognition, and successful private practice and consultation also condition the extent to which the counselor is free to pursue his calling. At least at the college center, the counselor's immediate supervisor is generally a professionally trained psychologist who usually assumes that he will perform in a professional manner. Nevertheless, he cannot long forget that he has a job and a place in the economy, much like that of other workers.

The more the demands of his position cause him to lose his sense of mission, the more he realizes his circumstances are very much like those in business and industry. Both the industrial worker and the counselor do what they must in order to survive. In an age of conformity (for example, the 1930s), conflicts between the individual and social institutions were either beyond awareness or too dangerous to job security to be openly discussed at conferences and in journals. Only during the 1960s did counselors become aware of the enormous capacity of institutions to level people, stifle dissent, and absorb for their purposes the staunchest deviants (Marcuse, 1968). Stewart and Warnath (1965) gave one of the first, if tentative, indications of this awareness within the profession.

As a staff member, the college counselor often lacks the protection of tenure and academic freedom and is not part of the committee structure of faculty governance, which protects the prerogatives of faculty. He also lacks the most fundamental guarantees of the unionized factory worker. To say that he is vulnerable to the whims and prejudices of an administrator is to state the obvious—and counselors have recently become all too aware of their vulnerability. It is rather ironic that the college counselor has recently been seduced by existential counseling with its emphasis on personal responsiblity, moral choice, and accepting the inevitable anxiety associated with such puritanic views of self. Perhaps, his acceptance of this emphasis illuminates how completely he can divorce his mode of serving clients from the stark realities of his professional existence. Existential counseling tends to live with the myth that the counselee is a free agent if only he would choose to exercise his freedom. Moreover, by elevating individual choice and responsibility to the level of sacred principle, the existential counselor need not examine his own and his client's powerlessness. Interviewing a faculty member on behalf of an inarticulate student or channeling a student's dissatisfaction into constructive participation in the affairs of the college requires a perspective and set of counseling skills different from those of the existential counselor.

A counselor's unwillingness to intervene on behalf of a client is sometimes rationalized by other theoretical positions. "My intervention would foster dependence" and "this is really the client's choice" deny the influence and power operating in the real world. One might attribute these attitudes to the counselor's counterdependence, his fears, or his lack of imagination. However, it would be a mere psychological ploy to assert that if the counselor would only develop the right attitudes and commitment and use his powers to the fullest, he would become a fully functioning counselor. Such a lopsided picture of what is wrong with college counselors would certainly betray a sociological naivete.

Whatever the counselor does or does not do occurs deep within the institutional matrix of the college. The counselor tends to be cast in a technological mold, and he cannot extricate himself singlehandedly from such entrapment. To say this need not imply that the college is an evil institution. It may be that the college is more benign and more receptive to change than most social institutions. But it is an institution. It has an authority structure and ostensible other values that do no necessarily coincide with the aims of counseling in fostering the fullest personal development of students. College counselors are not usually faculty members; nor do their aims necessarily coincide with them.

One need not be Machiavellian to recognize that the college as an institution may develop aims and modes of operation that are not in the best interests of its students. The college includes real people who covet power and status, and have objectives at odds with the humanistic goals of the college. When counseling is wholly dependent on such persons, it can be diverted from its professional aims. In order to have some hope of achieving those aims, the counseling service must be free to serve the students' needs (Kirk and others, 1970, p. 586). It is time to stop pretending that the college counselor can operate effectively in a no man's land. The duality of job and calling, the conflict between college counseling as a means of earning a living and as a mode of advancing student development, deserves more than tangential consideration. This duality is at least as significant as the counselor's diagnostic and therapeutic skills.

Being in a Large Institution

The college counseling center is generally viewed uncritically because it is in an academic setting. The traditions in higher education of openness, academic freedom, and research, as well as the constant renewal provided by new waves of students, surround the counseling center with attitudes that tend to protect it from the legitimate examination to which off-campus agencies are subject.

Until recently, psychology as a profession has been little concerned with the organization as an independent variable in human relations (Katz and Kahn, 1966). As far as most psychologists were concerned, the power relations in hierarchical organizations were part of a rational system for producing goods and services and modes of distributing rewards. But their impact in diminishing freedom and their effects on morale and job satisfaction were recognized only in recent years.

The relationship of the individual to the organization is important to the counselor in two ways. First, the college determines the functions of the counseling center, even though the individual counselors usually do not participate in these determinations. Second, increasing numbers of socially conscious students have begun to raise questions about their own roles in a world dominated by large organizations. The paradigmatic problem for the counselor, "How can I realize myself through college training and ultimately through a self-fulfilling occupational role in the economy?", has changed to "How can I survive as an individual in a world of gigantic corporate and public organizations?" In short, students are becoming more aware of organizational power as a significant dimension in their lives.

The traditional view of dynamic psychology concerning power in human relations is no longer satisfactory. According to this view, power is sought for pathological needs generated by peculiarities of personal development. In the course of normal development, no inordinate need to dominate others would arise. When industrial psychologists tried to introduce human relations into business organizations, they brushed aside power issues with the explanation that when workers are happy and satisfied in their work environment, questions of power do not arise.

We might expect counselor educators to be interested in the role of power in the nature and delivery of counseling services (Graziano, 1969). In other spheres of life, organizational relations —for example, trade associations, labor unions, and political alignments—reflect an awareness of the importance of power. However, in academia, the taboo against openly discussing power issues has broken down only since the end of the 1960s, with a number of college and university faculties accepting essentially labor contracts in which their power is spelled out and guaranteed. College counselors and other academic personnel believed that the legitimacy of our institutions made power an irrelevant dimension in the resolution of conflict. They believed that there were ample provisions for the redress of injustices without the use of power. This view is no longer as widely held as it used to be, but, generally, faculty and counselors engaged in wishful thinking—that in a reasonable academic world, reasonable men in power would ultimately make the necessary corrections.

The college counselor's lack of power is reflected in the ideological givens within which he must operate. Let us suppose that a number of students complain to a counselor that they feel lost on campus, that they find their professors inaccessible, that when they finally do encounter them, they seem hurried and distracted; too frequently they are sidetracked to a teaching assistant and feel themselves an inconvenience, almost superfluity. As a rule, the college counselor treats the complaint as a failure of individuals to adapt. He is condemned to this view both because of his original professional indoctrination and because defining the problem as a social-institutional one would bring him into conflict with the college power structure. The college counselor may know personally that the professors of which the students complain are seldom available for consultation and that they are engaged in various remunerative outside consultative activities which take them away from campus for extended periods of time. Nevertheless, he is not free to act on the basis of this information; at the least, any attempt to do so would be widely regarded as an affront to the whole faculty. A politically sensitive director of a college counseling center would feel obliged to sidetrack this kind of activity.

The counselor's position in a well-oiled large institution induces in him a sense of alienation (Levi, 1967). He must reduce his client's problems to matching youth and curricula, to lack of social skills and study habits, or most generally to individual existential problems. But if the counselor is a reasonably open person, he knows that this limited perspective does violence to his client. He is forced to regard his client as a scientific object which is not functioning fully. Yet he may recognize that it makes more sense to regard his troubled client as a spinoff of a malfunctioning college environment; he wants to have a full relation with the student, to share in the student's desire to humanize the learning process, and to relate it to the troublesome issues of the larger society. But these ideas are incompatible with his desire for security on the job, with the loves and hates engendered by his institutional ties, and with the ultimate possibility of moving from this situation of conflict to the more serene position of a regular faculty appointment.

Ultimately, he falls back on an attitude of scientific detachment with his clients, fellow counselors, and supervisors—a position which further splits and atomizes the unity of his experience. Whenever the counselor participates in student sensitivity groups, he experiences a vague sense of guilt and duplicity since he knows that he is viewed as a more integrated and courageous person than he is. Finally, he experiences a sense of alienation because he knows that being a counselor in a large institution is only tangentially related to student welfare. He is caught up in the spirit of capitalism, and his production is seen as comparable to the production of industrial workers.

The counselor is not alone in feeling alienated. He shares it with all whose occupations have been influenced by the advances of technology and bureaucratization. However, because of his ties to behavioral science, we might have expected the counselor to have more insight into the social forces that shape his own identity. Though the college counselor may have studied Freud, he has not had a proper regard for Freud's concept of the id. No picture of human behavior is complete without taking into account the far reaching influences of the irrational, the destructive, the blindly biological urges, and the capacity of man to distort and deny their existence. Counselors and psychotherapists have tended to shrink from the implications of this side of human nature, preferring to postulate a social impulse as more fundamental. At the social level, the analogue of the id is power. Power is undoubtedly used in the service of a coherent, functioning society and its institutions to ensure the survival of the state. But power also can be used against others for self-serving ends, for exploitation, and to maintain injustices. College counselors cannot properly evade the uses of power in their institutional web, for to do so is to evade their role in maximizing the freedom of their students.

Are college counselors deserving of greater self-determination vis-à-vis the administration? Autonomy is not granted a profession simply to satisfy a claim. The moral legitimacy of autonomy is based on specialized knowledge, the sanctity of the relationship with the client, and, we might as well admit it, a mystique regarding the special judgments that only duly trained practitioners can make. College counselors hopefully do not desire increased autonomy primarily for greater status, but for the social value which accrues from it. College counselors who wish the freedom to regard either the student or the university as the patient and to act on their diagnosis can scarcely avoid facing the issue of power and what must be done to legitimate it, and doing so with scrupulous attention to the interests of both students and the institution.

Current Ideologies

The college counselor is caught up in a number of contradictions which can be understood in the light of his ideology. The mental health principles which underly his operations place high values on independence and initiative, but he typically does not exercise much of either in his job. He subscribes to greater openness and candor in human relations than generally prevail in society, yet he is constrained in dealing with college and university authorities. In brief, in the waking hours of the early dawn, he is not much of a model by his own standards—until he reconciles what he does with what he professes by some rationalizations.

Counseling has not been much concerned with the ideological and metaphysical underpinning of its whole enterprise. Counseling literature is largely concerned with technical issues. Books such as Barclay's (1971) on the philosophical bases of counseling and Weinberg's (1969) on sociological foundations have had little influence. Counseling's technicism was taken uncritically from the various social sciences, and its humanism was drafted from conventional and popular wisdom. In the twenty-five years that I have been in the field, I have found the prevailing intellectual climate populist in its simplicity. Like the populists of the late nineteenth century and the technocrats of the 1930s, counselors followed simplistic formulae, such as matching youth and jobs, psychological and vocational testing without regard to development inequalities, and client-centered therapy. As a movement committed to self-realization, its history, catalogued in past issues of *Occupations* and *The Personnel and Guidance Journal,* is one of followership and accommodation with regard to the opening of new vistas of personal freedom for sections of the population denied it. Counseling has had no part, except a reactive one, in such national upheavals as school desegregation, civil rights, the struggle against racism and sexism, and mental hospital and prison reform. Yet all these issues impinge on the work of counselors, who often have little awareness of their implications.

Likewise, counseling has been relatively untouched by sociological and social psychological theory. Social psychological concepts such as bureaucracy, organizational roles, social class, power, leadership, and status are rarely invoked in the counseling literature (Katz and Kahn, 1966). Although college counselors are mostly of middle-class origin, there has been little exploration of the relationship between a counselor's social and class origins and the beliefs and attitudes he brings to counseling.

The obverse of Marxist and sociological disciplines has provided the prevailing climate in college counseling, as in the field of counseling generally. Briefly, it is romantic individualism and social Darwinism (Hofstadter, 1955) in the realm of psychology. This theory arose as the growing popularity of the theory of evolution in the nineteenth century was exploited by the apologists of laissez-faire capitalism. The social Darwinists postulated a principle of the survival of the fittest to explain inequities of wealth, education, and power. Just as natural law doomed certain species to extinction because of their failure to adapt, so, too, poverty and ignorance were natural outcomes of differences of ability and character. Social Darwinism and rugged individualism had two faces. The social face tried to explain and justify the status quo; it asserted that social arrangements were about as good as they could be and that governmental attempts to change them would be for the worse. The individual face extolled certain virtues as leading to success, such as hard work, loyalty to one's employer, initiative, and self-interest. The exponents of social Darwinism made no convincing attempt to relate its social and individual aspects. The attack on rugged individualism started early in this century, gained momentum at the hands of the muckrakers of the 1920s, and was dealt a coup de grace by professional economists (for example, Keynes, 1936) and political scientists in the 1930s.

The tradition of social Darwinism is implicit in individual counseling and psychotherapy. As Warnath (1971) points out, until recently the questions of how the high cost of such services would be met and their appropriateness and availability to the underclasses had not been seriously discussed. Actually the counselor and student who sought long-term counseling entered into their commitments conditioned by their respective ties to a middle-class world that had already guaranteed basic economic securities. When the counselor was confronted by a working-class client, he first had to face the probability that his client was not accustomed to dealing with his problems by reflection and self-examination, or to visualizing improving his present status by a change of perspective. Even after having won over his working-class client to the value of individual counseling, the counselor then had to stack his healing powers against the enormous power of the family, the ghetto, the leveling effects of impersonal institutions—in short, against the layers of social reinforcers (Bandura, 1969) that might have generated the student's problem in the first place.

Professional dyadic counseling is declining. It fell short because it promised too much, even to those whose social background made them aware of its benefits. And it promised far too much to those who were too disadvantaged to re-create themselves in a socioeconomic system that effectively froze their positions in the hierarchy. The shift to group counseling is a major step toward recognizing the limits of personal growth within the laboratory conditions of one-to-one counseling. As college counselors gain further experience with group counseling, they may move toward other environmental approaches, including concern for the total university as a growth milieu.

Partly as a consequence of their designated roles on campus and partly as a consequence of an anachronistic individualism perpetuated by their professional training, college counselors find themselves out of phase with the changing ideology of their brightest and most articulate clients. To college counselors, the most important arena for self-realization is work. Indeed, the college itself has assigned to the counseling center a prime responsibility for helping students in their vocational orientation. Having attained middle-class status by dint of hard work and self-denial, the counselor is likely to be impatient with those who do not share his views on industry and productivity. The unmotivated client embodies for him many of the indulgences and instant satisfactions which he had to repress to achieve his ambition.

The counselor's view regarding the central place of work in the life of the individual is being called into question, which poses a threat to the counselor's ties to the college. If he is to be true to humanistic values, he cannot invest any and all work with spiritual value. He ought to recognize that the spiritual view of work which has come down to him from a puritan past misrepresents most men's feelings about work. Cannot the counselor acknowledge that much of work continues to be an arena of exploitation? Getting out from under populist conceptions of work is not necessarily incompatible with viewing work as socially necessary in an interdependent society and attributing to it such positive values as these social aspects warrant. In closing his eyes to the destructive and wasteful aspects of work, the counselor is positing that the student can realize his full stature as a human being regardless of the social value of his work. The counselor's neutrality is one thing when invoked as a strategy for establishing rapport; it is something else when it is held as a basic principle. Then the counselor's neutrality moves toward an acceptance of the popular morality of an industrial civilization and a betrayal of his responsibility to help youth to distinguish between the trivial and essential in life, the human and depraved, and the beautiful and ugly (Roszak, 1969).

Since he must believe himself a model of self-realization for his clients, he must experience or beguile himself into believing that his own work as a counselor is useful and genuinely satisfying. But, as I have developed above, many factors deprive him of this satisfaction. Many of the problems and misgivings brought by college students to the counseling center are remarkably like those suffered by the counselor himself. College counseling should seek that middle ground between helping the client to adapt to and helping him change both the college and the larger world of work. After all, what other institution provides more congenial traditions and ideals for helping persons to become fully functioning individuals with due regard to social considerations?

Counselor as Change Agent

I write this chapter in the spirit of social criticism and do not intend to evaluate individual counseling outcomes with college students. Since the American pragmatism tends to ignore social criticism unless it is combined with suggested alternatives, the rest of this chapter is devoted to new relationships between the counselor and the college.

Beginning in graduate school, the counselor must be made aware of the entrapments and cooptations that await him as an employee of a college. A course in organizational psychology should make him aware of the gap between formal and informal structures, the politics of getting things accomplished, and the traps that await those who allow their good intentions to becloud the difficulties on the social scene. These ends can be furthered by giving preference for admission to graduate school to candidates with significant community and leadership experience. Preference can be justified on the ground that leadership abilities are required to deal with the increased use of group counseling, counseling aides, and outreach methods. Those most in need of counseling are the least likely to present themselves voluntarily. All these emerging functions add up to a set of traits and aptitudes somewhat different from those of the sedentary, reflective counselor who has prevailed until now. There is no evidence that candidates with a flair for the politics of counseling are intellectually inferior to those who are more individual- and feeling-oriented. On the contrary, some of the present younger candidates show a trait syndrome which combines antiintellectualism, an emphasis on the expression of feelings without regard to realities, and a tendency to privatism. They are not the type to provide the leadership necessary for a new direction in college counseling.

Graduate education should require membership in the counselors' professional association, as an important arena for the exercise of leadership and for influencing one's colleagues, and as an instrument through which counselors can reach a broad constituency. The college counselor has yet to build an identifiable professional organization free of the contamination of faculty and administrative interests. Those who work as counselors are typically junior members of professional organizations. These organizations are not quite company unions since they do afford scope for discussion and dialogue in the tradition of higher education. But it is difficult to determine which occupation any one of them represents since counselor educators, agency administrators, researchers, and general student personnel administrators may all be bona fide members. To recognize this situation is to recognize the vulnerability of the counselor in a service position, a vulnerability that is particularly crucial to his role as change agent.

In graduate school, the counselor-in-training should begin to make contact with his larger constituency, the student body. He should work with student committees, helping to channel their grievances into constructive ways of working with faculty and sifting out the emotionally immature demands of the students from the just ones; the experience will give him many opportunities to interpret to students the unique functions of the college counseling center. He should also have ample opportunity to practice the delicate role of ombudsman, resisting the temptations of playing to the students' gallery and of being corrupted by the influence of cynical faculty. There is such a middle road and there is an art of the possible which the agent of social change must travel and practice.

The counselor who moves out of his office is venturing into uncharted waters. But the inducement to do so is particularly high now. College administrators have become sensitive to the value of having a professionally trained intermediary between themselves and the students. If the counseling psychologist can demonstrate to students that he is truly free to express his professional opinions without fear of administrative retaliation, he can be a significant moderating influence on the campus with benefit to all parties. But he can hardly pass as free when his primary concern is meeting the institutional requirements for faculty appointment or with gathering data for a publication to bolster his promotional opportunities.

The financial retrenchment in higher education and the resulting freeze in personnel levels can provide an unexpected incentive to the college counselor to move into these new roles. The realization that the possibility of moving out of his present position has declined sharply may increase his incentive to make the most of his present position. There is no question that those counselors most likely to serve as change agents in the past were the ones who obtained more attractive positions elsewhere. Hopefully, today's poorer prospects for promotion will help retain them for more active roles.

When a counselor recognizes his role as that of change agent, he must reexamine his notion of neutrality. He must accept that his supposed neutrality was simply accepting functions assigned by the administration. For instance, when probationary or expelled students are referred to the counseling center, the student is told in effect: "This is quite a humane institution. We care about you; therefore we are referring you for counseling. Maybe a counselor can help you salvage something from your college experience." The counseling center is assigned the business of fishing sinking bodies out of the stream. But professionally trained counselors must be free to consult with the administration about moving upstream to discover the possible causes of student failures. It does make a difference where a counselor's time and efforts are deployed. To visualize alternatives to his present function the counselor must have a positive image of how he can serve college students; and he must get into the habit of thinking through problems independently of faculty and bureaucratic considerations.

The counselor's middle-class belief in work must be expanded to encompass the aspirations of youth who have new feelings about time, about repression of instinctual pleasures in the interest of achievement, and about the need for material goods—youth who see no need for a vocational objectives. Their views of work may not fit within any existing occupational title. These young people have injected a new dimension into counseling, yet their new values and priorities do not exempt them from the irresponsibilities and selfishness of earlier generations. The kind of counseling dialogue that can aid their personal growth cannot take place within the confines of a traditional therapeutic relationship. To begin with, the college counselor must be aware of the divided loyalties posed by humanistic and institutional demands, and he must be free to visualize his function as broader than being an adjunct to the teaching process. Some of today's students understand better than their counselors that in the most vital issues there often can be no neutrality and that neutrality itself may be a strategy in the service of some other well-defined purpose. A social injustice can be ignored, defended, or condemned. When a wise professor does none of these, he is neutral —not because he lacks a position but because he senses that the cause of justice may best be advanced by encouraging dialogue and enabling both extremes to understand each other.

Counselors can engender similar dialogue through the personnel services program. Ultimately, the "great refusers" must take their places in society and it is not too early to start while they are students. The counselor must visualize many meaningful, participative roles for his clients beyond the traditional work role: in social reform, community activities, nonremunerative intellectual and esthetic pursuits, and active participation in recreation. The counselor may come into conflict with the administration which defines his functions narrowly. As an occupational realist, however, the counselor knows that many of his clients will have to discover their essential identities through avenues other than work in the economy.

Counseling texts generally mention neither the critical counseling problems posed in this section nor the social context of counseling in general. As far as the texts are concerned, counseling occurs in an antiseptic vacuum. It is curious that a text such as Truax and Carkhuff (1967) has generated considerable interest in the personal qualities of the counselor that contribute to the growth of clients. But neither the book nor the discussion it has generated has explained the organizational ties of counseling and their potential for reinforcing such qualities as warmth, empathy, and authenticity.

A New Balance

We have now come to the point where we must bring together the several threads of this chapter. I have expressed disappointment that the college counselor has not employed a wide range of disciplines to study his situation. I have challenged the common conception of the counselor as a humanistic, scientific functionary in a rational institution. I have used the term *throwness* to trigger with the reader varied ways of examining the college counselor's employment. To repeat: He is not only that person trained in psychodiagnostics, counseling theory, and practice. He is that person who seeks to realize himself through such activities, to have a part in the economy, to satisfy his needs for status and recognition, and even to have some insight into the ways in which these sometimes conflicting needs influence each other. Throwness also connotes that his "thereness" could be taken for granted and therefore did not have to be properly analyzed. One aspect of his thereness is that he is in a profession and a situation that draws a sharp distinction between what is inside and what is outside. The counselor might believe that he chose this profession as a career, but he might be only vaguely aware that his choice was influenced by his middle-class values of neoromantic individualism.

That which is inside can, by that shake of the head that reverses foreground and background, be viewed as outside the counselor. The counselor's racial origin is not only the attitudes that he carries about with him—for example, that others might devalue him. If, for instance, the counselor is Mexican-American and was raised in the Southwest, his attitude correlates with that of other persons. The counselor's job is outside—it exists in the college. But what holds him to the job is inside if that is where we wish to locate his responsibility for his family and his self-concept.

Counseling psychologists have been obsessively concerned with being objective about their clients and justifying their procedures with supporting empirical data, but in the process they have been unaware that they lack a paradigm by which to inform others about their relations with the social environment. Is it not timely to recognize a politics of counseling and a social psychology of practice? By facing away from the client, and toward our institutional and societal ties, we could develop theories, practices, and research methods that would make us relevant to student needs. The data generated may bear no resemblance to or have any basis of comparison with those currently in our professional journals since their basic assumptions are different. The building-block theory of knowledge accrual is valid only within a given perspective. But Kuhn (1962) asserts that a scientific breakthrough occurs before the relevant data are at hand and that innovators are willing to go their own ways without requiring a higher order concept that explains why the old was wrong and the new was right. The latter theory typically emerged late in the evaluation of competing theories.

I hope that a case has been made for the college counselor in his setting as an interesting subject of study. I have tried particularly to state the hypothesis that the counselor's modus operandi cannot be adequaely interpreted in terms of his theory. The principles of learning which have proven so generative in understanding students can well be applied to the counselor. I have hypothesized that the counselor is rewarded for operating on the assumption that the student is the patient. Precious little on the college scene rewards him for regarding some other part of the college structure as the patient.

I have tried to steer clear of painting the college counselor's professional dilemma as a shortcoming of character and will. The spirit of social criticism demands that the counselor be properly identified in institutional and ideological space. The counselor is the doctor of the student's ego because the college frequently does not allow itself to be treated. But the counselor's professional training, the protestant ethic of work, and his counseling theories all make this assumption viable.

The suggestion that the counselor try out the role of doctor of the milieu opens the door to his possibly being all things to all people. The counselor can not be concerned with many aspects of the students' environment, however, the modern college is a complex ecology which requires the expertise of many others than psychologists if it is to function properly. The counselor can recognize the interdependence of students and various aspects of the college without getting lost in the woods. As for the institution, it has self-serving reasons to keep the counselor where he is.

The alternative to broadening the counselor's role to encompass the pathogenic aspects of the students' environment is to continue in the groove of romantic individualism, the self-made man, and the belief that the road to success is paved with traditional virtues—an alternative in the image of the inner-directed man of the nineteenth century (Riesman, 1950).

In an age of conformity such as in the immediate postwar years, the counselor's concerns were more or less clearly defined and were substantially the same as those of his clients. Currently, however, many students are asking questions about healthy human development and about lifestyles—questions that cannot be answered through the counselor's repertoire of technical methods. The counselor can deal with the question "Am I healthy or sick?" But students are also questioning university procedures and their relations to the larger society. Such students would like to view the counselor also as an environmental mental health specialist. It requires reeducation for the counselor to feel comfortable as doctor of the milieu. He is not accustomed to being in the center of controversy, he lacks the arts of leadership, and he certainly does not have the power base from which to launch this new role. Nevertheless, a declining number of the new waves of students entering colleges and universities will place high priority on the counselor's individual psychological services. They will be expecting counselors to lead them in humanizing the environment of higher education.

II

Education for
Human Development

Burns Ballantyne Crookston

Those who have worked to move higher education toward the philosophy and idealism of general education have had little if anything to cheer about in recent years. The reforms generated by a decade of turbulent change had shown great promise. At long last, it was hoped, higher education might in practice begin to accomplish what it had exalted in theory: the intellectual and creative development of the individual and the utilization of knowledge, not as an ultimate end, but as a means to individual growth and societal development. Under this banner the founders of general education saw the full, rounded, and continuing development of the person to be the first goal of education for democracy. "The discovery, training, and utilization of individual talents," declared the report

of the President's Commission on Higher Education (1947, p. 5),
"is of fundamental importance in a free society. To liberate and
perfect the intrinsic powers of every citizen is the central purpose of
democracy, and furtherance of individual self-realization is its
greatest glory." But general education was to become hopelessly
ensnarled in the same academic specialization and proliferation that
had figured so prominently in motivating its creation. And, although
the etiology of the student revolt of the sixties was replete with social,
political, economic, and scientific factors, a leading cause for the
assault on education itself appears to have been the failure of higher
education to accomplish the goals of general education.

Paradoxically, although the goals of general education remain more viable than ever, it is difficult even to get a discussion
of general education going in colleges and universities these days.
Instead, attention has been focused on the dramatic shift of public
interest and public dollars to vocationalism and career development.
Student response to educational issues generated in the colleges
during the sixties had typically escalated quickly from verbal confrontation with college administrators to physical violence. As the
disobedience of the child focuses the parent's attention on the
behavior rather than upon the stress which produced it, so the
institutions of higher education, pressed by an angry public, put
down the rebellion and punished the offenders. Made uncomfortable
by an investigation of the causes, institutions, under the convenient
cover of an economic crisis and public disenchantment with higher
education, have quietly filed away the investigative reports and gone
on to deal with the immediate concerns of dwindling enrollments,
money shrinkage, jobless graduates, academic retrenchment, and
faculty unionism. Tragically, these problems are also consequences
of the failure of higher education to accomplish the goals of general
education. Even more tragic is that the energy expenditure on these
problems will bring, at best, only temporary relief. This relief will
further delay, perhaps fatally, the essential task of making general
and liberal education fulfill the goal of enriching lives and gearing
society to accommodate and enhance the enrichment.

Despite this gloomy scenario, indications are that the move
toward a more student-centered higher education, while temporarily
derailed, will continue and transform undergraduate education. Of

particular importance are two related developments. First, an increasing number of college teachers have discovered that the goals of general education probably will never be achieved by continued preoccupation with subject matter; the focus must be on the student in a world of accelerating change. Such a shift in emphasis requires not only different teaching methodology but the acquisition of many new teaching skills. Second has been a parallel discovery by college counselors that effective practice of their art with contemporary students must include skills that go far beyond those required in the privacy of the consultation room. Like those of the new teacher, the skills of the new counselor focus on helping the student grow and develop in a changing world. These new approaches have much in common. A convergence of teaching and counseling into a collaborative teaching-learning model provides a basis for an emerging theory of human development, which could help achieve the outcomes that have thus far largely eluded the proponents of general education. How such a theory of human development can be applied is better understood with some brief perspective on what went wrong with general education.

Transforming General Education

While it is tempting to place the blame for the decline of general education on external forces, the principal difficulties were within the movement itself. Dressel (1961) attributes the decline to conflict in philosophy, accommodation to the existing organization of the college, and separation of student personnel work from instruction. To these factors should be added the problem of inadequate methodology that underscored all the other difficulties.

Conflict in Philosophy. To understand the nature of the conflict in philosophy of general education it is necessary to define terms. Recognizing that a pure educational philosophy rarely can be identified as descriptive of a given institution, Taylor (1952) describes three generally accepted types: rationalism, neohumanism, and instrumentalism. To the rationalist the sole aim of education is the development of intellect and reason. Neohumanism, while recognizing the primacy of cultivating the mind, assumes a dualism of mind and body, reason and emotion, thought and action. In

contrast to rationalism, in which truth and knowledge are the ultimate end, and to neohumanism, which separates the mind from the
body, instrumentalism emphasizes the full and creative development
of the whole person. Knowledge is applied not only to the growth
of the person but to the development of society as well. While
general education was clearly rooted in instrumentalism, the application of knowledge toward the fulfillment of man and society, the
teachers of general education were predominantly rationalist in the
liberal tradition, concerned with intellectual, esthetic, and moral
values, and timeless truth found in the great works of man over the
centuries; or they were neohumanists, concerned also principally
with developing the intellect and rational processes, but recognizing
the additional value of personal, social, emotional, and physical
development. Dressel (1961) notes that personal and social development as concepts were unacceptable to the rationalist because the
very word *development* suggests the instrumentalist view that
morality is relative to time and society. Consequently, instrumentalism, upon which general education was conceptually based, was,
ironically, rarely taught.

   Inadequate Methodology. An equally devastating conflict
in general education existed (and still exists) around teaching
methodology. While the controversy raged over what to teach, the
technology and the skills required to teach instrumentalism were yet
to be created. The rationalists saw teaching general education purely
as an intellectual exercise and readily, if not a bit smugly, concluded
that only the more able students were capable of mastering it.
Millions of first-generation college students, motivated by vocational,
economic, and social mobility considerations, found themselves enrolled in general education only to find "seeking after the truth" to
be both bewildering and sometimes humiliating in the face of
academicians who did not hesitate to communicate their disdain of
having to teach students with such pedestrian minds. The approach
to knowledge was theoretical, leaving to the student the task of
translating theory into practice after college. The function of higher
education, declared Bettelheim (1969), is "preparation for something you do later." The instrumentalist would argue that the
student learns to understand and cope effectively with human
problems by getting directly involved with them while a student,

relating what he learns in the classroom with direct experience and vice versa. Such a person, responded Bettelheim (1969), is "no longer a student at all, because he clearly rejects knowledge as a precondition of any meaningful activity." Thus the scenario had been drawn for the stressful sixties in higher education. The acceleration of change had created a sense of urgency in the students that rendered this insular, contemplative style of the academy an obsolete luxury. Writing at the height of the stress Bettelheim (1969, p. 6) observed, "Students bring the problems of society with them through the gates of the campus into the classroom. So do the faculty. The overwhelming urgency of the urban crisis, poverty, the Vietnam war, the omnipresent threat of nuclear war, inhumanity, disease, pollution of our streams and atmosphere, and other human-linked problems, the students say, just will not wait four years while we search for the truth and learn how to think!"

Primacy of the Department. Those who attempted to establish general education programs were confronted immediately with the vested interests and power of the academic departmental structure and its highly specialized teaching faculty. It was extremely difficult to find a teacher with sufficiently broad knowledge, interest, and perspective to teach general education successfully. When such a professor was identified he was often unwilling to pit general knowledge against that of scholars in specialty areas. So deals had to be made, and a holistic concept became fragmented and was parceled out to separate departments. By 1960 the system at many institutions had deteriorated so that students chose six to eight courses from as many as eighty specialties in four areas, such as humanities, social sciences, biological sciences, and physical sciences, in order to complete their "general education" requirements. Thus, the seeds of irrelevance, which was to become another battle cry of the sixties, had been sown.

Separation of Student Personnel. The fourth principal difficulty that led to the diminution of general education was the historic separation of student personnel work from the academy. At one time student personnel work was defined in instrumentalist terms as education (Clothier and others, 1931). It is interesting to speculate what might have happened if the leaders of the early student personnel movement had been able to join forces with those who led the general education movement in the late twenties and early thirties, instead of proceeding toward further separation from the curriculum. Certainly the knowledge of student growth and development, student culture and the campus community, and the skills of counseling, appraisal, advising, and group processes that were to be developed in the student personnel sector could have been a great asset in strengthening general education programs, particularly effective developmental teaching in these programs. But sufficient knowledge and skills were not then in existence. Student personnel workers were functioning largely as benevolent parent surrogates or as nondirective counselors. They had not yet learned to be catalysts and facilitators of learning.

Unfortunate Terminology. Like the term *student personnel* —a descriptive anomaly that has created widespread semantic difficulties, misunderstandings, and misperceptions for a half century —the term *general education* has suffered a similar fate. There have been many noble and lofty attempts to define it philosophically and educationally. Yet to academicians, students, and public alike, general education has continued to symbolize the watering down of solid disciplines and a glossing over of areas of knowledge, which presumably must be pursued with depth and rigor. And, despite eloquent appeals from leaders of the movement itself, like McGrath (1972), in a period of public support for career education and technical training, general education seems even more nonutilitarian and remote. Although McGrath reminds us that general education is still alive and well at a number of institutions, one must seriously doubt that either the universities or the liberal arts colleges will update themselves under the banner of general education. The image is perceived too negatively to remodel it.

What is needed is to transform education so that it neither focuses on subject matter requirements and syllabi, nor attempts to fit the student into a cultural heritage, but becomes a model of human development that teaches students the processes of discovering what is known and applying that knowledge to a deeper understanding of self, of enhancing the quality of relationships with others, and of coping effectively with their world. The teachers of human development are likely to be developmentally trained counselors and other applied social and behavioral scientists, liberal arts and humanities faculty who have become student-centered teachers.

Toward Developmental Teaching. During recent years much has been written of the trend in undergraduate education away from "irrelevant" subject-matter learning toward empirical, first-hand experiential learning. In the late 1960s only a handful of institutions were experimenting with living-learning programs, inter-disciplinary courses, student-initiated learning, free universities, student-teacher learning contracts, or off-campus learning designs, but today such innovations are commonplace. Many of the most successful learning experiences have focused on the individual student, his own development, or his interaction with physical and social environments. While critics have noted that many experimental programs are expiring, this should in no way minimize their impact on existing undergraduate education. Experiments are designed to create new knowledge whether they succeed or fail. If experiments succeed they become legitimized and institutionalized, thus losing their experimental quality. As history tells us, to invoke change from an established order it is sometimes necessary to propose or experiment with radical departures, often viewed by the majority as revolutionary. In the process of putting down the revolt, the established order often finds itself giving some ground, making certain concessions, or compromising. The resulting "failure" thus brings about some change in the established order, which describes not only what happened to a number of experimental colleges and free universities, but also the substantial gains made in response to other familiar revolt issues, such as inadequate teaching, irrelevant course work, ivory tower insularity to immediate problems, and recognition of student rights and freedoms.

While the spotlight during the revolutionary 1960s was focused on demonstrations and disruptions, other dramatic changes were quietly taking place within the classroom, much of it in the direction of human development methodology. Existentialism, the focusing inward on the self, the beliefs that existence precedes one's essence—and that the individual must take responsibility for one's life, had had great impact, not only on faculty and students, but upon society as well. As the examining of one's own life becomes academically legitimate, the pedagogical focus must necessarily turn from the subject to the student. The slaughter and carnage of the first war in history to be viewed live and on camera from the living room, the legacy of the Nürnberg trials (from which emerged a morality that one cannot escape the responsibility for killing others, even in the line of duty), the awesome awareness of man's nuclear capability of world destruction, the pollution of earth, air, and water, combined with the telescoping of time and distance into accelerating change, have brought about a new wave of humanism, of interest in human values, human relationships, and world community. Self-examination must include making sense out of a seemingly senseless world and forming a means of coping with it.

The changed relationship between the student and the university also has had dramatic impact on teaching. The end of the parental role of the college, the enfranchisement at age eighteen, and the legal and institutional recognition of the rights and freedoms of college students have cumulatively shortened the period of adolescent dependence. From the time they enter the gates of the campus, students now are to be treated as adults. The drive toward attaining adulthood at an earlier age is reflected in the current boom in career training. Learning a trade is the way to financial independence, thus allowing students to express their new-found adult status earlier than before. On many campuses students have not only been given primary if not complete responsibility for their own governance, but also are afforded greater opportunities to participate in the governance of the college as a whole. There is a further trend toward student policy or operational control of such student services as residence halls, student unions, student activities, bookstores, and commissaries.

Despite signs of return to traditional pedagogy, instructors have been learning new teacher-student relationships. As the new adult student takes increased initiative and responsibility for his learning, the instructor must become versatile and serve as catalyst, expert, critic, facilitator, collaborator, consultant, negotiator, or contractor—all functions of human development teaching. New instructional technologies have emerged: experience-based learning approaches, the laboratory method, small groups and student teams which involve instructors in group processes and group development methodology. The use of electronic devices for skill practice and multimedia approaches to information dissemination have added new dimensions to learning that extend far beyond the traditional teacher at the head of the classroom, students at desks, paper and pencil work, and other conventional classroom approaches of the past. Often the best instructors are young professors who have successfully negotiated the research-oriented, specialized graduate schools without losing their determination to make undergraduate learning far more creative than the alienating, compartmentalized curricula and obsolete teaching methods to which they themselves were subjected as undergraduates.

Sometimes the instructors are students. Mead (1970) describes the present culture as prefigurative, meaning that, for the first time in history, the old learn from the young. With the increased involvement of the students in defining, participating in, and evaluating collegiate learning experiences by means of differential arrangements and interactions or in utilizing those experiences of his own which are relevant to the learning task, the student on occasion does indeed become the teacher and the teacher the student.

A number of liberal arts colleges have been experimenting with new developmentally oriented courses, particularly at the freshman and sophomore levels—courses that focus on the application of knowledge to the student's own growth and development as a person and to enhancing his ability to cope in a world of accelerating change. They have thus been able to hold constant or increase their enrollments while colleges with more traditionally taught courses watch their entering classes dwindle. The emphasis on effective teaching that seems to be gaining momentum focuses heavily on teachers capable of working effectively within the developmental frame—facilitating, consulting, collaborating. With more imaginative teaching and a human development focus at the elementary and secondary levels, students increasingly will be able to develop the skills to set their own learning goals and behavioral objectives, negotiate with a teacher on the use of his knowledge and expertise, and through creative interaction with the teacher and work successfully carry the learning contract through to completion. Such teaching-learning interactions are not likely to occur under the rubric of general education, although such may well be the case at those few institutions which developed and applied instrumentalist methodology. The conditions and technologies of learning that focus on the student should appropriately be called human development.

Counseling and Student Development. While classroom teachers have been creating a new teaching form and expression directly applicable to the developing student in a changing environment, an even more dramatic metamorphosis has been taking place outside the classroom. As the seeds of student unrest spread from campus to campus in the mid-sixties, staff in college counseling centers discovered that many of the most pressing issues confronting students could not be resolved through traditional one-to-one interviews in the counseling office. They became convinced that this historic, passive, reactive, remedial counseling stance must give way to an active, preventive, collaborative, and, later, encountering or confronting relationship with students (Ivey and Morrill, 1970; Hurst and Ivey, 1971; Warnath, 1971, 1972). Joined by other student affairs staff, counselors moved out onto the campus, into the community, into the drug scene, actively seeking out students, encountering, consulting, facilitating, confronting, and otherwise influencing them toward effective resolution of their problems. But these newly adopted roles created new difficulties. The skills required were rarely included in the training programs for counseling psychologists or other counseling center staff and consequently were possessed by few practicing counselors (Warnath, 1971). In response, writers in the field urged various new counselor training models, adapted in part from the fields of community mental health and community psychology, to provide such skills and competencies (Koile, 1966; Oetting, 1967; Morrill, Ivey, Oetting, 1968), but of necessity those on the firing line had to experiment with campuswide counseling approaches of their own creation. The combination of theory with trial-and-error practice soon became known in the field as the student development movement.

Student development is defined here as the application of human development in the college setting. Its aim is to move the student toward fulfillment as a realized person and as an effective, contributing citizen of a community and of the world. In student development the old classroom-extracurricular dichotomy no longer exists. The entire academic community and beyond is a learning environment in which teaching and learning can take place, whether it produces academic credit or not; hence, the teacher of student development teaches in multiple situations, including the classroom (Crookston, 1972a).

Human Development

Human development refers to the knowledge, conditions, and processes that contribute both to the growth, development, and fulfillment of the individual throughout life as a realized person and effective, productive citizen, and to the growth and development of society. The relationship between the individual and society should be symbiotic, that is, mutually growth-producing. As the individual contributes to the enrichment of society, so the society is able to enrich the individual. Human development is based on the belief that for life to have meaning and purpose it must be examined by the person who must live it. *Education for human development* is the creation of a humans learning environment within which individuals, teachers, and social systems interact and utilize developmental tasks for personal growth and social betterment (Crookston, 1970). A *developmental task* is any experience that contributes to individual development (Oetting, 1967) or which helps individuals or groups function effectively in their world. Developmental learning can include inquiry, growth, experience, analysis, and personal synthesis. It can be based on such questions as: Who am I? Why am I here? Is there a purpose or meaning to my life? If so, what is it? If there are purposes and meanings in my life, how can I best fulfill them? What is the significance of other persons in my life? What have others contributed to my life? What should they contribute? What distinguishes me from others? How do I relate to the physical world? How should I relate to it? What do I need to learn and accomplish to fulfill this relationship to the physical world? How do I relate to my community, to my country, to humanity? How should I relate? What parts of me need further development? How do I accomplish this development?

In relation to each of these questions a series of developmental tasks emerges: First, collecting basic data: What is there in history, philosophy, culture, tradition, science, or technology that can be brought to bear on the question? What can be applied to this question from my own experience, from the experience of relevant others: teachers, parents, friends, enemies, siblings, grandparents, employers, employees, coworkers, peers, playmates, counselors? Second is analyzing the data and applying them to the problems at hand. Third is planning action steps: What experiences will give me further insight and understanding? What expert knowledge and assistance will I need? What additional knowledge and skills must I acquire? Next is taking the action steps; then collecting data on the action and evaluating the outcome. Then comes analysis: What has been learned? And, finally, synthesis—incorporating the learning experience into a definition of the self or redefining the self as a logical consequence of the learning experience.

Implicit in the above series of developmental learning tasks that would describe the human development curriculum is the necessity that the relationship between teacher and student be carefully defined. The teaching of human development includes any experience in which a teacher interacts with students as individuals or in groups that contributes to individual, group, or community growth and development and can be evaluated (Crookston, 1970). Teaching is organized around the student, not around the subject; therefore, the student must accept at least equal responsibility with the teacher for the quality of the learning content, process, and product. Human development learning takes place not only in the classroom but outside as well—on the campus, in the residence halls, in the community, even in other countries. Evaluation is based on competence and goal achievement, rather than on requirements and prerequisites. The awarding of credit, if used, becomes flexible and negotiable between student and teacher. Those who interact with the student in ways that yield to evaluation, whether as facilitators, consultants, experts, counselors, or masters of knowledge, are all teaching faculty, all contributing in differential ways to the intellectual, psychological, emotional, cultural, moral, physical, professional, and humane growth and development of the student. These teachers come from many disciplines and professions, but principally from the applied social and behavioral sciences. Developmentally oriented counseling psychology can and should emerge as the principal preparation and training ground for many teachers of human development in the college.

Affective Rationality. The recent legitimation of experience-based, affective learning, when combined with intellectual processes, can lead to affective rationality, a central expression of human development. *Affective rationality* is the capability to recognize and understand feelings and translate them into rational action. What is known about repression indicates that the less one is in touch with one's feelings the more irrational the "rational" actions become. Education for human development should help the individual use his brain to deal with his feelings; to put emotion to work; to recognize creative, growth-producing impulses and be able to set them free; to recognize destructive impulses and learn not only to understand and control them but perhaps even to convert their energy into growth-producing experiences. The function of the teacher of human development, therefore, is to help create a humane learning environment of affective rationality.

Human Development Teacher. Four interrelated competencies are needed for human development teachers: student-centered teaching, training, consulting, and evaluating. The most effective human development faculty are competent in all four. In practice, individual talent and interests, combined with the necessity for a division of labor, would undoubtedly lead a number of faculty to expend more of their efforts in a given area. The student-centered teacher would be the formal guide, advisor, and teacher of the student along the complex journey toward the examination of self, self-others, self-others-group, self-others-community-world, self-nature-society, self-science-technology-society, and self-life-death. Ideally this principal relationship would continue over the entire period the student is in college, helping the student design, complete, and evaluate developmental tasks, and integrate into himself experiences initiated by others in which he participates. Teaching skills emphasized in this role would be basic helping skills, individual and group counseling, problem-solving, and application of the scientific method in designing, completing, and evaluating developmental tasks. Depending on the nature of the relationship with the student, the teacher could be expert, catalyst, critic, facilitator, mediator, consultant, negotiator, counselor, collaborator, and contractor for developmental learning contracts. The setting could be any place required for the successful completion of a developmental task—classroom, laboratory, library, residence hall, gymnasium, ghetto, downtown, uptown, in or out of the country—depending on the nature of the task and the resources needed. As the student grows in awareness he will need to acquire new knowledge and skills related to such areas as man, human behavior, nature, science, good and evil, which requires reading, listening, and discourse with experts and, where indicated, training in a variety of fields. The knowledge becomes incorporated into the student's definition of himself, which undergoes continuous reexamination. By means of systematic evaluation, the student is able to develop a life plan and to assess progress toward its fulfillment. The hoped-for outcome would at last be the accomplishment of the goals of general education cited earlier: to liberate and perfect the intrinsic powers and further the self-realization of every citizen.

The training, consulting, and evaluating functions would sustain and support the principal teaching function and at the same time provide the means by which institutions could engage in a continuous progress of self-renewal, as suggested by Parker (1971). Training activities would include work with individual students, faculty, staff, parents, and others who have relationships with students as they work on their developmental tasks. Skills to be developed through training would include leadership and member skills in groups, organizations, communities; counseling and other individual helping skills; training people to train others; and, most important, training faculty from diverse disciplines and professions the skills required for teaching human development. Consulting activities would focus primarily on renewal functions such as helping groups, organizations, departments, administrative units, program units, and service units to change as needed: to assess goals, collect data, make decisions on action, take action, evaluate effectiveness, set new goals, plan new action. The consultant would help organizations improve effectiveness by means of team building, improving communication skills, and other organization development and human development technologies. The function of evaluation would be twofold. The first is to contribute through theory and research to the knowledge base about students in higher education (Parker, 1971): how they best learn, grow, and develop; the type and quality of learning environments; and organizational models most conducive to such growth. Studies could include human development, organizational functioning, status, power, values, and culture as they occur in the higher educational community. The second is to assist students, faculty, and staff in developing their own evaluation procedures and in designing research.

The late Abraham Maslow stated that such human needs are hierarchical. Concern for self-actualization (which is the ultimate goal of human development) gives way to the expression of lower level needs, such as those for food or for security. One finds it difficult to be concerned about actualization when one is hungry or one's job is threatened. Vocationalism also can be looked upon as the beginning of a brave new world, a giving up and "dropping in" of the present generation by plunging into work in much the same way the beat and hippie generations before them dropped out from the meaninglessness of the workaday world. Work has the advantage of keeping mind and body occupied, thus avoiding the necessity of thinking about the sorry lot of man and having to deal with the guilt of doing nothing about it. However, the motive toward acquiring the skills for a job most likely is linked to the shortening of adolescence, as noted above. In a utilitarian society, where persons are valued for what they do over what they think, it is important to one's sense of worth to have a skill that can produce something. The newly acquired status of legal adulthood at eighteen has a hollow ring unless the eighteen-year-old also has achieved economic independence.

In any event, the need for human development has never been greater. The acceleration of change, the awareness of a timeless and endless universe, the stark reality of world citizenship simply do not allow most people to escape long into the false security of making a living by day, watching TV by night, and recreating on weekends. If technology and science were capable of solving the basic developmental tasks and dilemmas of humanity, the problems should have been solved by now. Those who fail to make sense, purpose, and direction for their lives while young most assuredly will find it difficult to do so later. Later consideration can also be much more traumatic, particularly when the realization comes at mid-life that many years have been wasted. But, for many, the temptation may be compelling to live in a regulated, physically secure, electronically managed world in which technological diversions or pharmaceutical nostrums enable one to successfully escape, or at least indefinitely delay, the inevitable self-confrontation. The behaviorists have demonstrated in the laboratory that such a regulated world is clearly within the realm of possibility, as Thorstein Veblen predicted and Aldous Huxley fantasized. But if man is conditioned to accept a managed life, so can education for human development enable him to become a thinking, acting, creative, interdependent being. In any case the underlying assumption is that some person or group is in a position to make such a decision. Presumably in a democracy the people themselves decide. Even though our historic concept of education has been pragmatic, we have also desired that education provide some "common sense" of morality and citizenship and an appreciation of the "finer things in life." People probably do not want to abandon these expectations and leave them to the chance of individual choice. The people have already turned over to the schools the responsibility for the teaching of moral values, of social relations, of citizenship, and of personal, social, and even sexual development—all components of human development. Human development is in essence a process of self-confrontation made possible by a conducive learning environment and interaction with skillful, expert teachers. Though the examined self can be an exhilarating, fulfilling experience, even under the best of circumstances self-confrontation is a painful, often threatening process, easy for many individuals to avoid and put off indefinitely. Thus education, as an expression of the will of the people, must build human development into the curriculum, not as part of upper-division or graduate work, but as a prerequisite for living a full and useful life in a democracy.

This is not to say that later examination of the self toward fuller development should not be encouraged; it is already happening via the continuing education opportunities of the public community colleges. Self-renewal toward fuller development and life enrichment should be a continuous process. The optimum time for an in-depth examination varies with the individual. Many older persons insist that because of immaturity or lack of motivation, they would have profited little from such an exploration during earlier years. To some who prefer the simple, uncomplicated life, the urge may never come, as they remain content to live out their lives free from fretting over the meaning of it all. But if education is based on the tenet that life has little meaning and purpose unless it has been examined by those who must live it, then education, armed with the knowledge that individuals often have a tendency to flee from such self-examination, should provide the means by which such examination takes place early and often thereafter. Thus a pattern of examination, or self-renewal, using Gardner's (1963) phrase, would be built into the lives of people, reducing the likelihood of the trauma of discovering later that one's life has not been well lived.

The current emphasis on vocational and career development is by no means incompatible with human development; the process of life planning becomes a necessary part of it. Discovering what one can do with one's brains and body in the service of society in ways that are satisfying and fulfilling is at the heart of the process of self-examination. Taylor (1952, p. 41) notes, "The factor which determines whether or not an art or a science is liberal is whether or not it relates to the enrichment of the life of the individual who learns it. Enrichment in this sense goes beyond the practical use made of it in earning a living or in altering the physical or social environment into its use as serving the interests and needs of the individual." The more advanced thinkers and planners in the field of career development are making self-development and life planning a basic component from kindergarten on. Hansen (1972, pp. 243–44) describes the concept: "It provides for exploration of self in relation to educational and vocational pursuits and in consideration of the place that work and leisure have in a person's life. It assumes that a career covers a variety of roles people play in life, including those of student, spouse, parent, and worker. It sees career development as one aspect of human development that forms a natural core for unifying curriculum and brings into consciousness what many teachers already are doing unconsciously."

Organization. Because it is the prime source of institutional change and renewal, the human development component should be given special status within the institution. The teaching and research functions of human development should give it the status of an academic subdivision, such as a school or college, with built-in protection against the exercise of status quo-motivated power being used to neutralize or destroy it. But unlike other more traditional academic units, human development serves as a resource for training in student-centered teaching skills and basic helping skills for all individual students, faculty, and staff and as a planned change and organizational renewal consultation service for all campus faculty, staff, and student organizations. Furthermore, depending upon the size, mission, and location of the institution, the human development unit could serve people of all ages in the surrounding community. (As a consequence, financial support for the human development program would have to be shared by the community.) Large institutions should give human development special status beyond an academic unit and other than a center or institute, which can be subject to political pressures. At the small liberal arts college, human development should be the principal academic component around which the college focuses its program for developing the student as an actualizing individual and contributing citizen.

In addition to being the prime source for change and renewal for the institution as a whole, the human development unit must have a built-in system for its own renewal. Regular rotation of faculty in and out of the center on four-year cycles can match the cycle of entering classes. Some faculty would receive training in methodology, teach human development, then move back into their disciplines or professions and apply human development concepts there. Others would do research and evaluation through the auspices of the human development unit. Those who utilize consulting, counseling, organizational behavior, or organization development skills in other settings could apply those skills for a period in human development. This constant shifting of personnel and clientele, together with regular goal setting, performance contracts, and evaluation would help perpetuate the planned change character of human development.

Along with the increased capacity of the institution to renew —owing to the impact of a human development component—such planned change efforts would be greatly facilitated by a systematic rotation of leadership from the presidency to the department level (Crookston, 1972b), long enough to accomplish goals and to remain goal-oriented and short enough to avert the corruption of power and resulting entrenchment.

In my review here of the philosophical and methodological difficulties that have beset general education, I have asserted that despite the current period of academic retrenchment and diversion of attention to vocational development, the move toward a human development orientation, both in and outside the classroom, has been significant. The phasing out of in loco parentis, along with other changes during the sixties, precipitated a dramatic shift in methodology from the paternal-control-remedial stance of the student personnel worker to the active-preventive-catalytic orientation of the student development educator. While general education, philosophically instrumentalist and methodologically rationalist, has fallen on difficult times, the extensive experimentation in classroom teaching and in creating learning environments, generated in response to widespread dissatisfaction with poor teaching and irrelevance of curricula, has brought about the rediscovery of the student as the central focus of teaching. Thus, general education and student development have both moved toward human development, the implementation of instrumentalist philosophy. The logical next step is to combine general education philosophy with student development methodology into a human development component of the college.

III

Confusions of
Counseling

David W. Palmer

The confusions of counseling are many. In the university, they fall into two general categories: confusions as to the distinctions among various sorts of counseling and confusions as to the place of each in the university and their contribution to education.

This chapter deals only with the first category. It will attempt to remove unnecessary and inappropriate overlays of meaning, and to clarify useful distinctions. It is a radical reexamination because it tries to return to the roots of the counseling function, which were once universally understood, if only at the intuitive level, but which today are poorly understood and in confusion. As a result, counseling has had a scattering of meanings, some misuse, and a great deal of uneconomical and sometimes tragic unuse. Only if we recover a sense of the fundamental human needs involved and the genotypic nature

of the function which once served them can we modify the present forms of the function to correspond to the contemporary world and its changed circumstances.

And certainly the world has changed in real ways and in the ways we conceive it. We are now a *self*-conscious society. We are increasingly aware of ourselves, each as individuals standing *out of* the society and culture. We are increasingly aware of many and different cultures, their different values and different effects. But we may have to return to an understanding of the sense of the village and the tribe to rediscover the necessary roles and functions they once offered and which the more slowly evolving nature of man still craves and needs.

The changes and confusions in the function of counseling are part of a phenomenon that pervades colleges and universities of any size. Students are uncertain as to what counselors offer. Is it therapy or advice? An answer or help in clarifying a question? They do not know how to tailor their expectations, and from this uncertainty comes much of their dissatisfaction. Faculty and staff are similarly confused and are not certain where to refer students—or when certain, find their expectations confounded. Even where palpable differences exist, administrators are as likely to equate counseling A with counseling B, or counseling C with either one. Legislators call for more counseling to insure more efficient allocation of expensive course work, but no one is quite sure which counselor should do it. Thus, tough-minded management consultants, the new architects of American higher education, are likely to cry, "A plague on *all* your houses."

The word *counselor* now has very little precise meaning. It has come simply to signify anyone who calls himself counselor and wants to be helpful, essentially through discussions in a one-to-one setting. The word is certainly used to suggest that its possessor has some particular understandings, that apply to certain areas of experience, sometimes, by implication, even to all areas of experience. Counselor is, of course, a more august title than adviser. "Counselor" and "counseling" imply more concern, less intent to direct or manipulate, and more important, carry certain connotations of the honorific or of the psychologically sophisticated.

Counselor is, of course, a useful and simple title. By now,

little can be done to differentiate its several uses by title change or semantic quibble. Were we to call certain counselors, say, consultants, to indicate a wider or different sort of experience, academic consultants, peer consultants, student consultants (meaning the consultant is a student), and student consultants (meaning the consultant offers counsel to students) would soon emerge. When all these in turn drop the prefix in daily use, we would be back where we are now: only everyone would be a consultant rather than a counselor.

There are real differences, of course; and, unhappily, students seeking counsel, at least in the United States, are confused about them. Most unfortunate, when they encounter a difference between what they have expected and what they are experiencing, they become confused and disappointed and may blame themselves for their unrealistic expectations rather than criticize the inappropriateness of the service they are receiving. Students deserve to understand the valuable differences that do exist between types of counseling and how to identify them. So do administrators and faculty.

To sort out a confusion of this sort is always difficult. One approach is through history. Whence come the counselors of today? It would be interesting to chart, linguistically, man's uses of the word, and the concept, *counsel*. One would presumably first trace the evolution of *counsel* to *counselor* (lower-case *c*)—the person who provided wise and friendly advice. Later, one further supposes, *Counselor,* became a formal social role, title, or profession in the ancient basic, generic sense, now rating a capital *C*. For example, the Councils and Councillors of princes.

It seems hard to believe that in the beginning, those who offered counsel carried a title; they were simply persons who could provide a sort of response. Between the *Councillor-at-state* or the *Counselor-at-law,* the latter is still the strong prevailing image in the word *counselor*. It would be safe to hazard that only in the late forties and fifties—did *counseling* and *counselor* take on the special connotation now associated with them. In this sense counselor becomes "a practice or professional service designed to guide an individual to a better understanding of his problems and potentialities by utilizing modern psychological principles and methods especially in collecting case history data, using various techniques of the personal interview, and testing interests and aptitudes." (*Webster's Third New International Dictionary*, 1969.)

In earlier usage, as in Shakespeare's "In friendship I do counsel thee," counsel is a centuries-old human function. "Counselor," the "practice or professional service," cited above, on the other hand, is a very late meaning, a very recent social variant— perhaps even aberration. I should like to call that earlier, older practice, *generic counsel*, and the latter, *psychological counsel*.

Today these two threads and their variants exist side by side. It is also safe to say that the psychological sense overshadows and obscures the older form, confusing those who try to provide for the discharge of that more ancient, fundamental role, even in the subtler, more self-conscious forms our age may require.

Before exploring these two threads and their variants it is useful to make explicit the connotations of the word *counsel*, as distinguished from *advice*. *Webster's New Dictionary of Synonyms* (1968), says: "Counsel often stresses the fruit of wisdom or deliberation, and presupposes weightier occasions than *advice* or more authority or a closer personal relationship in the one who counsels. . . . The noun sometimes suggests instruction or advice of a lofty or ideal character . . . Wisdom . . . deliberation . . . weightier occasions . . . more authority . . . a closer personal relationship in the one who counsels [one might infer a quality of concern] . . . suggests instruction or advice of a *lofty* or *ideal* character." Reading these elements, the word *counselor* today seems in contrast to these definitions to have suffered from attrition—or, like the currency, from inflation.

What are the uses or variants of *generic* counsel today? First are the resources that bring wisdom, deliberation, authority, and concern to occasions where some action is contemplated and understanding and advice are sought. A matter of law could be an example. The focus of the action and the counsel is external, although he who offers counsel will take certain aspects of the person into account. The critical skill or resource of the counselor is knowledge and wisdom in this *arena*, the probabilities of success and the hazards of certain courses of action, the probabilities of other men's behavior and the like. In this context, the counselor-at-law particularly the English solicitor comes to mind, or the councillor to princes. On campus one might imagine an experienced faculty member providing wise counsel to students about his field of his specialization. Perhaps we may simply call this *situational counsel* or _____ *counsel,* filling the blank with the arena of action involved; for example, *legal counsel, financial counsel, career counsel.*

Second among the variants of generic counsel are the forms that bring perspective and experience to internal considerations of the counseled. These include the sorting out of the individual's own searches and speculations, his intuitions and intimations, his fears and doubts, his uncertainties, anxieties, and feelings about himself or those closest to him, and a host of other concerns and questions. We might call this form *personal and private counsel.*

There are several ways to establish the distinction. The concept of distance is one of the most useful. This may suggest the distance between the individual's inner and vulnerable private self and the focus of his concern. Thus in situational counsel, the focus is more on the area: the legal setting, the workings of the law or the job market, the process of job choice. The individual's private self comes under less scrutiny. He is less vulnerable to others and more distant from the process of his examinations.

Personal and private counsel, by contrast, focuses on the individual's inner self. He is more vulnerable because he is more exposed, and his defenses are the subject of concern; his methods of dealing with the world and of keeping it at a distance are in the spotlight. There is less protective distance between him, the inner core of his being, and the focus of inquiry. He *is* the focus. Clearly, the expertise, the sophistication, the understanding, the ethics, of the counselor—the inner constraints and awareness he must employ—are of much more moment. The individual who seeks his counsel is much more at the mercy of the ignorances as well as the actions of him who provides counsel.

In situational counsel, feelings, vulnerabilities, confusions, and inner dynamics are at a distance for both parties. By contrast, in personal counsel, feelings run much closer to the surface—and feelings are contagious; they much more easily arouse their counterparts, or opposites, in him who seeks and him who offers counsel.

The close, often intense arena calls for sophistication in him who offers counsel—the experientially forged sophistication of the awareness of one's own self and feelings, needs, drives, mechanisms, vulnerabilities, irrationalities. He who offers counsel must be less the victim of his own unconscious workings. He must regain the element of distance lost in the shift from the external to the internal, from situational to personal and private counsel. He requires it as a dimension of wisdom, hammered out in the sufferings, the informed resolutions and the resignations of experience. It must also be, not just a kind of folk wisdom alone, but informed by some conscious knowledge of the subtle new awareness of man, his dynamics and of the workings of society, culture and institutions that study and formal learning have accrued.

The distinction between external and internal foci, between situational and personal, is of course arbitrary. No counsel can leave out consideration of the self; nor can the self leave out externals. But the distinction allows differential patterns of qualification and thus differential patterns of staffing.

There are tremendous difficulties with distinctions—and especially so with the word personal: everyone would insist that his work and attention were personal, and justly. But the word, in their objection, would have shifted in meaning from the precise denotation I have given it to the sense of friendly and concerned attention to the person. The shift, while understandable and human, obscures a relevant distinction. I have tried to strengthen that distinction by adding *and private:* personal *and private* counsel.

What is at stake is a recognition of a real continuum between two extremes (which might be called "external focus" and "internal focus"), and this leads to different or differentiated behaviors. It is a continuum from a greater concern for *normative* statements of objective fact or probability, on the one hand, to a concern, on the other, to listen to, recognize, help raise to consciousness, and help to deal with the idiosyncratic thoughts, intuitions, and feelings of a given individual. The differences between points on the continuum also carry implications for the professional and personal qualifications of the individual offering counsel and for the social safeguards that need to be provided (all men being in some measure and at some time fallible in areas of close personal relations). People's desires as to how they are called (employees, staff, "professionals") may well be observed in the titles of positions on the continuum. But such naming should not confuse the expectations of potential users of counsel.

The expectations of "potential users" are critical. In a simpler time, names or titles did not matter: people and their capacities became known through daily experience. Counsel was chosen by personal and communal knowledge. But today, names and titles must give partial indication as to expectation. And we should do more to have potential sources of counsel seen publicly, in other roles, where they may be tested and come to be known, as in the past.

There are several considerations as to names and titles, particularly in respect of personal and private counsel. First, they should *not* be psychological in connotation: forms of "counsel" offer an alternative to persons who do not want the psychological or psychiatric. Second, they should not connote mental health. Counsel offers an ancient and central social role, educative, developmental, and social, not healing, therapeutic, or medical. (There should be other resources called "psychiatric" and "mental health" for those who prefer these terms and their connotations.) Finally, titles should give some indication of broad primary areas of focus or at least initial entry significance. Such titles as Educational and Career Counsel, Financial Aid Counsel, Curriculum and Course Counsel, Foreign Student Counsel, are easier to identify and easier to understand.

The closest I have come for a title for personal and private counsel is "counsel for living." Like Socrates, I have also called it maieutic counsel. It is existential. It is educational. It speaks to a real need of man to achieve the higher levels of differentiation, integration, and sentience that make for adaptability (and survival) in our world. In personal counsel, one senses also the link with the ancient role of confidant, the intimate alter ego "to whom secrets [as of personal or professional matters] are confided . . . an intimate with whom one feels free to discuss private . . . matters . . . [to] seek advice or help [as in secret distress or perplexity]." (*Webster's Third New International Dictionary*, 1969.) The origin of *confidant* itself is revealing: from the Latin *com* plus *fidere*, with trust. A confidant was a trusted and intimate friend—one whose friendship and trust was the product of a long history of mutual and intimate experience. The time involved has inexorable implications for anyone who would be an instant confidant. Trust takes time.

Most of our worst confusions accrue from this second variant of generic counsel. And it is to this personal and private counsel that the attitudes and executions of psychological counsel bring their own particular historical and cultural connotations.

The logical distinction between situational counsel, whose focus is external, and personal and private counsel, whose focus is internal, is only possible in the light of the history and the contributions of psychology. With the coming of psychology, we have all become more acutely aware of the intricacies of man's *inner* world. We are out of the Garden of Eden and into Pandora's Box. And that realization has profound implications for him who would offer personal and private counsel: he must understand himself; he must have wisdom, experience and perspective; but he must also have considerable learned and conscious sophistication about the nature of man and the nature of culture, society, and institutions and their state in our chaotic, unstable time.

The psychological practices of interview and therapy grew up to meet some of these new needs, perhaps out of new recognitions, certainly to operate in a wholly different world. Part of that novelty was a world enthralled by science. It was also a world of strangers, of relatively isolated individuals, broken social and communal institutions, mobile population, transitory relationships, nuclear and even broken families, and loss of extended-family resources —a world where institutions, bureaucracies, specialists, anonymity, and anomie took the place of communities, real persons, close relationships, stability, continuity, a fabric, a sense of belonging, and a sense of personal identity. This is not an extreme interpretation. It is middle-class U.S.A.

Effects of Psychology on Generic Counsel

The contributions of psychology to counsel—if by that is meant academic and professional psychology, especially in the

United States—have not always been fortunate. However, if psychology is taken to include the work of thoughtful biologists, zoologists, poets, ethnologists, historians—all those who reflect on man and our changing society—and to exclude most American academic and professional psychology, then the effect has been tremendous and most fortunate. It has greatly sharpened our awareness of our present and our past. But psychology in this definition covers all man's study of man.

The effects of the narrower psychology have been roughly of two kinds. The first derives from the claim of professional psychology as guardian discipline of counsel; the second is the heightened interest in the psychological.

By the fifties, American psychology had already laid claim to the practice of counseling. It was soon to establish a professional subdivision, counseling psychology. The most expert counsel was implied—sometimes stated—to be in the hands of professional psychologists. This association began harmlessly enough with the introduction of a mechanistic quality—an increasing tendency to think in terms of techniques and methods, statistics, experimentation, manipulation, and gadgetry. The client, subject, or patient gradually became more of an object, the process more and more a matter of techniques. This mechanistic, behavioristic strain blends with an unreflective, pragmatic quality in the American character to make counsel seem to many only a single matter of technique to be learned quickly and practiced cleverly: a kind of more altruistic updating of an American classic.

In the forties and fifties another stream, the clinical movement in American psychology, blended into the main currents of counsel. It introduced the whole apparatus of concept, attitude, and practice which clinical psychology had derived in turn from its ultimately psychoanalytic prototypes and exemplars. Unhappily the model was a medical or psychiatric one, and basically psychoanalytic in derivation. The mode of psychoanalysis and psychiatry is therapy. Therapy, however, in concept and in origin (*therapeia*), is "medical treatment . . . the treatment of disease and disorders." (*Webtser's Third New International Dictionary*, 1969.) *Counsel*, which had historically been a general resource, a natural act, a resource for living and an educative act now took on the aura of the quasimedical. It still bears this stigma and many students still refer to the counselor as *shrink,* slang for psychiatrist.

Even more subtle and longer lasting was the tacit accrual of the psychoanalytical model of the form of practice. If one thinks of the word *counsel,* one thinks of such sentences as "I had better take counsel with my lawyer," with no inference of fifty-minute hour or regular visit or prolonged treatment. But with the preemption of counsel—now counseling—by psychology there accrued all the psychoanalytic model derivatives—the fifty-minute hour, the frequent regular appointment, the prolonged sequence of regularly spaced interviews, the whole panoply of conceptual entities such as beginnings and terminations, transference and countertransference, and the like. The *form* of therapy changed the practice of counsel. Those who offered counsel no longer simply did so on request; they set up tacit expectations of hour and interview, appointment and treatment, of therapy or its adaptation or relationship—and above all, of doctor and patient. Then, finding that prolonged psychoanalysis or psychiatry would be unacceptable in many institutions, they modified their expectations down from that tacit model, rather than imagine new ways in a new world, to meet an ancient need out of the forms and attitudes man had used for centuries. The question became not, "How can one respond to the need for counsel," but "Can our fifty-minute hours be less than a year in sequence; less frequent than twice a week; fewer than twelve; less than once a week at the same hour," and so on.

The growing resistance of the public was not only to the concepts of psychological, treatment, therapy, and to the idea of the diagnosis, care and retraining of emotional and behavioral problems. It was perhaps basically to the length and expense, in an educational context, of what was fundamentally a psychoanalytic model for the treatment of disorder. For all these quiet, unexamined accruals, these adventitious accidents of history, the provision of counsel as counsel suffered and is now suffering.

My purpose here is not to criticize psychiatry or psychoanalysis but to recover the social function of providing counsel and to distinguish it from therapy and thus to recover some of its lost contributions. I have sought to separate (and deplore) the psychological effects on this different function, counsel. Therapy has an honorable place in our society; its practices may well be different. One frequently refers from counsel to therapy. When pain is deep and inner distress profound and neither yield to counsel, one may well wish to seek therapy, and when the pain *is* so profound, it is appropriate that the therapist be a doctor, with the full range of knowledge and resource of medicine made available. The dignity of counsel and therapy should each be preserved but the differences must be kept clear and precise.

There is another related consequence or development—the sometimes explicit identifying of the highest form of counselor with the psychologist. It was an additional effect of the emphasis on the role and title of counselor rather than on the process of counsel. There then further accrued the distinction of psychology between the professional and the nonprofessional, between the lay counselor and the paraprofessional counselor and all those conditions of less than professional. These distinctions were unnecessarily invidious: they seemed implicitly to downgrade those who gave counsel but were not formally accredited psychologists. And because those who might provide personal and private counsel were now associated with psychological counsel, and psychology was professional, it seemed that those who provided situational counsel, to whatever area of concern, might not be as professional as those who worked in the area of the personal. It should be asserted that those who provide situational counsel may be in every way as professional, however the standards are defined, as those whose area of concern is the personal and private. The useful distinctions are between the areas of concern and the differing emphasis of functions that may characterize each. The concern for excellence and for ethics can characterize any area, and is not the implied province of only one. And all the baggage of "professionalism" has less to do with qualifications than with titles and status hierarchy and man's need to belong to associations.

Similarly, in this tacit ordering of all counsel to a vertical or hierarchical ordering of levels of which it was the peak, psychology confused those who practiced in other areas of counsel. It led them to feel they needed to know things psychological that they did not need to know. The emphasis on the psychological frequently distracted the exponents of situational counsel from their primary task of expertise and service, and to be unnecessarily concerned with practices peripheral to their central responsibility. All this wasted their time and energy, deflecting them from what they could do and vitiating their ability to serve well more numbers in the area of their expertise.

Of course there are responsibilities which all of us who offer any form of counsel must bear. All of us must learn to be more aware of the individual before us, the person whom we counsel. All of us must learn to listen better and to hear better. All of us can learn to recognize and acknowledge better the uniqueness and hence the dignity of the individual before us. All of us can be more aware of ourselves, our strengths, our limits, our fallibilities—especially those we are likely to exercise at the expense of others, their dignity, self reliance, growth, and sense of achievement. We can all be more aware of when we are likely to serve our own needs at the expense of others in this very complex and subtle relationship whose very nature allows the beings of each person to overlap the other.

Finally, all of us who offer counsel must become more tolerant of ambiguity. Counsel has more to do with questions than answers. It has to do with clarifying the uncertainties, and then exploring the possibilities. It may well have to do with accepting that there are no answers, only decisions to explore and to one day commit oneself. And that takes tolerance of ambiguity. But these are aspects demanded of anyone who would offer counsel well. They are not the concerns of the psychologist or psychiatrist alone.

Interest in the Psychological

The second major effect of psychology on counsel was the fascination, curiosity and excitement in things psychological encouraged by the media. Some of this was inevitable. Man in the twentieth century had again come into focus, this time supposedly through the lens of science. To this natural interest, intensified by the presures and upheavals of the times, there accrued the fascination with all things hidden, mysterious, bizarre, secret, monstrous. To the understanding of man, Freud had opened the door into the unconscious. Man's fascination with horror and the dark in a more naive century found its focus in the gothic novel—in Dr. Frankenstein and his monster—and placed the sense of dark things safely in the "out there." Perhaps it was only natural, in our time, with the help of the discoveries of Freud and Jung, that this fascination would shift to the even more terrible shadows *within*.

Inevitable or not, the act of counsel has been affected and shifted out of its traditional place in the process of education, socialization, living, growing, and aging. Thus we find that a large segment of those who wish to offer counsel are themselves motivated by a personal interest, however unrecognized, in abnormal psychology. (It should be added that interest in the psychological is not the only motivation for the role and title of counselor. To some, the attraction is political: both young and old have a fascination with the implicit power in the role. The unworthy as well as the fallible in man is never to be ignored, especially in contexts which seem so manifestly pure and altruistic.)

Not all the motivations that move people to practice counsel can be attributed to dark and psychological, of course, or even political, interests. Many persons are clearly motivated to "help." They are not always sophisticated, unfortunately, as to the role of that "help" in filling their own needs. Among the young, seeking to affect the dehumanized and fragmented quality of our present society, seeking to help free and integrate the expression of feeling in individuals constricted by an overrationalistic society, and seeking to build bridges across the gulfs of isolation, the helping motivation seems more external to their personal needs, and more appropriate. The motivation to offer peer counsel is certainly less clouded among those students like the blacks and the chicanos whose peers face substantive, economic and social problems, which they know to be real and external to them. The concern and the practice of these persons is clearly to help their younger brothers and sisters and one who offers counsel in this case is more concerned with situational or special counsel.

The task and motivation of middle-class white students is often less clear. It is more likely conceived of as being to provide personal and private counsel, even a kind of instant confidant, and the whole effort is thus more likely to be clouded with the confusions derived from the psychological. These confusions can be somewhat clarified by conceiving of much of counsel, particularly peer counsel, as situational counsel, with an external focus. This frees the role somewhat from its psychological overtones.

The difficulties that affect much of the practice of counsel can also be ameliorated by shifting the focus from being a counselor to considering *how* one may provide counsel. Our task is then to assist those whose counsel is sought by their fellows to recognize their capacity to offer counsel, to increase their sophistication in its discharge, and better to understand and bear the burdens of its responsibilities. Such an emphasis on counsel rather than counselor shifts the focus to the act away from the title and helps avoid the latter's tempting connotations of status and authority.

The final criticism of the effect of academic and professional psychology on the practice of counsel is less a criticism of these institutions than of American higher education generally. American social science, both in its academic and in its professional forms, has been a well-trained but poorly educated movement. Its graduates are poorly lettered with little breadth in understanding and little depth in their temporal and cultural perspectives. It has been narrow and parochial, which has affected these forms of counsel which social science and psychology in particular have preempted.

This same parochialism may be the reason that psychology has been so slow in recognizing in its own affairs its central dilemma best expressed by the metaphor, "The light of measurement alters the path of the particle," and the related phenomenon of the self-fulfilling prophecy. Psychology has also been slow recognizing the limiting and even distorting effect of its preoccupation with the models and methods of seventeenth century physical science, and its preoccupation with behaviorism, operationalism, and positivism. Part of the problem of course lies in the newness of American psychology. It has the self-centeredness of adolescence and the need to compete for status of the newly arrived. However one would wish to temper these criticisms of American psychology, one must admit that it has had its effect on counsel and it has tended to limit the perception of that function.

The sum, it seems to me, is that no one discipline nor profession should preempt or be identified with so central, fundamental and pervasive a social function as counsel. In a pluralistic society, a pluralism of relevant disciplines and understandings should be available. Standards should obtain and qualifications defined; but the definitions should be so broad that a community may understand them and apply them in identifying for itself, those whom it would wish to test, validate, and call to the discharge of such functions. I have suggested elsewhere that it may be well to include, as necessary but not sufficient, formal academic standards and accreditations. But these should not be limited to one discipline or profession. They should come from a host of related disciplines and professions devoted to the understanding and service of man, his society and his relation to society. The only proviso should be that a person must also fulfill the necessary generic qualifications: the qualities of wisdom, experience, perspective, self-awareness and self-acceptance and objectivity that larger experience, temperament (and good fortune perhaps)' alone can provide.

The concept of a pluralism of resources for a pluralistic society is not just born of a need for logical tidiness. It reflects a central assumption noted earlier: if ours is a time in which man must hammer out his own identity, his own unique pattern of values, resources and relationships, his own pattern of commitment, then he needs exposure to a number of models and a number of kinds of answers to each of the kinds of major questions he must decide for himself. If awareness and objectivity of and toward the self, societal forms, cultural forms, and value forms is necessary for such a process, *then* differences in each must be available. Cross-cultural experiences are the critical events in the fashioning of objectivity. Academic disciplines are in effect subcultures and the concept of cross-cultural experience applies to them when it comes to an individual's understanding and fashioning of his own identity.

Thus the potential public for counsel—which means everyone—must have not only an ability to choose their resources for counsel, but the informedness that makes such a choice true and free. Those concerned about the provision of counsel must insure such informedness. Similarly, in a stable and simple society expectations were specific and tacit, consonant and understood by both performer and recipient of a social function. Not so now. There is perhaps no single social function today in which there is so much variation in expectation among both performers and recipients. The result is frustration, dissatisfaction, and actual suffering. Those who are puzzled and disappointed may even then lay blame on themselves for the failure, doubling their original pain.

There is no more important task within an institution than to insure that everyone knows what counsel is and what legitimate expectations there may be of it, especially of such an ancient and central function.

Confusions in counseling are many. This chapter has sought to address only one set, those arising out of the associations with and the effects of academic and professional psychology, particularly American psychology. Until counsel can be freed from the obscuring and distorting effects of this association, it can not be restored to its simple, central, and crucial function to which everyone must at some time have access. This access is critical today when so much burden is placed on the individual in the forging of his own identity and of his existence. Generic counsel should be of ready and simple access to everyone, to chancellor or student, when they need it and for whatever support, small or large, businesslike or profoundly personal.

IV

Counselor as Double Agent

Seymour Halleck

There was a time when counselors could convince themselves that their only role was that of helping clients. Today such self-deception is impossible. Rigid scrutiny of the practices of counselors has created new information and a new consciousness regarding practices once taken for granted. In the light of the new consciousness we can no longer deny that we sometimes have put the interest of the college ahead of the interest of the student. Nor can we deny that the counseling role has political implications and that our interventions can hurt clients by diminishing their power in relating to the college.

Some of the ethical pitfalls of the counseling role can be clarified by the following case vignettes.

An applicant for admission to a college is asked to fill out a form which asks whether he has ever sought psychiatric help. He answers the question affirmatively. Because of this response he is asked to see an admissions counselor. In the course of the interview the student reveals that he has many anxieties and that in the past he has been troubled by prolonged depression. He also admits a suicide attempt. The counselor fears that the applicant will not be able to handle the stresses of the college without becoming emotionally disturbed and recommends that he not be admitted.

A student is picked up by the campus security police after he has been caught for the third time peeking in windows of a girls' dormitory. A report is made to the dean who insists that the student be interviewed by a college counselor. During the interview the student reveals that his voyeuristic tendencies are deep-rooted. He talks of wanting to hurt and humiliate a woman and reveals that on one occasion he stopped a coed with the intention of assaulting her but ran in fright when she screamed. The counselor then reports to the dean that the student is a threat to the community and the student is asked to leave school.

A student voluntarily requests counseling because of difficulty studying. In the course of a series of interviews he develops a close relationship with his counselor and begins to talk about personal problems. He eventually reveals that he is quite disturbed, with a variety of psychological symptoms, one of the most serious of which is a compulsive desire to set fires. He tells the counselor that he once set a small fire in his dormitory which was found and extinguished before it did any damage. The counselor after much soul-searching and discussion with his client reveals this information to the housing office. As a result the student is allowed to remain in school but is required to live off of campus.

A student is referred to the counseling service by the School of Education. He is known to be unstable, with a history of psychiatric treatment, and is prone to argumentative outbursts in class. He is told that if he does not see the counseling service he will not be granted a teaching certificate. The counseling service is asked to comment about his emotional maturity and his competence to be a teacher. The counselor decides that the young man is indeed disturbed, but does not feel competent to assess his capacity to teach. He therefore reports to the School of Education that the student is emotionally disturbed but makes no further recommendations. His report is used as a basis for dismissing the student from the School of Education.

A student who has voluntarily sought assistance reveals to his counselor that he has homosexual tendencies. This is noted in the counseling center's records. The student does quite well in counseling and in college but ten years later the counseling service receives a request for information about him from a federal agency. In applying for a sensitive job in government the student has admitted that he had once experienced emotional disturbance. By this time the student's former counselor has left the university and the new director of the counseling center must decide how to respond. The new director knows that if he reveals the material in the former student's records he is not likely to get the job. The director also knows that to ignore the government's request may cast suspicion upon the student's credentials. He is faced with the choices of risking the former student's employment opportunities by doing nothing, of seriously compromising the student's opportunities by telling the truth, or by somehow fabricating a response that will not damage the student.

A student is having difficulties with the material in one particular class. He talks with his professor and it soon becomes apparent to both that theirs is a personality clash. After some discussion the professor persuades the student to visit the counseling service. The counselor helps the student clarify some of the reasons for his conflict with the professor. With the student's permission he talks with the professor about the student's problems. As a result the two develop a better relationship and the student manages to master the material of that particular course.

A highly militant radical student comes to the counseling service for help with sexual problems. During the course of treatment his problems are alleviated. The student also discovers that with less sexual anxiety he is able to enjoy life more fully and he gradually loses interest in radical activities. He becomes more an armchair radical than an active militant.

On one or more occasions in fourteen years of student health psychiatry I have been the counselor in each of the above case situations. I am not proud of all the things I have done and know that I would not do all things in exactly the same way today. At the same time, I know that all the counseling practices I have described above are still utilized at most colleges in the country.

With the exception of the last example, the counselor in each of the above cases is functioning as a *double agent*. That is, he has allegiances both to the client and to the college community. His position is different from that of a physician in private practice or that of a psychotherapist operating on a private contract basis, both of whom hold allegiances only to patient or client, and do not, except under very unusual circumstances, reveal any of the information obtained in the course of counseling or therapy. The college counselor, however, is not allowed such privilege. He wants to help his client but he is also employed by the college and has a commitment to help create a smoothly functioning college climate.

Sometimes, of course, the interests of the student and the college community are compatible. The latter two vignettes illustrate this point. The student who gave information which was later used to help him overcome his problems in a particular course was probably grateful. The student who received relief from his sexual problems not only felt better afterwards but the college was probably also grateful to the counselor for helping create a more cerebral, less visceral, radical. Even in the latter two instances, however, the counselor's influence in helping create a stable college community is considerable.

There *is* a complicated ethical problem in the latter two cases but it does not involve any direct harm to the client. Even when intervention has apparently benign consequences, it is important that counselors be aware of the political meaning of their work. Actually, there is no way for a counselor to intervene in any client's problems without exercising some political influence. People are part of social systems and intervention in the life of any element in the system will effect the total system. Any counseling intervention will either help stabilize the status quo or help change it. Partly because of the nature of the counseling process and partly because of the counselor's commitment to the prevailing college structure, the counseling relationship more often than not is a stabilizing agent.

In all but the last two situations, the counselor's interventions may simultaneously serve the needs of the college community (or in some cases the needs of the general society) and actually hurt the student. Of course, it can be argued that the disturbed student who is denied admission to the college might be better off in the long run. Or the student who is asked to leave school because of difficulties in controlling violent impulses might be better off, too. But no one can say this with any certainty. And the student client rarely sees it this way. He usually wants to stay in school. The student's needs and the college's needs are often incompatible.

The ethical political problems of the counselor placed in a double-agent role are explicitly described by Dr. Thomas Szasz (1961) in his eloquent critiques of institutional psychiatric practice. Szasz describes how physicians employed by mental hospitals, courts, and prisons are mistakenly viewed by their patients and the public as operating just like other physicians. The patient believes that the state-employed doctor will respect the patient's needs and protect his confidentiality. Szasz then documents how a patient, assuming that he is protected, might provide the doctor with information which could be used to deprive him of liberty or of privileges. More recently, Szasz (1970) has argued that any therapist or counselor not explicitly hired by the client and employed by the state or an institution can similarly hurt his client.

The major fear of Szasz (1970) is that the counselor as double agent may hold more allegiance to the institution than to his client. At its worst, the counseling situation may be visualized as an alliance between the university and the counselor to control or socialize the client.

Indeed, profound political pressures urge the college-employed counselor to act as an agent of conformity. Every agency, including a college, wants to retain a degree of stability. The college community is not eager to train nor graduate those who wish to bring about drastic changes within the college structure. College administrators are more than willing to use counselors to help maintain community stability. Insofar as counselors can be used to keep those who are different or deviant from achieving power or privileges, they will always be under considerable pressure to help preserve the status quo.

To be more than just an agent of conformity, the college counselor must eventually confront the ethical pitfalls of his double-agent role. He can do this in several ways. First, he can refuse to participate in certain kinds of counseling practices. He may, for example, point out to the college administrators that his skills in weeding out emotionally disturbed students are minimal or that admission screening is not a proper function for a counselor. He may also refuse to examine students when professors or deans are questioning their capacity to fulfill a professional role. These positions, however, are difficult for a counselor to take. College administrators and deans can argue persuasively that it is in the student's own interests not to be admitted into situations which might prove too stressful. When professors and deans ask for evaluations by a counselor they usually insist that they only want reassurance that it is safe to allow a disturbed student to remain in school. Usually they maintain that the primary reason for referring the student is to insure that he or she will receive help. While the counselor may be suspicious that these are a convenient rationalization for weeding out troublemakers, it is likely that in most instances the college officials are quite sincere in asking the counselor for assistance.

One of the less disruptive ways of dealing with this situation is to try to educate college officials as to the counselor's limited skills and to the ethical pitfalls of the double-agent role. In my own work as a student health psychiatrist, I eventually convinced the administrators of the University of Wisconsin that I had no skills to offer in weeding out students for admission. I was also able, but only with prolonged and arduous efforts, to persuade administrators of professional schools that involuntary examination of disturbed students is, except in rare instances, an improper use of the counseling function. The education function in this situation must be an ongoing one. There is a rapid turnover of professors and deans at any college or university and it is essential that new people understand the limitations of the counseling process.

When the counseling agencies are faced with requests from college officials for information about clients, the counselor usually has the option of refusing the requests. Maintaining this option also requires continued educative efforts as professors and deans have a hard time understanding why they cannot know more about their students. When requests for information come from government, industrial agencies, or insurance companies, the counselor's problem is even more difficult. An outright and tactless refusal can hurt the client. So can an honest report, even if the report might have little relevance to the client's current situation and capabilities. The counselor can lie, of course, but this is hardly desirable. Some counseling centers have solved this problem by developing a form letter which is actually a polite refusal to report information and an admonishment to the agency not to construe that refusal as any indication that the client's problem is serious. If such a letter is sent in all cases, the agencies eventually appreciate that it does not mean that the applicant is disturbed.

Still, in some instances the counselor has no other option but to respond to the requests of university officials. The emotionally disturbed student thought to be violent must be evaluated by someone and the college has reason to use its own counselors to protect its interests. In some instances, the counselor may want to see the person referred simply because he may feel able to help him. Once the client has been interviewed it is difficult for the counselor to avoid providing some opinion to college officials since reluctance might be interpreted as a sign that something is seriously wrong with the client. The counselor may also be eager to give information to college officials if he is convinced it can be used to help the client.

Ultimately, no college counselor can completely avoid facing the dilemmas of the double-agent role. Sometimes the counselor can do nothing but deal with the problem as honestly as possible. I believe that one of the main obligations of the counselor in the double-agent role is to be absolutely explicit in spelling out his role to his client. In actual practice this is rarely done. Ordinarily the client is not aware of, or chooses to ignore, the possibilities that the counselor's communications may be used against him. People think of a doctor, a therapist, or a counselor as someone who will provide total confidentiality and who is primarily interested in his client's welfare. People in trouble who are looking for help are especially likely to be oblivious to the possibility that the alleged helping relationship may actually be a harmful one.

Ideally, the counselor should begin his evaluation with a clear statement to the client of the counselor's obligations. The client should know what records will be kept, and the limits of confidentiality. He should know to whom the counselor might report details of the client's case, either formally or informally. He should know if the counselor will express opinion about him to any other person. It is extremely easy for the counselor to lapse on these issues and become careless in how he presents himself to his client. This, I believe, is a grave error. The only protection the client has is a clear understanding of the nature of his counseling encounter. In my experience, such honesty does not diminish rapport or communication. In fact, the client may be so disarmed by the counselor's frankness that he may say more than he intended.

I believe that it is also critical that the counselor, wherever possible, put his client's needs ahead of those of the college. This, of course, is tricky, requiring complicated value judgments in almost every case. Certainly when a client is violent and is not motivated to control himself it would be difficult for a counselor to ignore the needs of the community. But, too often, counselors do not support clients strongly enough against institutional arrogance and too often they fail to look at the details of the client's problems in ways that reflect more favorably on the client than the institution.

Actually, the counselor can frequently be quite helpful in aiding the client to deal with an insensitive organization. The following case illustrates one way this can be done.

Several years ago a dean of a professional school of education asked me to evaluate a student who was threatening suicide. Her professors were apparently worried about her behavior and had serious doubts about her potential as a satisfactory teacher. Primarily, the dean maintained, he wanted me to help the girl, but he also asked that I give an opinion on whether she was capable of continuing her education. I did not promise that but felt I should see the girl since she was allegedly suicidal. The patient had been told by her dean she could not continue her classes until she had been evaluated.

The patient appeared in my office as an angry, resentful, and quite spirited young woman. She told me she had been having a battle with one of her professors for several months. They had disagreed violently about her teaching methods. She had taken a much more radical position on educational issues than was generally favored by her school. As the conflict escalated the patient began to feel that the professor was giving her lower grades than she deserved. She argued with him about this but he insisted she was being paranoid. When she talked with her adviser and her dean, they backed the professor and pointed out that she might be emotionally disturbed. During one session with the dean, she broke down and admitted that she had had extensive psychiatric treatment in the past and said that the entire situation had so troubled her that she was having suicidal thoughts.

I found the patient to be quite intelligent and aggressive. She had definite ideas about teaching her classes which obviously conflicted with the views of her professional school. She seemed quite capable of carrying out her professional intentions if she were in an environment which would tolerate them. She freely admitted that she had experienced considerable emotional distress in the past. At the time I saw her, however, she seemed reasonably self-confident and comfortable. She was certainly not the type who might injure others, and she gave no indication that her suicidal threat had been anything more than an hysterical and manipulative outburst.

I called the dean and told him that my examination had shown this girl free of serious psychological disabilities and that any decision regarding her continuation in school would have to be based on other than psychological criteria. I put the statement in writing and further suggested that I felt a political rather than a medical issue was involved, and while I had not heard both sides I felt that my patient had presented a strong case for having been discriminated against because of her political views. The dean responded with disbelief. When I suggested that he might be using psychological consultation in an inappropriate manner he was also skeptical. He accepted my recommendations with cool politeness, but the patient was allowed to finish school and was graduated with above average grades. I have kept in touch with her since, and she has had an outstanding career in education, held a responsible administrative post, and contributed several important papers to the educational literature.

It is extremely important for the counselor to disabuse himself of the notion that his unhappy, complaining clients may be paranoid. Many who are seen involuntarily, or voluntarily under great pressure, do feel that they have been wronged, whereas those who have referred them are convinced that the student has not been wronged but is misperceiving the situation because he is emotionally disturbed. In my experience, the student's perception is as often correct as that of the person who referred him. Unless the counselor tries to empathize with the student as much as possible he may do great harm to his client.

Other forms of nonmedical labeling by counselors also may be unfair to the student. Some students are labeled by counseling centers with such words as *troublemaker, slow developer, immature,* or *underachiever.* These terms may actually describe the student's behavior but they usually are applied to the student without any description of the environment in which the behavior occurred. In some environments, troublemaking is quite understandable, even laudable, and underachieving may simply be a natural response to bad teaching. Again the counselor's obligation is to define both the individual and environmental factors without putting the total blame for undesirable behavior on the student.

In recent years, more and more college students have become aware of the dangers of seeking help from college counselors, so they have begun to seek help elsewhere (Warnath, 1971). For many years, of course, students have consulted private psychologists and psychiatrists. But now they are developing their own free or low-cost counseling centers. Rap centers, peoples' offices, drug rescue centers, abortion and draft counseling offices are now thriving on almost all large campuses. Some of these organizations were created and are being maintained independently by students. Others are indirectly supported by college funds. In either case, these counterculture or radical counseling groups are not accountable to the college structure. They are generally located off-campus. The counterculture counselor can always feel free to put his client's interests ahead of the college's, since he owes no allegiance there. These types of counseling arrangements offer an interesting and sometimes highly effective solution to some of the problems I have discussed. They are effective even when the college stays involved by indirectly supporting the counterculture clinic, as long as college officials do not interfere in the counseling process.

The major defect of counterculture counseling, of course, is the inexperience of the counselors. Counterculture counseling centers are frequently staffed by graduate students or other nonprofessionals who may have great natural talents for helping people but who have little skill in the techniques. Such clinics often lack permanence and personnel turnover is rapid. The student who seeks counterculture counseling will unlikely see a person with experience or skill. Also the student who seeks free counseling may expose himself to massive political indoctrination. The client may find that receiving help is contingent on his adopting certain radical values.

In all fairness, it should be noted that college counselors also impose certain values on clients. After some sensitivity work with athletes and coaches two years ago, I discovered that counselors at one of our major liberal universities were counseling all black athletes into physical education curricula. The coaches and the counselors shared the myth that blacks could not retain athletic eligibility unless they took easy courses, so that the black athlete was often denied the opportunity of seeking a nonathletic career. And the record of college counselors in advising women, as indicated in Berry's chapter, is certainly not admirable. Women have been subtly counseled out of masculine fields for decades. All in all, there may be as much danger of political indoctrination in the college counseling center as in the rap center.

I have learned while drafting this chapter that some colleges now require new students to participate in sensitivity groups. These groups, sometimes led by college employees, may encourage the student to reveal information that could be used to hurt him. It is hard to believe that in this day and age, administrators would be so insensitive as to force students into counseling, or that students would be passive enough to accept it. There is little doubt in my mind that such compulsion is illegal, as well as unethical, and that colleges which utilize it will be subject to court actions.

Of course, the college can use the powerful pressure of the peer group to encourage reluctant students into sensitivity groups. However benevolent the motivation of college administrators, there is no ethical justification for even the most subtle pressure to push previously untroubled students into self-revealing situations. Sensitivity groups can be both psychologically and politically harmful to clients yet only an enormously self-confident student can resist the pressure of the college and his peers.

Students need, and will actively seek, guidance in making

decisions that effect their academic and personal lives, thus it is unlikely that the counseling function will ever become irrelevant. If the counselor is to provide maximum assistance to his client, he must know that his own values influence his work. And he must always be willing to wrestle with, rather than deny or ignore, the ethical dilemmas of his work.

V

Credibility and the Counseling Center

Lenore W. Harmon

Credibility is more noticeable in its absence than in its presence.
Once it is lost, people begin to coin terms such as "credibility gap."
It may seem heretical to propose that the credibility of college
counseling centers be examined since to do so implies a lack of
credibility. We all know that counseling centers are staffed by people
who are warm, concerned, open, and sincere. However, it is possible
for good counselors who act in essentially the same way counselors
acted ten years ago to lose credibility with some clients, just as the
Urban League or the NAACP have lost credibility with some
blacks.

Since counseling centers were developed to help alleviate the
problems which keep students from maximal performance both as
scholars and as persons, the counseling center must appear credible

to students with debilitating problems. It needs credibility in two major areas. The first is the ethical one, the second concerns the type and quality of services offered.

Students in 1973 understand very little about the ethical stance of counseling psychologists. They went to high schools when dress codes were strictly enforced, students newspapers were censored, and students were expelled for alleged misdeeds without any semblance of due process. They remember the student strike of 1970 when many college and university administrators refused to listen to student outrage over the Cambodian invasion and appeared to be more concerned about physical plants than about students. Whether students acted logically in striking against colleges as a protest against governmental action is not at issue; the message students received about their personal worth from administrators *is*. Many students learned that society holds their civil rights in little esteem and their feelings in even less. Students see themselves powerless with administrators. They have become wary of confiding in anyone who might use their confidences against them. College counseling centers, often housed in close proximity to such administrative offices as Admissions and Financial Aids and staffed with obvious professionals, have become suspect.

While numerous counseling center staff meetings each year are devoted to the ethical problems of keeping student confidences in the institutional-legal situation of a specific college, students rarely know about them or about the personal commitment of individual counselors to ethical behavior on behalf of students. A research assistant interviewing a counseling center director as part of a study of student services confided that she and her husband had agreed that neither would come to that office no matter how pressing their problems. Asked why, she replied that both needed financial aid in the form of assistantships to meet their educational goals. Despite the fact that she was an intelligent, sophisticated psychology student she really could not imagine how improbable and unethical any communication between her counselor and her prospective employer or employing department would be if she had used the counseling center. In that specific counseling center, even the fact that she had been a client would not have been routinely disclosed to her prospective employer. She would have had to tell the employing profes-

sor or department where to look for information as well as authorize
its release before any information would have been made available.
She did not know about the counselors' strong commitment to
protect the confidences of each student. Rather, she was reflecting
the generally pessimistic views of her peers toward the institutional
loyalties of counselors employed by the college.

Another counseling center director was contacted by a
clergyman who had been receiving requests for information regarding abortion. Since the clergyman was part of the campus community he began asking the callers why they did not seek help from
the campus counseling center. He reported that the majority responded that they did not want their pregnancy to "go down on my
record." The belief that an all-encompassing record exists for each
student seems hilariously naive to anyone who knows the real state
of recordkeeping in large colleges and universities. The tragedy is
that many young people believe that the college possesses just such
an interlocking web of both academic and personal information
garnered from the whole college environment which may be used
against them in various ways. They do not believe that their confidence would be kept, despite the elaborate plans of counselors and
counseling centers to protect their clients—plans that could actually
flout either institutional or legal authority. The prevailing spirit of
distrust among students is self-perpetuating; the previous experience
of new college students supports what they are told about the
loyalties of college counselors by older, more experienced students
whose distrust, by the way, has kept them from using the counseling
center.

A second area in which counseling centers must be credible
is in the services they perform. The technical competence of counselors is not as much at issue as their values and characteristics. The
student who brings a problem to counseling must enter into a tacit
or formal agreement with the counselor about what is to be accomplished. Some students do not feel this agreement can be reached,
because they assume counselors will not agree with some of their
values and will attempt to change them even though they are not
necessarily a part of the problem. Thus, political radicals, homo-
sexuals, drug-users, minority group members, and conscientious ob-
jectors, to name a few, do not expect much understanding. Again,

the students assume that the counselor shares the prevailing societal attitudes and worse still, many students assume that the counselor's goal is to lead the client to conform to those attitudes.

Few counselors would admit to trying to change the personal values of their clients; most have grown up professionally with too many prohibitions against coercing clients. However, some subtle issues are involved, and the student is often more sensitive to them than the counselor. The student sees his or her position as powerless and the counselor's as powerful (usually more so than it actually is). When an unconventional client senses that his or her counselor assumes the client wants to work within prevailing societal norms and that is not the case, the client has two options. First, he may leave and decide that counseling cannot be helpful. Second, he may confront the counselor. While Kell and Mueller (1966) point out that this approach benefits both the client and the counselor, clients who perceive themselves to be powerless and vulnerable are not likely to initiate it. The most likely result of a values conflict between client and counselor is that the client leaves with negative feelings about the counseling process which he does not express in the counseling situation, where they could be constructive, but which he expresses outside, thus destroying the credibility of counseling services. In this area, and in the ethical one the lack of credibility of a counseling center multiplies geometrically as one student tells many others, who each tell many other students, of real or supposed counselor inadequacies.

The case of young women and their problems provides an illustration. The fundamental thing most young women need to discuss with a counselor today is the breakdown of the traditional women's role, and how it will effect them. Many coeds grew up expecting to adopt a way of life that may not exist in the future. They expected to marry, bear children, and maintain as large a household as their husbands were able to provide. Yet children and extensive real estate holdings are economic and social liabilities today. They no longer play the important economic part they did in agrarian life. In 1972, the United States reached a birth rate which if continued, would insure zero population growth, while construction and sales of condominiums became big business. Thus, child-rearing and housekeeping may not take up the lifetimes of women in the future. For many women the whole lifestyle which surrounds marriage may become entirely unnecessary. Since the Equal Rights Amendment will change some of the protections women enjoyed almost automatically under the old divorce laws, women will have to become more self-sufficient.

Bronowski (1955) says that living things have a way of sensing the future clearly and Freedman (1967) notes that student unrest is related to the phenomenon. Most young women see quite clearly the potential changes in their lives. Some are frightened, others exhilarated, but both report troubles in the counselor's office. The former, concerned about what will happen to a woman who holds the traditional values of the early 1970's after they become non-traditional, may find that the counselor can do nothing more than assure her that traditional values will always triumph. Although she wishes she could accept the counselor's predictions, she tends to come away from her counseling experience feeling unreassured. What she needs is to explore her strengths according to her traditional values. She senses she may soon be out of step but she is not sure about her capacity to march to another drummer. A counselor who could entertain the possibility of societal change could help such women by separating societal pressure from personal, well-reasoned value systems. With some help from the counselor, these women might emerge with an awareness of personal strengths that they were unaware of because their ideas were immersed in the mainstream of popular thought.

The young women exhilarated by the possibilities of tomorrow have different problems. They expect very little encouragement from counseling centers staffed and administered by counselors who are predominantly male. Kirk (1972) pointed out that in 1970 only 15 percent (302) of the members of the American Psychological Association Division of Counseling Psychology were women. The 1971–1972 Counseling Center Data Bank (Magoon, 1972) showed that in 201 counseling centers, only 30.4 percent of the full-time professional staff (including testing and reading personnel) were women. Kirk identified only eleven women counseling center directors among the 35 percent (110) of women members of Division 17 who responded to her questionnaire.

Vocational counseling has been discouraging for some

women because occupational information available in counseling centers portrays only men in leadership positions. When women talk with counselors about becoming oceanographers, architects, or administrators, the results are likely to be discouraging, because counselors routinely dissuade women from such aspirations. Friedersdorf (1969), Pietrofesa and Schlossbert (1970) and Thomas and Stewart (1971) document the negative attitudes of counselors of both sexes toward nontraditional careers for women. When women are tested, they are disappointed to discover that the results reflect the bias of the society which produced them (Harmon, 1973). Only the most inventive psychologists can devise tests useful for women in making appropriate vocational decisions (Cole, 1972).

Discussing personal and sexual relationships can be discouraging for women counselees, too. Broverman, Broverman, Clarkson, Rosenkrantz, and Vogel (1970) have demonstrated that mental health workers attribute traits which they evaluate as healthy more to men than to women. Chesler (1972) has documented cases in which women have been hospitalized merely because they refused to play the housewife role. Young women today, with some reason, expect counselors to believe that a woman's place is in the home caring for her children and being supportive of her husband. The counselor of the husband of one of my clients pleaded with me to convince my client to suppress her feelings and stop her attempts to express her independence even though what brought her to see me in the first place were the problems created by suppressing her feelings and her independence for the sake of her family. The other counselor was firmly convinced that the needs of the husband were more important than the needs of the wife, and he really could not understand my position that the needs of my client were just as important. I never mentioned this discussion to my client, but she reported that after she and her husband visited both a marriage counselor and his special consultant, that both counselors seemed to be more sympathetic to her husband's needs, expecting her to adjust to the lifestyle most comfortable for him, despite her own discomfort. She began to feel guilty about her attempts to develop a more satisfying lifesyle for herself because they suggested that she should feel guilty. I believe that the induced guilt delayed her progress toward personhood.

Personality theories have not always treated women as well-developed human beings. Doherty (1973) and Sherman (1971) point out that Freud really did not expect girls to resolve the Oedipal complex, hence leaving them with weak superegos, and that Erikson really does not expect women to find identities except in their husbands. When I visited an undergraduate class to talk about counseling, one young woman told me and the class that she had seen a campus counselor for most of a semester regarding some serious personal problems. Finally, she dropped out of school. When she stopped at the counseling office to tell him, he was enraged and told her she had no right to drop out because women never knew what was good for them. Perhaps his theoretical position did not allow for a woman who could control her emotions and understand the consequences of her actions. Luckily, for the image of counseling on the campus, the woman also reported that she transferred to another male counselor whose attitude was "beautiful, he respected my ability to find answers that would suit me." Unfortunately, many women are not willing to give counselors a second chance.

Some young women want to discuss with counselors their rage over their lack of control over their own bodies. They must choose among contraceptives whose safety and effectiveness they doubt. If the contraceptive fails, they must choose whether to go alone through the frightening and sometimes dehumanizing procedure of an abortion or to go alone through birth and parenthood. They perceive the medical profession as male dominated, and failing to take women's needs into consideration. When psychology and counseling follow the medical model, women expect no better from psychology. In fact, some of their rage is directed at counselors. While many counselors might enable women to honestly explore their feelings about their bodies, few get a chance because of women's mistrust of male attitudes.

On the area of women's changing roles and values, one can hardly expect the counselor to remain without an opinion. Certainly, the counselor's values will affect his service often more than he realizes. The same can be said of his attitudes toward the use of drugs, alternative life styles, homosexuality, radical political tactics, and extremely conservative political stances. Whatever the counselor's values, they are likely to offend some subgroup of students, and given the human nature of counselors, it may be impossible to establish credibility with all subgroups. In some areas, such as feminism, radically oriented counselors may set up the same kind of credibility gap with their more traditional counselees that the conservative counselor sets up with students holding radical attitudes. All counselors know that an ability to live and let live is valuable in accepting any kind of client, but every counselor also knows that at some very personally defined point he is unable to preserve this attitude. This dilemma contributes to the credibility crises in counseling services.

Given the current conditions on many college campuses, even those counseling centers with the most competent and concerned counselors are likely to have difficulty establishing credibility with some groups of students. Assuming that the subgroups who mistrust counselors have as many problems as those who trust counselors, a search for solutions becomes imperative. The bread-and-butter issue of college administrations continuing to support counseling centers that many students do not use is less idealistic, but it motivates a search for solutions. In fact, the success of off-campus counseling services which offer specialized services such as drug counseling, abortion counseling, draft counseling, and veterans counseling is an index to the credibility of the official counseling center. This may also serve to convince college administrators that compared with the campus, the community is better able to serve the counseling needs of students than the campus is.

A search for solutions to the credibility problems of counseling center staffs requires examination of two assumptions usually unspoken, thus unexamined. The first is the belief that, as Freud dictated, all counselors should remain as unknown as a blank screen to provide an ambiguous facade on which the client can project his transference, thus his neurosis. While sometimes this may be important in the counseling process, I believe that many counselors have accepted the prescription without considering how often, in their own caseloads, the development of a transference relationship is necessary if the client is to be helped. Often counselor ambiguity is assumed to be good mainly because it provides the counselor with a more comfortable professional stance than a nonambiguous position which implies personal choice and commitment. The latter always imply values sure to be incompatible with those of some clients. Since counselor values do come into conflict with client values anyway the solution is hardly to hide behind an assumption broadly misapplied and impossible to implement. Even a Freudian analyst transmits to his patients his faith in psychoanalysis and its procedures for solving personal problems. Adherence to an assumption of counselor ambiguity is a self-deception which contributes to the credibility problem.

The second assumption that should be examined is the applicability of the medical model to college counseling situations. Most clients are not sick, even in the disputed psychological sense of the word (Szasz, 1961). If counseling center clients could be identified as sick and their illnesses properly diagnosed, psychologists would still disagree about treatment strategies. College students do not want anything done *to* them, but to participate in changing their own lives. Indeed, the wish to have changes made in his life without active participation is often an indication that a college student has problems. Neither do students wish to have attempts made to change their values, even if they do not match those of society.

The ambiguity of counselors and the authoritarian implications of the medical model fits in with the students' (sometimes justified) mistrust of authority fostered by the events on and off campus over the past few years. These have indicated to the student that his rights, feelings, and values count for little in our society. Because the counseling center is ambiguous, the student projects into the situation the qualities he has come to expect from institutions in general. Because counselors are presumed to believe they can "treat" clients they are suspected of wanting to change clients into the molds prescribed by society. Whether student expectations about counselors are accurate is less important than whether students believe them and thus cut themselves off from potentially helpful services.

This analysis suggests a potential solution for the counseling center faced with a credibility problem. It is, simply, to become less ambiguous. If the counseling center staff is, in fact, trustworthy in an ethical sense, then students deserve to know it. Some counseling centers make their ethical stance available in writing to students, but another approach is for counselors to get out in the campus community and allow students to know them as trustworthy human beings rather than to remain ambiguous unknowns in their office.

Any campus involvement by a counselor implies his values as an individual. For instance, if a counselor becomes involved with a radical political group, a feminist group, or the campus conservation club, his values and personal priorities become apparent to students. During the late sixties on our campus a counselor who was active in Students for a Democratic Society attracted a kind of client who had seldom utilized counseling services before. They trusted the counselor not to attempt to change their political values when they talked to him about their personal problems. When the counselor later left our campus, the number of radical students who felt free to use the counseling center was substantially reduced.

Students seek help from persons whom they consider trustworthy whether or not those persons are qualified to give the required help. Thus, feminist students will often go to older women involved in the feminist movement for help, in preference to professional counselors, even women counselors, who have not been visibly involved. Professors of women's studies and staff members who have helped to organize campus women appear more trustworthy to young women than counselors.

The implication of reducing counselor ambiguity seems clearcut; involvement along the lines of one's interests can help establish personal credibility for a given counselor with some groups of students and collective credibility for counselors among several groups of students. However, the implications for counseling centers and individual counselors are more complex. Obviously, one cannot staff counseling centers so that each subgroup on campus feels its values are accepted. Some students are likely to feel alienated by the personal stances of individual counselors. Thus, a varied staff is important but its variety will necessarily be limited by fiscal reality.

Another important implication of reducing ambiguity for the counseling center is that administrators as well as students will view counselors more clearly. Stubbins (1970) notes that counselors usually avoid the use of power within their institutions to protect themselves from administrative scrutiny. Such scrutiny implies a very real problem. Administrators may, in fact, view some of the counselors' values as expressed in his activities as a form of disloyalty or a threat to the university. For instance, if a counselor has been instrumental in organizing a campus women's group which agitates for gynecological services and the administration considers these illegal, the constructive aspect of the counselor's involvement may be lost on administrators, even though the counselor may have increased the credibility of the counseling center and its impact on this group of feminists. That involvement may be seen as disruptive even though the counselor understands the administration's position and attempts to interpret it to the students. The significant help that a woman counselor may be able to offer feminists will not be apparent to administrators while her seemingly disloyal activities will be. Thus, dispelling ambiguity and presenting themselves as real people with values—people whom students can accept or reject— may result in reducing the credibility of the counselors and the counseling center with college administration.

This problem calls for a courageous counseling center director willing and able to convince his superiors of the value of involvement with student concerns. Later, he should be prepared to back up his assertions with data showing that students from previously alienated subgroups now use the counseling center in greater numbers. The current word for this process is accountability, and college administrators have a right to expect it in such a situation. Academic appointments with the possibility of tenure for counseling center personnel can afford some measure of freedom to senior staff members who attempt to reduce counselor ambiguity and establish credibility with students.

Another implication of reducing counselor ambiguity for the counseling center is a redistribution of time spent in the counseling office and out on the campus. Here, too, the director may need to support his counselors against administrators who think they should be spending their time in counseling activities.

Abandoning the medical model and reducing counselor ambiguity opens up new possibilities for the individual counselors. With the support of the counseling center director, the counselor now can afford to set up preventive programs based on his counseling observations. Thus, the counselor who hears woman after woman tell about the subtle discrimination employed by job interviewers can attempt to set up a program to inform women of their employment rights. In fact, some of the enraged or discouraged clients may be glad to help, while simultaneously learning how to take action personally in problem situations. Individual counselors who are aware enough of student problems to set up preventive programs or to intercede with college officials in the role of advocates can add considerably to the collective credibility of the college counseling center.

In summary, college counseling centers do have credibility problems both in their ethical stance and in the acceptability of their services to students. The prevailing societal attitudes toward student rights and values cause students to distrust any institutional affiliate as ambiguous as a college counseling center. They also mistrust any institution whose goal seems to be treatment for the purpose of adjustment to the values of society.

The suggested solution is a concerted attempt to reduce the ambiguity of counselor and counseling center on the campus. Counselors should become actively involved on campus in the areas of their own interests. This should ultimately lead to counselor intervention in preventive and advocate programs. However, while this program may increase credibility with students it may decrease credibility with administrators unless the counseling center director takes a strong position to back it up with data as soon as possible. The rewards for both counselors and college students seems well worth the institutional risks.

VI

Relevant Training for Counselors

Richard W. Thoreson, Charles J. Krauskopf

Counseling psychology first emerged as vocational guidance. Its major methodology and techniques were derived from applied psychology with particular emphasis on individual differences. It flourished during the thirties when the emphasis was on the measurement of a wide variety of individual aptitudes, abilities and interests related to the criterion of successful job performance. The forties brought a reaction against the rational, trait-factor approach and a turn toward affective problems. Client-centered therapy gained instant popularity, positing a procedure in which a client could become a better person through his own efforts. It was both optimistic and simple in application, fitting nicely with the liberal, humanistic traditions in the United States. The sixties brought another reaction and attacks on the state of the art. The current charge was irrelevance. The thrill was gone from the romance. Traditional psychotherapy did not work for most, and those for whom it appeared to work, usually the affluent middle and upper class, had capriciously journeyed to new temples to share in the arcane mysteries of small group experience. Our under-thirty generation is openly disenchanted with the one down, doctor-patient relationship found in traditional service delivery systems (Warnath, 1972). They appear more or less amused by the 1940 concept of an exact fit into the proper vocational slot.

An outline of proposed functions for college counseling centers (Kirk and others, 1971) is a jarring reminder that many services traditionally offered survive as principles of faith and do not seem to change when data appears which definitely suggest change. Their proposal highlights two such services, "psychotherapy" and "expert consultation." Astin (1961) termed psychotherapy functionally autonomous in referring to its amazing persistence in spite of a lack of evidence to support its effectiveness. Bevan (1971) admonishes us to take heed of society's growing disenchantment with the so-called expert and the resulting dehumanization of the consumer that it engenders. We believe that unless counseling centers do more to reconceptualize their functions and their personnel they may become like buggywhip factories—interesting and nostalgic but totally useless.

Our review of current issues in theory and practice of applied psychology coupled with findings from our study of counseling psychologists provided the stimulus for this chapter. The findings of the study and their implications for counseling are worthy of review and serve as a precursor to our discussion of issues and predictions.

The study, conducted with the approval of the American Psychological Association, Division 17, was launched to collect information on the training, professional identification, and activities of a large sample of recent graduates of programs in counseling psychology. Briefly, the methodology was this: from the 121 departments with doctoral programs in counseling, counseling psychology, counseling and guidance, etc., more than 1,000 doctorates were granted during 1962–1967. From these graduates, a stratified sample of 200 was selected, eliminating all programs granting fewer than five doctorates.

Our sample was asked to provide a wide range of personal data on educational experience, professional identity, reading and research habits, areas of competency, and occupational functions and preferences. A number of general characteristics and patterns have been previously reported (McGowan, 1970). Some of the findings and their interpretations appear significant in considering the issues facing all areas of psychology.

A summary of our findings indicates that counseling psychologists are an amalgam of many different professionals performing a wide variety of tasks, very few of which appear in descriptions of counseling psychology. The apparent circularity of that statement results from the fact that if we define counseling psychology by what the professionals are doing, we can hardly define it at all. Young psychologists appear to have been well educated only to move promptly away from direct application of their knowledge. They tend to move out of counseling into administration and teaching, most frequently in academia. Few are engaged in what counseling psychologists are presumed to do, namely, direct service to clients. The role of the counseling profession with regard to current and future needs would appear to be ill-defined.

A recent survey of clinical psychologists in academic settings (Thelen & Ewing, 1970) suggested that the scientist-practitioner model is most generally advocated by those who teach clinical psychology. The inference is that student clinicians will be exposed to this viewpoint and can be expected to adopt a similar position on graduation. This inference was supported by Clement and Sartoris (1967) who surveyed clinical graduate students and found that 59 percent preferred the Ph.D. degree and 32 percent favored the Psy.D. degree. Tyler and Speisman (1967) traced the historical development of the role(s) of psychologists and concluded by advocating a highly functional model for operating within the scientist-practitioner paradigm. The report of the Greystone Conference (Thompson & Super, 1964) is titled "The *Professional Preparation* (our italics) of Counseling Psychologists," but the report goes on to say that "in accordance with the principle that counseling psychologists are members of the discipline of psychology, the professional preparation of counseling psychologists should include training in the foundations of psychology as a behavioral science."

The position that seems dominant among professionally oriented psychologists in training and in academic settings, then, is that the practitioner must be both professional *and* scientist. Somewhat less popular is the position that applied work can effectively exist without the rigorous scientific background of the Ph.D. and that man cannot serve two masters (i.e., solve practical problems and simultaneously collect scientific data), as suggested by Miller (1969).

The basic scientist-professional issue is reflected in the development of models for training applied psychologists. One emerging trend is the development of professionally oriented schools. The California School of Professional Psychology exemplifies such development. In defining its rationale Pottharst (1970) stated that "we simply propose to reverse the priorities and train psychologists who are professionals first and scientists second . . . we are proposing a concept of training which recognizes that professional psychology no longer solely represents an outgrowth of academic psychology departments."

Another program likely to be emulated is that of Claremont graduate school. This program is academically oriented, yet proposes a different emphasis on practice. Brayfield (1969) described it as the "demonstration of appropriate roles for psychology and for psychologists in the development and use of psychological knowledge in the formulation and implementation of public policy." The above models have the distinction of freedom from a psychology department struggling to meet diverse training needs. Traditional psychology departments seem torn by intradepartmental jealousies, and within this context a multitude of questions have been raised. Among them are: Should schools of applied psychology operate outside the traditional arts and sciences areas? Should psychologists in schools of education, business, home economics, and so on, have appointments in the psychology department? Should they be considered psychologists at all? Or, perhaps, should there be no psychology department, but rather a school of behavioral science with a multitude of divisions?

Many of the above questions have been recently examined in the literature, with a considerable difference of opinion evident. For example, Webb (1970) proposed a universitywide department of psychology model. The basic premise would be to encourage and support (through joint appointments) psychologists in as many departments and colleges as possible and to accept the extradepartmental psychologists as peers. On the other hand, Sears (1970) advocated a multiple-department model, essentially a collection of numerous departments which operate with formal independence, such as the programs at Stanford and Harvard Universities. Still other writers (Coffey, 1970; Pfaffman, 1970) envision a school of behavioral sciences which would include many interrelated disciplines under one administrative umbrella.

These issues, however, transcend the limits of psychology. A perspective on such general trends and issues in higher education was offered by Toynbee (1968), who pointed out that until post-Renaissance days, life and education were considered static. That is, knowledge was held to be constant and circumscribed. For educated persons, life consisted of two stages: professional preparation in which education was imparted as a complete package; and professional practice, in which this circumscribed, complete knowledge was applied. Toynbee further pointed out that knowledge is dynamic, but, professional preparation has not kept pace with changing emphases. Students still endeavor to master a complete package of knowledge, but, in order to do so, are forced into increasingly narrow niches of specialization because of an implicit assumption that the world is static and, therefore, does not equip one with the breadth of knowledge necessary in a dynamic world.

Toynbee's answer is deceptively simple: education, even professional education, must be liberal and it must be lifelong. For applied psychology, recognition of this concept might lead to changes in graduate training toward a multidisciplinary model. The products of such training would have interests and loyalties transcending the professionalism of psychology.

Another pervasive issue in psychology during the past decade is that of relevance. Current literature concerning relevance tends to emphasize community psychology and the consultant role, with special emphasis on minority and disadvantaged populations. The literature also suggests a growing awareness of the ramifications of behavioral engineering.

The concept of community psychology seems particularly to

be receiving increasing support as a necessary direction for the practice of psychology. The phrase "community psychology" typically elicits the notion of medically oriented inpatient-outpatient mental health programs. Such programs are an important part of the community mental health movement. However, the effective practice of psychology must move beyond this limited concept. (See chapters by Crookston, Southworth & Slovin, and Rose.) As Brayfield (1967) suggested, the ideal program should find expression among the major social arenas of the community. For counseling centers this should include teaching, academic advising, influencing administrative change, and provision for psychological services to students where they are and not just in an office where some students might drop in. The trend, then, is toward involvement in social action programs which transcend the traditional definition of community mental health. Tyler and Speisman (1967) pointed out that the psychologist now sees himself as a problem-solver with skills relevant to the needs of society at a variety of levels and in multiple directions. These authors see the applied psychologist contributing to the community in many different ways and not restricted to the specific, perhaps narrow, functioning of the mental health center.

Kelly (1970) articulated an additional concern by suggesting that few psychologists have been "trained to cathect to a locale." He wrote that if psychologists can broaden their definition of therapy they then "can help to build a psychology *of* the community." The emerging role of the community psychologist, then, is that of a consultant who may direct his expertise to other professionals in a community health effort or to any of a broad range of persons, or problems, at a variety of levels. Counseling centers can be seen as a psychological agency to a community. But are they fulfilling this role? Are counselors trained for the consultant role?

One area which has received tremendous attention in recent years is the application of psychology to the problems of divergent groups—exemplified by the large number of governmental programs for the disadvantaged. According to Kunce (1969), these programs arise from either a social humanitarian or an economic viewpoint, and these differing perspectives contribute to different emphases: education and training, counseling and motivation, eradication of squalid living conditions, developing jobs requiring minimal skills, improving overall health, and so on. Kunce further pointed out that these basic economic and humanitarian viewpoints often conflict, and although all the proposed solutions may have merit, the result frequently is uncoordinated and ineffective programs.

Another confounding factor is that many programs of service for the disadvantaged are built around traditional service paradigms, and training programs are designed to fulfill the traditional roles. Unfortunately, as Thoreson and Haugen (1969) observed, traditional systems, although congenial to the style of middleclass America, are often inappropriate for the poor. It is becoming increasingly clear that the problems of the disadvantaged cannot be solved by a direct transposition of methods developed for other purposes. Psychology can make major contributions to human welfare, but appropriate training must be developed which will prepare counseling psychologists to fill roles for counseling centers and other psychological services that will not be invented until long after the new graduate has completed his training. We must not confuse relevance with specificity in training for currently useful roles.

Behavioral engineering, or the direct application of psychological principles to the manipulation and control of people, either individually or in groups, has occasionally been subtly advanced as representing the epitome of relevance for the behavioral sciences. Skinner's *Walden II* (1948) is the classic example of literature which advocates it, and many nonpsychological literary works have dealt with it (e.g. Huxley, *Brave New World*, 1932; Orwell, *1984*, 1949; Rimmer, *The Harrad Experiment*, 1966).

Although it may be comforting to ignore the ramifications of this issue, the opinion is widely held that applied psychology (e.g., psychotherapy) does involve the direct application of behavior control (Krasner, 1961). Many therapists or counselors deny that they manipulate behavior, as expressed by Rogers (1955) and Jourard (1959, 1961). However, the denial is of little consequence when we recognize that behavioral modification techniques with individual clients have been in rather general use for some time. The cogent ethical consideration, then, should concern the possible application of these psychological principles to the control of society at large, as suggested in *Walden II*. Krasner (1962) pointed out that the techniques of control are not sufficiently refined *at this point* to modify behavior in any way we should want, but that science moves at a rapid pace and we must therefore "concern ourselves with this problem before basic knowledge about the techniques overwhelms us."

Our research findings and extrapolations have led us to some observations, both factual and speculative, concerning future training in psychology and the fate of its applied aspects. Predictions are that training programs in psychology will divide further along lines already developing (Albee, 1970; Marx & Hillix, 1963). Trends in this direction are currently visible. The prevailing cry for immediate relevance in all forms of education, including applied psychology, is an additional pressure to abandon the scientist-practitioner model. This could mean further splitting of professional training, both within and outside the university, leaving the present APA-approved programs to take on a more specifically scientific character and the current programs preparing Ph.D.s for administrative positions in schools and colleges continuing pretty much as they are, with perhaps some tendency to abandon the need for peripheral identification with psychology which many have today. Our data further leads us to suggest that every division of psychology develops a circular communication system with its own language (jargon) which the incumbents publish for other incumbents and the recipients read primarily from journals within the circle. Our data are from counseling psychologists, but we assume they are not different from those of other applied psychologists.

While the functions of past clinical and counseling psychologists will remain of value, there is an apparent disenchantment on the part of funding agencies. Perhaps psychology has promised more than it could deliver. A great deal of money has been accepted from various federal agencies to train applied psychologists which has gone into the training of professors of psychology and education. This may be an artifact of the marketplace of the Fifties and Sixties. The future of employment in universities looks bleak indeed (Cartter, 1971). Whatever the cause, there are cutbacks in the funding of psychologists, and the money is going into other programs.

These things lead us to predict, albeit reluctantly, that in the name of relevance and changing with the times, we will soon achieve

Toynbee's (1968) model of a static education in separated professional programs. The Boulder model of the scientist-practitioner was an attempt to preserve the dynamic aspects of training professional psychologists. It is a difficult ideal which the discipline has often failed to meet. Psychologists would appear to be no better than other mortals at tolerating differences within the tribe. We think the baby is about to go out with the bath. Academic training programs do not seem to have created the dynamic training envisioned by the Boulder conference. As a result, many aspects of training have become irrelevant. Now, in the name of relevance, some would have the training changed to reflect the current situation, and, in twenty years or so we will have another round of fighting irrelevance.

What should we propose? An alternative model for the professional psychologist is that of translator-teacher-evaluator, a bridge between the discoveries of the scientist and the work of the practitioner. Ideally, this is a two-way street. Many discoveries of the practitioner have direct relevance to theoretical research; for example, Binet, Murray, Kelly, and many more, probably, should be brought to the attention of researchers. We have ample evidence that many of the current functions of the applied psychologist can be carried out by persons of more limited training (Magoon, 1966; Rioch, 1966). Someone is still needed to provide the training and evaluate the results.

Several promising examples fit our alternative model. Goldstein, Heller, and Sechrest (1966) examined the practice and rationale of psychotherapy within the framework of research from laboratory, clinical, naturalistic, and manipulative sources. Bandura (1969) provided a systematic presentation of social learning procedures that can be used by applied psychologists to achieve psychological changes. Goldiamond (1966) offered an account of the applications of behavioral analysis for psychotherapy with detailed attention to the ongoing behavioral transaction, or how to create a psychotherapy for a particular situation. Dawes, England and Lofquist (1964) presented a theory of work adjustment culminating a decade of research at the University of Minnesota, which shows how persons and jobs fit together. All these authors provide testable research hypotheses and precise implications for professional practice.

In the training area, Truax and Carkhuff (1967), Carkhuff (1969a; 1969b), Rioch (1966), and Magoon (1966) described the training of paraprofessionals and demonstrated their ability to carry out specific tasks in applied psychology. These people are showing us a way of multiplying the usefulness of our knowledge through the traditional methods of scholarship: translating, teaching and evaluating. Counseling centers could become an agency for these activities on the campus and a few have. On closer examination, this may turn out to be the scientist-practitioner model which we have neglected for our ingroup circle reading of directly "relevant" literature and writing for an ingroup audience. The role of the doctoral level applied psychologist will be that of translator—to change the dynamic, changing knowledge of psychology into programs relevant to their time. And teacher—to show others how to carry out the programs. And evaluator—to take back to the academy the conditions of the outside world (Bendix, 1970).

VII

Campus Community
Mental Health

Howard C. Kramer

This chapter represents a form of allegiance to an approach to mental health services characterized by Schulberg and Baker (1969) as the "belief system of the 1960's." Adherents of a community mental health paradigm, however, have no shortage of things that ought to concern them, a few of which I would like to mention. The adoption or promotion of any approach ought to be predicated on demonstrable attainment of specified objectives. In the case of mental health programming, too often the programming has outstripped the verifying, a situation of dubious value for effective long-range program development. A question of genuine concern is how long those who pay the fare will allow this situation to continue.

Wagenfeld (1972), in tracing the advocacy of the concept of primary prevention by community mental health personnel, notes

116

how easily ideology may replace empirical evidence as the major means of program substantiation. A sizeable component of the community mental health model is dependent on the notion of primary prevention—that is, of counteracting harmful forces before they have a chance to produce harmful effects. The notion of prevention is appealing, and, like the boomerang, one finds it difficult to discard. Even the loyal opposition find the concept intriguing. Chu and Trotter (1972) writing in the Nader Report, "Community Mental Health Centers" suggest, "Programs aimed at genuine alternatives to the customary labeling and segregation of people with emotional disturbance or other problems that inhibit an individual's self-sufficiency are to be encouraged. Furthermore, efforts by mental health professionals to act as advocates in order to help their individual patients gain self-control over their lives is desirable: effective outreach work in satellite clinics is also desirable. But all this should be aimed quite clearly at helping individuals: if mental health specialists want to call it prevention, that is all right too." Among their recommendations are two that seem related to future developments in campus mental health programming. They recommend public support of training programs for paraprofessionals, volunteers, and citizens in how to run their own human service agencies, and suggest that community mental health centers be converted into help centers or human service centers to assist with problems in living.

As college mental health staff become more active in their outreach and intervention efforts in the campus community, their expansionist tendency becomes a concern. Wagenfeld points out that community mental health has been increasingly broadened in definition so that just about all aspects of the human and social condition are grist for its mill. At the extreme, then, everything may be interpreted as a problem in mental health and under the purview of the mental health specialist. This suggests that staff must carefully define and articulate to the campus community the functions for which they are accountable and guard against unsanctioned expansion of that commitment.

A related aspect of accountability concerns the responsibility of the staff to a greater variety of clients. Will staff be responsible to individuals, to consultee groups, to populations in the institution, or to the institution? In the area of organizational consultation this question is particularly difficult. An extension of the question has to do with the amount or degree of influence, and perhaps direct control, exercised by the community. Decisions concerning allotment of funds, agency policies, program priorities, service delivery styles, and other questions will require discussion and negotiation. They represent only a few of the issues agencies must face in the future.

Perhaps one of the major contributions of counseling and mental health staff is fostering and maintaining climates that can facilitate efforts to solve the difficult questions of the time. Michael (1970), writing about the value of feedback for long-range planning efforts, commented, "the capacity to adjust depends on effective use of error. But we do not now have an error-embracing ethos, nor do we know how to design organizations that have a capacity for continuing redifferentiation and reintegration as a function of what the feedback from the environment requires." This notion of the tremendous need for, yet extreme difficulty with, organizational growth could accurately portray many of the delivery systems in the college. The urgency—and the opportunity—is no less significant for counseling and mental health delivery systems. As we strive to provide appropriate preventive education, counseling, and mental health care on the college and university campus, a community-oriented model—in short, campus community mental health—may provide a reasonable alternative.

The college setting, representing one form of community, has characteristics that lends itself to the use of a community mental health paradigm. The campus community has, for instance, the traditional sociological elements of a community such as territorial entity, functional unity, shared common destiny, centers of activity or community business, systems to achieve various functions, and sources of stress and strain (Banning, 1971). The community paradigm or community mental health model will continue to grow and be shaped by time and experience. It may even be incorporated into new forms or models of comprehensive health care such as the community center plan discussed by Morrill (1972). While the intent of this paper is to favor a community approach in campus mental health programming much remains to be done in terms of adapting, using, and evaluating the community mental health paradigm in the university setting.

The community paradigm, only partially described here, is an idealized version of what might be. While present conditions in higher education such as financial stringency, accountability, long-range planning, and other forms of institutional pressure may militate against development and change, such conditions may also facilitate institutional or agency renewal. These ideas draw, in part, on the concepts of social planning as discussed by Mayer (1972). In his presentation, Mayer reviews three basic ways of conceptualizing social planning. One way is by providing organized services to individuals to help them overcome deficiencies in the present system. In a college setting this may mean providing direct services such as information dissemination, counseling, medical care, or other services not provided by the institution.

A second view of social planning is that of integration and coordination of the component parts of the total system—Mayer calls this comprehensiveness—to a set of higher criteria or superordinate goals. This means trying to piece together the specific objectives or goals of smaller units to achieve the general or major goals of the total system. Attempts in the college to coordinate efforts of various agencies or departments to achieve the general institutional goals of educating and developing persons may be an example. The third concept of social planning is that of advocacy planning—equipping the disadvantaged groups so they may develop ability to exert pressure on centers of power for a more favorable distribution of available resources. In the college these efforts may include designs facilitating the development of new organizations and assistance to the membership for the process of achieving changes. For instance, the mobilization of persons interested in creating special programs of assistance for certain populations, such as teaching assistants, drug-users, or transfer students are to be examples of this concept.

My assumption is that future colleges and universities will have some type of center on campus and its mission will be partly directed toward the mental health needs of the college population. Since the parameters are by necessity vague, I will refer to it here as "the Center." This paper discusses selected aspects of the Center's future programming pertaining to the adoption and implementation of a campus community mental health model. The topics include the college organization, or the institution as client; activities in research, assessment, and program evaluation; and the use of volunteers and paraprofessionals. While it may be assumed that the Center may have additional objectives, responsibilities, and attendant programming, the full scope of the Center's potential operation will not be discussed here.

Institution as Client

Within the community mental health or human services model the structural pattern and network of liaisons are such that a center is only one of a variety of resources that cooperate to serve the mental health needs of the population (Schulberg and Baker, 1970). The relationships between the Center and other community or college agencies serve administrative as well as therapeutic purposes. According the Gruenberg and Huxley (1970) organization and coordination of services is important in combating chronic deterioration in social functioning. Given the complexity of most colleges and universities, such coordination is also vital to the efficient delivery of effective services. One of the characteristics of a broad mental health system is that it is by nature large (containing a great number of elements), complex (made up of many connections, relations, or interactions among these elements), and dynamic (subject to change or movement over time [Holder, 1969].) Thus the institution or the mental health or counseling programs cannot be simple, fixed structures. The population to be served is constantly changing; the activities designed to meet their mental-health and individual-growth needs must also change.

Consequently, I think future Center staff will view various portions of the organization as appropriate target populations and with this perspective become agents of change and development in the organization. As applied behavioral scientists, staff may assume roles as resource person, therapist, consultant to the organization, trainer, disseminator of behavioral science knowledge, or professional liaison (Moses, 1970), organization diagnostician

(Levinson, 1972), or transducer or energy link between scientific knowledge regarding principles of organizational functioning and the particular organization or group with which he is working (Bowers and Franklin, 1972). This perspective leads to a diversity of activity. Three possibilities are: professional staff of the Center engage in efforts that focus on the efficient delivery of existing service; the redefinition of therapeutic service, or the modification of the community as a social environment.

In dealing with concerns surrounding the efficiency of existing college services, Center staff provide a common linkage and coordinating function. They participate in interagency meetings, consult with agency staff and directors, assist in gathering appropriate feedback data, intervene as third parties to resolve communication and conflict issues, and assist with planning and assessment. Much time is focused on those natural work groups concerned with providing direct services to students. The objective is to use the skills of Center staff to facilitate service delivery. As one example Schmuck and others (1969) describe a setting in which consultants helped natural work groups in an educational system—public school administrators and faculty—develop problem-solving skills relevant to job-related tasks. Similarly, some of the staff of the Center become teachers, trainers, and consultants, assisting others to acquire knowledge of human behavior relevant to the natural work requirements in the institution. Thus, staff facilitate the development of skills important to the delivery of adequate and relevant service to members in the institution.

In the redefinition or development of therapeutic service, Center staff are involved in exploring new approaches of facilitating personal growth. As a counselor or therapist, Center staff may experiment with organizational variables that might have an impact on individual growth. One might expect, then, that new programs and methods of therapeutic intervention are developed and tested to determine their impact and potential usefulness. To say it another way, staff carry on research and development programs with the aim of systematically varying institutional procedures, structure, or format to meet existing needs. To develop programs that combine in creative ways the institutional and personal variables in the learning environment, the residential setting, or the student union may lead to preventive as well as therapeutic benefits. For example, continued exploration of models and methods of orienting students to the college would be research and development work with a select sample of variables present in the college. Though activities to develop revised treatment methods exist, a substantial effort is also expended in developing programs and activities that might be described as health promoting. The preventive goal is not to avoid or remedy disabilities but to create positive strengths (Bower, 1972). Drawing on available models of the developmental sequence of college-age youth, programs are designed to assist individuals in mastering specific skills and facilitating the transition from one level or stage of personal development to the next. The earlier example of orientation programming seems to lend itself well to goals that may be either remedial or preventive.

The third area of consideration for staff is that directed toward modifying the social environment of the institution or the systems within the organization. Some staff members of the Center, using their knowledge of systems theory and organizational dynamics, find themselves involved in teaching, training, consulting, and research activities, as well as other forms of intervention. These activities, carried out at various organizational levels and locations in the college are part of a systematic effort designed to impact organizational dynamics. A conceptual map of the organization and its inner workings are used by staff to design a network of interventions to effect change in the organization. Social-structural change is premised on the assumption that one solution to problems may be found in rearranging the social environment of community members. Through an interface or liaison function across organization levels or subgroups, staff provide one means of organization development. This liaison activity by Center staff becomes part of the organizational structure for sensing internal and external changes that demand the development of new procedures. In his discussion of a healthy organization, Miles (1965) points out the need for structures and procedures for detecting problems, creating alternative options, choosing solutions, implementing them and evaluating their effectiveness. He discusses the special properties of educational systems that distinguish them from other types of organizations and suggests several interventions to improve organizational health.

The point is that Center staff use their knowledge of interpersonal and organizational dynamics to facilitate intraorganizational change sequences.

While consultation and intervention may be useful in the general procedures or work activities of the college, primary focus will likely be toward those persons, functions, agencies, or networks that impact the health care services. This means chaining together interventions in some systematic fashion to accomplish objectives at various organizational levels. Thus, efforts directed toward existing service delivery practices are designed with an eye toward changes in the means of therapeutic intervention. For instance, an attempt to provide better care for test-anxious students may lead to exploration of the use of various group procedures or outreach activities rather than freeing, or finding, more staff for individual counseling.

In the same vein, efforts designed to redefine service or provide a new or modified form of service may have potential contributions for the modification of the institutional environment. A program providing special assistance or information to, say, faculty advisors to train secretarial staff in certain human relations skills or to provide appropriate consultation to key committees may have much to do with altering perceptions, attitudes, and behaviors.

The foundation of such consultation activity is the conceptual framework and organizational map created by Center Staff. As they become involved in dealing with the organization as client they are called on to identify, conceptualize, and analyze the linkages or relationships that now exist. As an example, Mann (1972) reports on a study exploring the relationship between the distribution of power in a university and the problems of entry and resistance to mental health consultation. In this case, conceptualization of the accessibility-power relationship provided the consultant with a useful working hypothesis for assessment and planning in the initial stages of consultation.

Activities that lead to creating a conceptual model of the organization may be as detailed as those suggested by Levinson (1972). His five-step procedure includes a detailed organizational history which will delineate both the forces impinging on the organization over time and its characteristic adaptive pattern as well as its modes for coping with crisis; a description of the organization including its structure, physical facilities, people, finances, practices and procedures, policies, values, technology, and context in which it operates; an interpretation of observations, interviews, questionnaires, and other information about the organization's characteristic ways of receiving, processing, and acting upon information, as well as the personality characteristics of the dominant organizational figures and the style of the organizational personality; a summary and interpretation of these findings with a diagnostic formulation; and a feedback report to the organization to establish a basis for organizational action toward solving its problems.

The diagnostic formulation and feedback report take on critical dimensions for organization consultation and the research activities to be mentioned later. Brown's report (1972) on data gathering followed by feedback discussions with organizational members and faculty and students in a private secondary school, underscores the point. The feedback served not only to improve upon the researcher's preliminary diagnosis but also broadened the organizational constituency for the change effort. The latter notion of broadening the base of sanctions available to the interventionist is also crucial. Clark (1972) describes a program that collapsed because the circle of those who sanctioned the program was not increased. The goal of expanding the sanction base must be kept in mind and gradually made more explicit to the client system and worked through with its members. The need for clarifying the role relationships between the consultant-researcher and the many systems and key personnel in the college exists, partly because few colleges have created organizations or centers that have social innovative research as their primary function. However, even with institutional history on his side, the consultant must be acutely sensitive to the issues of ongoing relationships with others and the degree or kind of sanction implied.

Activities designed to impact growth and development in the organization are ongoing, integrated, and context-based, using whenever possible the natural work unit found in the organization. My experience may serve as an example. Students in the university had been critical of services available to them and of the pervasive "campus gloom" relative to personal concerns and individual needs.

A committee of faculty, university staff, and students were invited by a counselor to explore the dimensions of the need. Early in the planning stage financial assistance was obtained from various university student affairs agencies, and a questionnaire was designed and administered to a representative sample of students. Summaries of the findings were then distributed to heads of all the general university student service agencies (Kramer, Berger, and Miller, 1972).

Following consultation with the counselor the vice-president for student affairs convened a half-day workshop for all student affairs staff. Data summaries were distributed and discussed. More importantly, workshop participants were engaged to determine the implications of the findings, which were assumed to be "true, real, and replicable," and to plan for changes within existing student affairs agencies to substantiate findings or to help agencies meet the expressed need. The workshop design followed the "images of potentiality" framework used by Ron Lippitt of Michigan. Sixty participants worked in small task groups to determine implications of the survey findings. Groups listed implications on newsprint and each task group presented their newsprint product to the total gathering. Next, task groups were asked to describe an ideal future where the conditions, concerns, or needs suggested by the survey data were being handled adequately. The "images of potentiality" created by each group were shared and discussed with another work group. Following the workshop, the images or descriptions of all task groups were reproduced and printed copies sent to all workshop participants.

The workshop created a learning situation where a diverse group of university student affairs staff interpreted the meaning of the survey data and suggested alternate methods of meeting the identified needs. Consultants to the staff of the agency most directly concerned with the data implications were other peers and colleagues, not only the counselor-researcher or other members of the original planning committee. Members of the agency, in this case the Career, Planning, and Placement Center, obtained input from all sections of the Division of Student Affairs and, in a sense, were able to "accept" responsibility for dealing with the expressed need in the presence of helping peers. Following the workshop Career Center staff continued the discussion in an effort to reconceptualize their mission and method of operation and plan to share and discuss these notions, as well as their implications for others in the university, with faculty, students, and general student affairs staff. I anticipate that the degree of freedom experienced by Career Center Staff will lead them to catalyze activity in other sections of the university that share mutual interests, concerns, and responsibilities. In fact the matter has been broached and is receiving vigorous attention.

The behavior of the counselor in this example may typify the role of consultant to an organization provided by Ferguson (1968). He describes the role of consultant as diagnostic and, if necessary, healing agent to release forces that move toward balance and health. The counselor's behavior also follows the basic requirements of an intervention activity as suggested by Argyris (1970). The basic processes are generating information, allowing the client to make a free and informed choice, and facilitating the client's internal commitment to his choices. According to Argyris internal commitment means the client is acting on the choice because it fulfills his own needs and sense of responsibility, as well as those of the system. It seems implicit that involvement with research, as well as the promotion of the utilization of research findings, are important areas to the practitioner of the future.

Research and Evaluation

Research, assessment, and evaluation are important responsibilities of the practitioners in the Center. Pressures created by demands for comprehensive service, coupled with the emphasis on accountability, underscore the need for sophisticated expansion of these functions. A significant proportion of staff time therefore is allotted to the design and execution of methods of data gathering and analysis. Primary areas of research activity are epidemiological description of the population; treatment-focusing research; program evaluation; and program facilitation or action research.

The comprehensive counseling and health care program provides for a variety of systematic efforts to determine the mental health needs and resources of the campus community. Epidemiological data is gathered through prevalence studies, user rates at the campus service centers, and users' reactions and assessment of these services. Data may also be gathered from students prior to their arrival on campus, early in the school year (perhaps we might expect to find modified versions of the freshmen testing experience), from selected samples of students followed in a cohort design, and through followup studies of students and alumni. A cohort study, as the term is used in epidemilogy, contains a sample that can be referred back to a given population or universe. This sample is then stratified or divided on the basis of a certain characteristic or a set of characteristics. All those in the sample found free of the condition being studied are followed over time, with members of the sample with and without the characteristic being examined to determine the conditions of interest. Assuming a sample of freshmen were categorized on the basis of certainty of long-range personal goals one condition of interest might be successful adaptation to the university. A cohort study would facilitate the exploration of possible relationships between the characteristic, certainty of goals, and the condition, adaptation to the college.

All of these approaches may be used to determine the specific needs and potential resources of the target populations. On a specific target population, the student dropout, extensive studies have been conducted at Harvard. One of the recommendations (Roche Report, 1972) was that colleges adopt a preventive psychiatric program. On the need for epidemiological research, the report suggested, "The first step in a preventive program lies in obtaining a detailed profile of the dropout-prone student. Such findings and resultant programming makes possible not only prevention but also early diagnosis to help stem the disorder before it progresses to the point of intellectual paralysis." The report appears to view dropping out as a form of personal disability on the part of the student. I prefer to view dropping out as possible symptom of disorder in the learning environment. In either case the intent would be to stem the disorder, or at least to alleviate it.

An example of a research activity designed to gather information about student needs and students' perceptions of available helping resources was alluded to earlier (Kramer, Berger, and Miller, 1972). A systematic random sample of university students were surveyed to determine the types of problems or concerns they experience, to whom they would turn for assistance, and if they perceive the university as providing means of help. For eighteen problem categories, respondents were asked to state if they had felt a need for help with the problem; list sources they would use or recommend to a friend; confirm their awareness of facilities on campus designed to provide assistance; and comment or provide suggestions about help. Survey results were used as input data by university student personnel staff to explore means of redesigning direct student services to accommodate the identified needs.

The second type of research activity, treatment-focusing research, illustrates most of the research now carried on in campus service agencies. Efforts are directed toward developing or refining knowledge with an eye toward creating effective interventions and behavioral change technology. One aspect is to develop and test hypotheses concerning possible associations between health of individuals and specific population characteristics. Research results then lead to designing program interventions that can influence conditions of disability or potential impairment known to affect selected portions of the population or to magnify or develop strengths already found. As an example Taube and Vreeland (1972) report an interdisciplinary study on the use of written reports of secondary school teachers to identify signs of faulty ego functioning in adolescents. They conclude that the direction of future development of adolescents in the sample could be predicted by data about their character structure available from the teachers' reports. Armed with analogous information Center staff may be in a position to design treatment interventions to support the students identified and to forestall the development of dehabilitating patterns or self-defeating modes of adaptation.

Other examples of treatment-focusing research are investigations desgned to map the stress-inducing characteristics of the community. Crisis theory suggests that various developmental and accidental stress-events provide pivotal points for the mental health of the individual (Caplan, 1964). In the college, a program similar to those described by Wright (1964), to determine the existing pattern of stresses in the institution will provide valuable data for designing programs and deploying resources to best advantage. In charting stress points, Miller and Aponte (n.d.) found few techniques for the monitoring of events at a social system level higher than that of individual life space. Their efforts at developing a monitoring system in a rural county may hold promise for the creation of methods and procedures to be used by Center staff in the future.

As risk-resistant characteristics of the population and risk-inducing characteristics of the environment become known, program planning is activated by Center staff. Smith (1971) suggests a design for a series of experiments to test the effectiveness of various intervention techniques with persons who evidence signs of positive risk in the community. In a pilot program, three populations would be identified: an experimental group with risk-marker characteristics would be exposed to a special preventive program; a control group having risk-marker characteristics would receive no special assistance; and a control group without the risk-marker characteristics would receive no special assistance. Risk-marker characteristics are factors associated with the development of an undesirable condition or consequence for members of the target population. Using Smith's notion of critical life-events as potential risk markers, developments such as a death in the family, moving from one college or curriculum to another, or facing major academic requirements such as theses or dissertations may predict impending difficulty. The results of the pilot study would be used to determine the efficacy of preventive programming on a larger scale.

Program evaluation studies, the third type of research activity, are notable for the large number of people who favor them and the small number who actually try (Zusman and Ross, 1969). In the future, though, the Center will be committed to evaluating programs they sponsor as well as carry on evaluation of those sponsored elsewhere in the college. Evaluative research, the scientific method for collecting data concerning the degree to which specified activity achieves its desired effect, will constitute one of the major contributions of the Center. In order to meet the demand for service suggested by the research activities, sponsored programs will be systematically assessed and will be continued only if they attain specified objectives. Shrinking financial resources and the ethos of accountability will require such activity.

Evaluation of Center programs by Center staff provides

benefits beyond the information necessary for decision making. Staff involvement provides an appropriate role model for other institutional members and makes visible Center staff as competent to carry out program evaluation elsewhere in the institution. One of the general goals of the Center is to generate programs for effective formal and informal affiliation between members of the various university subpopulations. These activities are consistent with the general strategies of the campus community mental health model and are found in the use of paraprofessionals, consultation to or with the organization, and the research efforts discussed here. With Center staff's visibility and resultant accessibility to community members, it would seem reasonable that they may become valuable resource personnel for others seeking assistance with program evaluation. It seems equally likely that some of the more research-minded staff in the Center may form consortium or consultant networks with other program evaluation specialists in the college to provide a broad-based resource team in the institution.

The fourth type of research activity supported by the Center are programs of data gathering and feedback to help shape developing programs and provide a continuing method of program monitoring. In this action research activity, the staff design methods of gathering information that are useful in planning, designing, implementing, and evaluating college programs. For instance, in the early stages of planning a specialized counseling program, data from potential consumers describing what help looks like would provide valuable information. Once the program has been initiated a monitoring procedure may be called for. This monitoring procedure would attempt to assess, in terms of outcomes from consumers who have participated, program benefits for those services rendered during a specified period. The procedure might also concern itself with the impact of the program on other help-giving agencies. For example, if a program were designed to assist students in dealing with interpersonal problems in a residential setting, a procedure to gather information about behavioral changes evidenced in that setting by program graduates provides information about effectiveness, as well as suggests possible alterations in design.

A form of program evaluation suggested by Zusman and Ross (1969)' may also be considered a type of action research. They discuss how process evaluation, that is, an assessment of the treatment or procedure used, may be used to upgrade services. Process evaluation, then, is a means of measuring or reviewing how well and how appropriately the specified methods of treatment or intervention were applied in the program.

Finally, activities designed to facilitate the utilization of scientific resources in the processes of educational change represent another aspect. Lippitt (1967) identifies six patterns of activities in the use of scientific resources: knowledge retrieval; feasibility testing; documenting creative innovations; data collection and analysis; organization or agency self-study, and training research consumers. Variations constitute a portion of Center commitment as staff strive to help others make use of available knowledge. A major consideration for staff as they increase research activities concerns support personnel. How are they to do all these things with tight budgets and limited staff?

Volunteers and Paraprofessionals

Counseling and mental health programming of the future will make extensive use of volunteers and paraprofessionals, and their participation leads to numerous benefits. First, direct involvement by community residents, faculty, students, university staff, or local townspeople facilitates a free flow of information and influence from the community to the Center and from the Center to a diverse sampling of the community population. Second, the use of volunteers opens up avenues for residents to meet a need of the community, a relevant personal need of the volunteer, and perhaps to test firsthand a possible future life's work. Third, adequately-trained volunteers provide sufficient manpower for the Center to attempt programming on a scale otherwise impossible. Fourth, training programs designed to assist community members in carrying out paraprofessional duties represents a part of a preventive education program. Finally, and perhaps most importantly, the paraprofessional network represents a step in the direction of matching community need with community resources.

Paraprofessionals will likely come from four sources: graduate and undergraduate students; spouses of faculty, staff, and students; emeritus faculty; and members of the local non-university community. Though fulltime faculty and university staff will also be involved, their regular commitment to the university leads me to take them out of the category of untapped resources. Students by and large have been, and will continue to be, the mainstay. Then as now, students will be involved for a variety of reasons—some because of a strong personal motivation to be of assistance, to help others, or to fill an unmet personal need; others to seek practical work experience related to formal courses in the helping professions, and still others to receive academic credit for experience analogous to practicum arrangements. For some students, paraprofessional duties will represent a form of financial aid since they receive payment for service rendered.

In many institutions spouses of the "regular" members of the university represent an almost invisible population. Though directly connected to and personally interested in workings of the institution, many have been only tangentially involved. Representing a wide range of backgrounds, ability, availability, as well as a direct connection and source of influence on the visible community members, faculty and staff spouses are an important resource.

Retired faculty represent another subgroup. As specialists who have dedicated their professional lives to teaching, research, and service, those who are sufficiently motivated to volunteer and participate in training programs are valuable assets. They provide not only a stimulating influence and a variety of sophisticated skills, but contribute a diversity of adult role models. The combination of experience, accessibility, and commitment may do much to foster the sense of community we hear so much about in the rhetoric of higher education.

Another potential resource are local community members not directly connected to the college. Engaged in all forms of endeavor, they can bring a multitude of skills, attitudes, and perspectives. Their participation may do much to enrich both the volunteer and the college community. Often, I suspect, local townspeople are not involved with the college less from disinterest than because no one thought of inviting them.

What are the reasons for participating in volunteer or paraprofessional activities? Some respond because they seek the experience, training and assistance they may receive. Personal gain may outweigh service to others, and once on the firing line they may decide to withdraw. Others may sincerely want to help but later find that other factors in their lives gain in importance and they, too, either withdraw or are selected out. The third group represent those motivated by sincere desire for self-improvement, education, and service to others. Members of this group make the entire program both functional and worthwhile. They participate in, and benefit from, the training program and proceed to carry out responsibilities with dedication, compassion, and enthusiasm.

The future will see paraprofessionals in a variety of activities at many levels in the institution. In the Center, paraprofessionals will administer testing instruments, assist in clerical functions, help with public relations endeavors, provide receptionist, intake, or screening functions, do individual and group counseling under appropriate supervision, and assist with program research and development. Other activities will include tutoring, "home visits," supportive therapeutic followup, case finding, carrying out predesigned need surveys, and teaching. Outside the Center, paraprofessionals will lead discussion groups, run workshops, direct programs, staff outreach clinics or centers, gather research and evaluation data, and represent the Center in the community.

Paraprofessionals will continue to be involved in orientation activities, programming in the residence halls or the student unions, and in other student personnel and helping agencies. In the academic sector, they will assist faculty in the administration of innovative programming, coordinating learning resources, and facilitating assessment efforts. Additionally, paraprofessional staff may provide specialized services for faculty team meetings, faculty committee meetings, and school and college faculty meetings. Even at the interface of broader system levels, say between segments of the college and the local community, between the college and alumni, or between college and prospective students, some of the paraprofessionals will be able to contribute to the general goals of the institution and the specific objectives of the Center.

An illustration of a program combining volunteers from two of the categories mentioned earlier may be helpful. At Cornell University we attempted to design an outreach counseling program staffed by paraprofessionals, bringing together students and faculty wives in a supportive counseling, information, and referral service for the campus community. Specifically, the service was directed at two target populations, undergraduates living in one sector of the campus and married graduate students and spouses. The program has not been operating long enough to permit any substantial conclusions, but experience to date does invite speculation regarding program development.

The two subgroups faced each other with surprisingly similar feelings, attitudes, and agendas. Most had little prior experience with members of the other group. They felt unsure of what to expect, attributed a host of characteristics to members of the other group, and felt uncertain of their own competence and acceptance of this new combination. It was difficult for some to see members of the other group as persons, and conversely, to represent themselves as they would in their own circle of peers. For example, faculty wives felt threatened by what they considered bright, able, sophisticated representatives of the student culture. Students, in turn, seemed to expect faculty wives to somehow mirror the "professor," and tended to be subdued and watchful in their early encounters.

The attempt at combining two resource groups created both positive and less desirable consequences. On the plus side was a total paraprofessional staff with skills, strengths, and talents far beyond what one group alone would have provided. We were thus able to consider types of program interventions impossible with a less diverse group of volunteers. In one of the forays into a graduate residence hall, the volunteer group was able to design and carry out a "food and friendship" microlab program that was warmly received and remembered by graduate students. In another instance, faculty wives aided in an outreach attempt with graduate student spouses. Difficulties arose, however, that frustrated both. One issue was program orientation. For whom were programs to be designed—for undergraduates, married students and spouses, single graduate students, others? Members of each group tended to promote programming directed toward persons much like themselves. A related concern was the domination or control of one group by the other. Regular weekly meetings typically had varying numbers of volunteers from each subgroup. At subsequent meetings those who had missed the prior meeting were likely to liven the discussion by saying, "Say, I heard that last time. . . ." Another tension producer had to do with questions brought about by differing perspectives and life styles, such as, Do we meet during the day or late in the evening? What types of program activities should we engage in? What type of training do we require? How should this group go about making decisions?

Most students were far more adventuresome and risk-taking than the older women volunteers. Individuals, however, generally learned from one another and as the year progressed, cooperation, trust, and affection increased. Mutual self-other education alluded to by many volunteers was evidenced by individual behavioral change and mounting group solidarity. Now the group is struggling to continue and perfect a method of operation to help circumvent some of the difficulties of newly created consultation and educational services.

Here, There, and Everywhere

Contemporary views of the role of counselors and counseling, such as that advanced by Kirk and others (1971), portray counseling as integral to the educational process, playing complementary developmental and remedial roles in regard to students. Additionally, counselors are presumably involved in academic and administrative planning and implementation in all aspects of student life. Thus the counselor is urged to embrace a broadened perspective of the contribution that counseling and counselors may provide the campus or educational community.

In terms of specific activities, Walz and others (1971) discuss seven types of counselor behavior to be encouraged and promoted in a training program. First, the counselor should be able to carry out a more complete diagnosis. He should make a systems analysis, whether dealing with an individual or an institution. Second, counselors should rely more on measurement by performance rather than by tests. Third, the counselor should reach out to potential clients rather than wait for his services to be solicited. Counselors have a responsibility to identify and interact with individuals who could make use of their services. Fourth, the counselor should be an advocate and initiator of specific changes in clients, in such areas as life style planning, destiny control, self-interest advocacy, participatory governance, significant group relationships and the effective utilization of human and physical resources. Fifth, the counselor should take direct action to change the environment on behalf of his client in certain situations. For some clients, such as the culturally distinct, it is often the environment, rather than the deficit in the individual that interferes with behavioral change. Sixth, the counselor should provide linkage with resources. Finally, the counselor should evaluate his own efforts and the resultant behavior of his clients.

I can only agree. Practitioners currently following the guidelines of Walz are already using an action-oriented, population-based, campus community mental health appoach. Questions and hypotheses about its general applicability in colleges and universities await formulation and examination.

VIII

Outreach Programing: Campus Community Psychology in Action

J. Alfred Southworth, Theodore Slovin

In community psychology we are concerned with new values, new theory, a new set of psychological skills (different from those most of us learned in graduate school) and an increased awareness of and sensitivity to the use and manipulation of power. Our values tend toward humanism as it applies to groups of people. We dream of a better human condition which, paradoxical to humanistic philosophy, we attempt to advance through the manipulation of power. Bloom's suggestion (1969) that we are dealing with a broad syndrome involving power, self-esteem, and human actualization is well taken.

137

Our theories focus on how one influences small and large groups of people (sometimes referred to as human systems and subsystems) toward valued goals (productive happy life, sound family relationships and structures, and so on). Skills in training, supervision, consultation, change agentry, and organizational development constitute the major armamentarium of the community psychologist. Community psychology addresses itself to a broader range of problems than those commonly associated with counseling and clinical psychology with their emphasis on one-to-one relationships, individual diagnosis, treatment, and remediation. A significant component of community psychology is a focus on the development and enhancement of positive attributes in man and his domain. Community psychology moves the emphasis "from a concern essentially with mind-body problems to a concern with a sound mind in a sound body in a sound community (Adelson and Kalis, 1970)."

The term *community psychology* came to the fore in 1965 at the so-called "Boston Conference" where a broad conception of the role of psychologists in community affairs was emphasized (Iscoe, 1970). In the context of that conference, community mental health was viewed a subspecialty of community psychology. *Campus community psychology* viewed in this framework, has the broad scope of community psychology but limits its target populations to those that participate in some significant way in the life of a college campus. Along with a concern for community mental health (which historically has focused on prevention), it includes a concern for enhancing human growth and the improvement of human systems and organizations.

Why are we no longer content with traditional one-to-one counseling as the sole human service in our centers? Cowen (1973) has presented a number of reasons. Traditional approaches to mental health problems are not meeting the need for services. Society is also changing rapidly and applied psychology is sometimes leading and sometimes scrambling to keep up. Warnath (1971) perceives a major need to be "in the training of selected students, faculty, and other campus personnel where professional counselors can make their most significant contribution to the campus community." Leona Tyler (1972), in her address to Division 17 of the American

Psychological Association, traced the shifting central emphasis from the Age of Anxiety of the fifties, when psychotherapy was *the* answer, to the redirections of the sixties toward behavior modification, small-group work, and social change as an equally viable approach to human problems. Tyler sees the seventies heralding a period of great confusion characterized by a sense of isolation for many. Crumbling social controls, plus the array of choices that most of us face, will account for many emerging psychological problems. Feelings of rootlessness and uncertainty are evident. In addition to being skilled in remediation, counselors now need on a grand scale to help individuals develop and use their own resources and those of society to enhance their lives.

We need to consult history in order to maintain perspective in a period of rapid social change. All that we include in community psychology is not new. Counseling centers have been involved in varying degrees in community psychology for a long time but many called it something else. In 1958, William F. Field, who then headed the Guidance Office (later to become the Counseling Center) at the University of Massachusetts in Amherst, initiated a summer orientation program for freshmen. It involved training upperclassmen to counsel and advise incoming students. We did not call these students paraprofessionals then, but their efforts were clearly directed toward preventing psychological and academic casualties in the fall. This program was and still is one of the largest and most highly developed summer orientation peer counseling programs in the country. It now eases the transition of over six thousand freshman and transfer students into the university each year.

We who mount outreach programs from college counseling centers are beginning to find them clearly productive. Through our influence and the influence of those we train, individuals and groups can learn to function better and move toward more productive and self-fulfilling lives than they would have been able to realize had we not come on the scene and deliberately intervened.

To begin to sense a potential for providing strong and positive impact on the lives of others is rather heady stuff. Counselors are not used to identifying with power. It is not so easy, however, to get carried away with our own importance and potency in community work when we examine what we have been able to accomplish. Many of our forward steps have been halting. For every successful outreach effort, we can find at least one community-oriented project that did not work out. Because we sometimes succeed—and falter more often than we like—we need to subject our work to frequent and careful scrutiny. We need to connect our zealous efforts to critical investigation. Careful evaluation of outreach programs offers one of our best means of developing sophistication and increasing successes in community psychology programs.

If our rhetoric sometimes sounds grandiose, our practices in counseling centers infrequently achieve the spectacular. Our dreams usually approach implementation through projects of modest proportions that we can mount with our limited manpower and other resources. For example, one ambitious project considered this year by University of Massachusetts Counseling Center staff was the training of sixty teaching assistants to conduct freshman rhetoric courses more effectively. We had visions of significantly touching the lives of over three thousand freshmen through a manageable number of graduate students. We were not able to implement this project and ended up turning our energies to more modest-sized undertakings.

Our successes this past year include developing and carrying out a human relations training program for seventy secretaries in student affairs, a pilot program for an undergraduate internship program, human relations and counseling training for forty heads of residences, and workshops in life planning for about a hundred students and a comparable number of nonstudent women. Descriptions of two of these as well as three additional programs appears later in the chapter.

Approaches

Many forces currently influence the direction of counseling centers. Counseling center directors represent one force for change. The Task Force on Training of the Counseling Center Directors Conference (Southworth, 1972) has identified a number of skills (and their relative availability) that counseling center staffs need. A recent conference on graduate student training in counseling psychology (Banning, 1972e) produced a number of social explanations why applied psychology seems to be changing and seemingly must change. Colorado State University Counseling Center staff did much in the sixties to advance campus community psychology by experimenting with so-called outreach programs (Morrill and Oetting, 1970) and other nontraditional programs of service delivery. Out of this experience and their familiarity with a broad range of counseling center services, they have developed a model of intervention strategies that include traditional services as well as broad community-based strategies (Morrill, Oetting and Hurst, 1972). Their model has considerable potential for analyzing and understanding intervention strategies. It seems to include all new and traditional approaches to psychological intervention and suggests strategies that have seldom been tried.

Golann (1970) indicates that the basic difference "between traditional clinical approaches and community approaches . . . are associated with strategies of intervention." His conceptualization of strategies focuses attention on a useful way of classifying innovative outreach programs. Helper-linked, occasion-linked, location-linked and service-linked strategies denote interrelated categories. Golann's approach clarifies "the relationship between the goals of a program and the strategies and priorities of choice used to approach them." Moore and Delworth (1972) have developed a detailed analysis of and procedures for initiating and implementing outreach programs. Their work further develops Morrill's (1972) and Golann's (1970) emphasis on making explicit the decision-making and conceptual processes that are involved in program development, delivery, and evaluation.

We will examine a number of significant outreach programs at the University of Massachusetts. Community-oriented programs developed by the human service agencies on our campus encompassed a number of innovative outreach strategies.

Peer Sex Education Program

An outreach program initiated and implemented by the Division of Community Health Education of the University Health Services which has received national recognition is the Peer Sex Education Program (Zapka, 1972).

The program had its informal beginning when a small group
of women students on campus requested instruction in birth control,
so they in turn could educate the women in the dormitory where
they lived. After some discussion and planning, the program was
broadened so that training would include other aspects of sexuality.
The first pilot group employing the peer education model was
started in September 1969. Responsibilities of the volunteer group
of students included not only educational functions, but also provision of a communication link between health professionals and
campus living units. Training sessions were held weekly. The original
PSE group decided to continue the project in the second semester.
Awareness of, and enthusiasm for, the project grew and groups
developed in additional dormitories.

Quite broadly, this program seeks to develop a model in the
use of trained students in an educational, counseling, and supportive
role in order to promote knowledgeable, responsible, nonexploitative
decision-making with respect to sexuality. Human sexuality is an
increasingly difficult emotional and medical concern on the college
campus. Students are struggling with decisions in an atmosphere of
increased activity and openness, of more experimentation, and more
awareness of homosexuality. The incidence of venereal disease is
rising alarmingly, problem pregnancies continue to develop. Yet,
much discussion among peers about sex is erroneous and steeped
in negative emotionalism.

The roles and responsibilities of PSE counselors are many
and demanding; they require conscientious and creative counselors.
Although each counselor shapes a unique program according to
her/his abilities and the needs of the target group, there are some
common PSE functions. First is information input or general consciousness-raising through posters, handouts, and other means.
Second is referral resource or directing peers to the persons or groups
which might best assist them. Third is liaison for helping groups,
paving the way for some groups to make contact with students to
establish open communication. Fourth is the role educator–facilitator, presenting colloquia, films, or other seminar formats in an
ongoing educational process in the dorms. Another PSE function is
as confidential counselor—being available to listen creatively to
personal problems of peers and suggesting solutions. The sixth

function is to provide a peer model of the kind of trained assistance which students can provide for students. In addition, the team approach is exemplified through cooperation with student counselors in other fields, such as drugs, race relations, or academic planning. The last PSE function is to promote the counselor's own personal growth. This last function is not incidental to the PSE undertaking, for anyone who seeks to be a helping person has a great deal of self-growth to achieve.

Male or female applicants must be at least second-semester freshmen, but not more than second-semester juniors, except that counselors working with married students and commuter groups may be first-year graduate students. No prior preparation is mandatory. Applicants must make a commitment to stay with the program for a minimum of one semester in training and two in service.

Those interested in participation send written application and a statement of their interest in the program. Each then has a personal interview with a member of the PSE Training Team of health, mental health, and counseling center professionals. Candidates must respond to a variety of prepared questions and are rated on subjective criteria. Awareness of vital issues related to campus life, ability to communicate with others effectively, empathy with the needs of others, and flexibility to ideas and beliefs of others are considered. Applicants must evidence relative comfort with their own sexual attitudes and behavior. In part, the basis of selection is comparison of the candidate to successful and unsuccessful PSE counselors in previous pilots. Qualities such as ability to organize and being a self-starter have proven important. Recommendations are sought from fellow students, a dormitory Head of Residence, a faculty member, or member of the administration.

It is felt that one-semester preservice training is imperative, as the role of a counselor in sexuality is extremely complex. It involves development of a sensitive awareness to one's own identity, value clarification, and accurate perceptions of others. In addition a counselor must develop educational and personal counseling skills. The training also provides the prospective counselors with experiences that can serve as models for some of the activities they might carry out. As part of preservice training, each counselor is required to enroll in one-semester, graded, three-credit courses offered through the University of Massachusetts Department of Public Health and coordinated by the University Health Services. It meets once a week for three hours. Students are responsible for active class participation, periodic quizzes and evaluations, and a variety of semester assignments and projects.

Included in the course is content-oriented material—the facts about various aspects of sexuality; information on helping or referral agencies and people; educational techniques and methods— audiovisual aids, handouts, knowledge of available speakers, and so on. The course entails introduction to course (expectations, evaluations, purpose, texts, importance of evaluation, project's historical perspective); introduction of group members to each other; group discussions (Why are we here? Reaction of parents and peers? Definition of responsibility to each other); reflection of attitude formation on sexuality; sex knowledge tests; interpersonal skill-building (nonverbal behavior, sensory awareness, and strength sharing); clarification of role definition and limits of the paraprofessional role; development of counseling and group dynamics skills; knowledge of factual material, referral agencies, psycho-social aspects as related to human sexuality.

To combine all these aspects of training in a meaningful way is a constant concern. New modalities and approaches are continually being investigated. We particularly emphasize the counselor trainee's responsibility for learning the content-oriented material outside class while emphasizing skill-building in class. Extra emphasis is placed on implications for the trainee's own feelings and attitudes.

Once on the job, three hours' group consultation time per week is required of each counselor. The inservice obligation is necessary in order to meet problems once they become real, to share successes, to develop new skills, and to continue to provide a support group. The training includes a discussion of problems, feelings, and reactions, using such techniques as videotaping, role playing, observer-participant exercises, and so on. Because the job seems to be complex and time-consuming, counselors receive credit from the Public Health Department for the actual field training experience and consultation.

It has become clear that paraprofessional work can only be

carried out with continuous supervision by trained staff. The staff associated with this program consists of an interdisciplinary team which meets, plans, and evaluates sessions regularly. The Counseling Center has committed consultant time for inservice training and provides consultation in preparing and collating evaluation instruments. The Mental Health and the medical staff of the University Health Services also provides consultants.

This past year, a first attempt was made to define the effect of the Peer Sex Education Program on the student population. The recently developed Sex Knowledge, Attitude, and Behavior Survey, now in the process of being standardized and validated, was utilized. A September 1971 pretest sample consisted of an experimental group (N = 457) and a control group (N = 464) from sections of campus without a PSE Program. The most obvious problem was the inability to control the multiple variables which could affect one's sexual knowledge, attitudes, and behavior—reading, exposure to mass media, invited lectures in residence halls, classes, and so on. A May 1972 posttest sample from the same areas and dorms consisted of an experimental group of N = 246 and a control group of N = 334. Within the understood limitations of the instrument, both control and experimental groups demonstrated an increase in knowledge during the academic year, but the positive increase was greater for the experimental group. At times this difference was dramatic, as in Question 39: How early can a pregnancy usually be diagnosed medically? The percentage of correct answers increased 21 percent over the year in the experimental group, as opposed to 7 percent in the control group. Indications also were that awareness of helping persons or agencies was higher in the experimental group. For instance, the percentage change of correct answers from pretests to posttests in Question 31—Can pregnancy tests be done at the Health Services?—was 22 percent in the experimental group and 17 percent in the control group. In terms of willingness to discuss a sexual problem with a counselor, 5 percent more of the experimental group people were willing to do so in May 1972 as opposed to 1 percent less of the control group.

We tried to get some grasp on the broad concept of "responsibility" and on sexual behavior patterns. Posttest data is presented in parentheses. In the control group, 54 percent (62 percent) of the respondents indicated they engaged in intercourse "sometimes" or "often" and 44 percent (52 percent) indicated they used a birth control method or device "sometimes" or "always." In the experimental group, 58 percent (69 percent) indicated they engaged in intercourse "sometimes" or "often" and 50 percent (69 percent) indicated they used a birth control method or device "sometimes" or "always." Future evaluation will focus on the training program and its effect upon the counselors as well as the impact of the counseling program on the recipients. Measurement will be done in at least four areas: knowledge of factual material, personal attitudes, awareness of social issues (for example, population and human ecology) and behavior change in such areas as utilization of contraceptives, degree of responsibility for own behavior, pregnancy rates, etc.

To summarize, the PSE program has a preventative as well as developmental emphasis which utilizes a variety of indirect interventions. In terms of strategies of innovation in the delivery of human services (Golann, 1970) the PSE Program exemplifies helper-linked (for example peer paraprofessionals), location-linked (that is, in the residence halls) as well as service-linked (sex education, referral, and counseling) innovative elements. Program development has progressed through Stage III-Implementing and Evaluating the Pilot (Moore and Delworth, 1972) and the current request for funding from NIMH represents progress toward Stage IV-Implementing, Evaluating and Redeveloping the Mature Program. The University administration at Amherst enthusiastically supports the program and recently expressed its support in a concrete way by providing tuition waivers for PSE counselors.

Counseling Center Undergraduate Internship

The undergraduate internship is a recently developed (Slovin, 1972) year-long experience which provides an opportunity for students to become involved in a learning experience similar to the VISTA and ACTION programs. It is a didactic and experiential training program focused on the development of personal and interpersonal competencies in these students and their peers—the kind of learning experience characterized as process education (Cole, 1970) and centered on "learned capabilities" (Gagne, 1967)—statements of what the individual can do—rather than verbalized knowledge. A major goal of the program is to involve students in the planning, delivery, and evaluation of human services. The target population is freshmen and the main delivery system is a new three-credit course in psychology entitled "The College Experience." "Our goal for the course is to help you make a smooth transition from home and high school to the college experience and self-directed learning. We hope to provide opportunities for you to develop and improve your understanding in the areas of interpersonal relations, 'learning how to learn' and decision making."

Interns have an opportunity to choose two three-credit courses from relevant offerings in human development, psychology, public health, education, and sociology per semester. The training, four to six hours per week, and supervised field experience, three to five hours per week, account for nine credits of academic work. The training focuses on the improvement and development of specific interpersonal skills (for example, attending behavior, reflective listening, empathic understanding) and conceptual understanding of interpersonal processes. We have utilized a variety of instructional approaches such as role playing, group discussion and encounter, audiotapes, and films. The contributions of Argyris (1968), Carkhuff (1972), Dyer (1969), Ivey (1971), Johnson (1972), Mager (1972), Maslow (1970), Mogar (1969), Rogers (1969), Thoresen (1970), and Watson and Tharp (1972) have been found stimulating and useful. The field work involved coleading at least one discussion group of ten to twelve freshmen enrolled in a psychology course for an hour and a half a week for each semester. There was usually a specific topical or interpersonal skill focus for each session. Groups met at a scheduled time, with membership limited to residents of the area in which the meetings were held. The design was intended to facilitate increased contact among group members outside the sessions.

Freshmen in the special psychology course attended a weekly lecture led by a Counseling Center staff member in addition to their discussion group session. Sessions dealt with congruence and honesty in interpersonal relations, roles people play, study skills, values, ways to live, and a taxonomy of educational objectives. Films were used. There were no exams, with grading on a contract basis. Students chose to work for a given grade by fulfilling specified requirements. To earn a C or better, freshmen were required to carry out a behavior modication project according to the steps presented in Watson and Tharp (1972). Projects included study behavior, eating, smoking, and listening behavior. We hoped students would become aware of at least one method of changing behavior patterns.

We attempted to evaluate the impact by using two instruments, Rotter's I-E Scale and an evaluative questionnaire, the I-E Scale during the second and again during the last week of class. We had anticipated freshmen who participated would have a greater tendency to believe that they controlled the reinforcements or outcomes in their lives. The results were in the predicted direction but not statistically significant. It is probably unreasonable to expect individuals to change fundamental attitudes or beliefs as a result of a single course. According to the results obtained on our evaluative questionnaire it was well received by the freshmen. Most felt it related to their educational and personal concerns, with the discussion meetings viewed as more helpful than the lectures. They valued the experience of preparing journals and behavior modification projects. Thirty students out of a class of 110 volunteered to help us offer the course the following semester.

Future plans include collecting data on the impact of the training on the interns; offering interns an opportunity to specialize in one of three areas (for example, individual educational and career counseling, group processes, and research) developing competency-based training modules; preservice training for interns; designing experiences for freshmen with both clearly defined behavioral objectives and methods of measuring knowledge, attitude and behavioral outcomes; and increased involvement on the part of counseling center staff.

In summary, the undergraduate internship is a developmentally oriented teaching-learning experience utilizing upperclass peers to help freshmen in their transition to college. Goals include helping freshmen make maximum use of their environment as well as "teaching the student skills he needs in order to modify his own environment so that it will better meet his developmental needs (Morrill and Hurst, 1971)." The rationale is based on the contributions of Bandura (1967), Guerney, et al. (1970), Miller (1969), and Thoresen (1970). The internship involves a number of innovative intervention strategies—helper-linked (peers), service-linked (educational), occasion-linked (freshman year), and location-linked (meetings held in their own residential area). We are currently in the stage of implementing and evaluating the pilot program. A number of significant questions remain unanswered. Among them are: Are we reaching those freshmen in greatest need of the program? Should we narrow the target to more specific groups—for example, the socially isolated, academically deprived? How can we involve academic departments in offering similar types of experiences to students other than freshman?

Room-to-Move

Room-to-Move, a student-run drug center at the University of Massachusetts in Amherst, represents an important concept for campus community psychologists. It also represents a successful community project. It demonstrates the positive effects that can derive when several community agencies collaborate to produce a service or meet an emergent need. Matters of territoriality and competition must be set aside if multiple agencies are to combine their talents in a constructive way. Room-to-Move is a fine example of the kind of payoff that can come from a truly collaborative effort.

Room-to-Move began in 1969 (LaFrance, 1971, 1972), generated out of consultation among a knowledgeable graduate student, a group of undergraduates, Counseling Center staff, the dean of students, and the Director of Health Services. It was initially funded with a small local grant, energized with much student zeal and the commitments of considerable volunteer student time. Many hours were spent training students in the Counseling Center on counseling process and how to counsel. Large investments of time went into improving student counselors' sophistication in the nature and effects of drugs and the management of drug-related problems. The Health Service was particularly helpful.

By the fall of 1970 Room-to-Move had received substantial funding from the university, the Student Senate, and HEW and opened its doors to the college community. During 1970–1971 it served more than 1600 students. It responded to requests for information from more than 800 students, arranged for drug analysis for more than 150 requests, counseled better than 600 students, and helped approximately 100 students through bad trips. Twenty educational programs were conducted in residence halls; a speakers' program was established; visits were made to more than forty high schools and adult groups in surrounding communities.

Room-to-Move went through considerable painful development during its first two most formative years. It was staffed largely by students who were sympathetic to the counter culture but resisted forming a structured organization. There was great affinity for friendship relationships among the members. They became a loosely organized community of workers, aiming to function through personal informal relations rather than formalized relationships. This method worked fairly well when only a dozen or so persons were involved. As the organization enlarged during its second year of service and took on fixed commitments, like running a 24-hour drug hotline, informality became less functional and reorganization became necessary. Also, in their zeal to serve, the staff found difficulty in setting limits on the kinds of services to provide. One time-consuming new activity had to do with providing a crash pad and related support for runaway teenagers. (This has subsequently been given up.)

Now in its third year of operation, Room-to-Move is a more mature organization—less exciting in some ways, but still highly functional and much more together. Its business affairs are administered by the University Health Service, but it has an informal but close liaison relationship with our Health Education division. It has restricted services to a more manageable area—it no longer runs a 24-hour, 7-day-a-week hotline, for example, but does provide an extensive drug education program for students, as well as helpful sophisticated services to those with problems. It also has an extensive inservice training program that enlists instruction from a number of different campus agencies. It is also beginning to develop and spell out its own code of ethics.

In brief, Room-to-Move is a tale of how an important and useful organization was born through collaborative efforts of many, how it survived a rather tumultuous adolescence, and how it is beginning to take its place as a relatively independent and mature organization. In terms of innovative strategies, Room-to-Move includes helper-linked (peers), service-linked (drug counseling and education), and location-linked (an informal setting) elements.

Along with providing an example of the value of collaboration, Room-to-Move also shows what can happen when a founding organization lets go. We in the Counseling Center feel we are much in the position of the good parent: we provided much support in the form of time, money, and administrative backing during infancy, backed away somewhat during a period of rebellious adolescence, and now take satisfaction from knowing that the child has become a successful adult. Counselors now collaborate with Room-to-Move more as peers than parents. We respect the organization and the services it renders, and enjoy its respect in return. We both take pride in our mutual accomplishment.

Secretaries Communications Workshops

The Secretaries Communications Workshops were started in the fall of 1971 with the specific aim of improving the interactions between secretaries in student affairs departments and the students they encountered in the normal course of their duties.

The model was developed the previous summer by two members of the Counseling Center staff and five secretaries. The result was a one-day workshop with a microcounseling approach (Ivey, 1971) to instruction. A typical workshop was led by a secretary and a psychologist from the Counseling Center, both trained in microcounseling interviewing techniques (Ivey, 1971) and both experienced with the workshop model. Four to six women were trained at one time. Workshops began with an informal coffee hour at 9 A.M., to acquaint staff and trainees with each other and help each secretary share the unique nature of her job and the kinds of communications problems it presented.

After thirty minutes' discussion, leaders directed the women to form pairs and develop role-playing themes related to typical incidents on their jobs. The roles were then enacted in usually two- to five-minute episodes and videotaped, then played back in a rather leisurely manner, with everyone encouraged to respond. Leaders guided the feedback so that it was not judgmental or threatening.

An open discussion followed. This usually shifted from the specifics of the videoscenes to other communications problems. Difficulties with peers and supervisors and role restrictions were common topics. The level of openness and willingness to share and be helpful was high and very gratifying to the leaders.

Next, a prerecorded set of videotapes was shown. These depicted extremely drawn examples of high- and low-quality communication between secretaries and students, and were followed by further discussion. Again, the atmosphere was one of openness, sharing, and mutual support.

At noon staff and trainees went to luncheon and informal conversation continued. The last part of the workshop repeated the first role-playing portion. Secretaries reversed roles, that is, usually each played a student at least once: scenes between supervisors and secretaries (or between peers) were sometimes depicted. Specific problems were discussed—"I tend to respond to everyone the same," "I have trouble because of divided loyalties—sympathy for the student—the need to enforce an unpopular rule," and so on.

Discussions tended to focus on day-to-day problems and concerns of secretaries, which often had little to do with communicating with students. The workshops typically came to an end between 3 and 3:30 P.M. following feedback from the secretaries on how they had experienced the day. A day or two later, a questionnaire asked for further evaluation. Responses were almost wholly positive: the day had been pleasant, the communication level high, and new acquaintances had been established. Many reflected seriously on the experience and viewed it as having contributed to self-improvement, to their own assertiveness, or in some other heightened capacity to handle relationships on the job. There were very few negative comments.

The last workshop in the initial series was held in the summer of 1972. Workshops were resumed in February 1973 with somewhat surprising results that highlight the rate of social change on college campuses today. Women's concern for their rights and self-expression were at least as important as the Center's concern for the level at which they could communicate. The open atmosphere of the workshop facilitated expression of concerns over opportunities for advancement, to learn information that was important to effective functioning on the job. Encouragement of assertiveness no longer seemed necessary.

The secretaries in the first workshop of the new series identified several different areas of personal development that workshops could serve: they were interested in more real communications workshops in which students would also be present; new secretaries wanted one devoted to providing them with useful information; still others wanted life planning workshops.

The workshop leaders concluded after the first of these workshops, "The energy generated in the afternoon session was considerable and indicated that people should not be called into a communications workshop on the assumption that they need it: choices must be available, and secretaries must be involved in the planning and designing." The leaders' recommendations have been followed. New workshop models are being developed as this book goes to press. Community psychology in action requires the kind of frequent program review and evaluation that is depicted in the evolution of the University of Massachusetts' workshops for secretaries.

The innovative strategies included in the secretarial workshops are: recipient-linked (secretaries) and service-linked (communication training).

Everywomen's Center

Everywomen's Center is a young and vigorous organization that is in its first year of development. Like Room-to-Move, it grew out of a collaborative effort. In the spring of 1972, the Counseling Center, Continuing Education for Women, and the Office of Community Development and Human Relations initiated the Center on a pilot basis. Women from each of the three organizations were given release time to test the need for such a center. In less than a year, on a somewhat limited budget, but with much zeal and volunteer effort from women in the community, Everywomen's Center has developed a strong educational program (for example, workshops on women's history, life planning, the image of women in literature and films; creative workshops on poetry and painting, and so on); launched a personal counseling service for women; developed ongoing self-support services for special interest groups; provided child care for women who attend its workshops; solicited and obtained additional financial backing from the university administration, and in general established firmly the need for its existence and has already furnished much needed direct service to women who live in Greater Amherst and surrounding communities.

Major strategies employed by Everywomen's Center are: recipient-linked (adult women); location-linked (central to a number of communities in the Connecticut Valley); service-linked (women's service needs determine programs); helper-linked (trained volunteers provide much of the service). In terms of Moore and Delworth's (1972) stages of development, the Center is moving into Stage IV as it continues to extend its programs to a wider population and in other ways shows signs of becoming a mature organization.

Freshman Preventive Intervention Program

Bloom (1971) developed a unique preventive intervention program for university freshmen which was somewhat successful in meeting some of its objectives.

The goals of the program included "the development of greater emotional maturity, more successful adaptation to the college community, less psychological disability, and fewer dropouts." We decided to implement a similar approach at the University of Massachusetts. Following Bloom's conceptualization we are attempting to find out more about the variety of tensions, anxieties, concerns, and uncertainties that confront freshmen during their first year in a large university and to determine whether anticipatory guidance would be useful in reducing these uncertainties. The research design involves an experimental and control group procedure (that is, random sample divided in half). Each group responds to questionnaires mailed directly from the Counseling Center. The questionnaires (a total of five over the entire academic year) deal with several major areas of concerns (for example, independence and interdependence with parents and with peers, coping with stress, career orientations, academics and heterosexual relations). Items with significant face validity in these areas were copied or adapted from the instruments used by Bloom or constructed specifically for use in our investigation. The experimental group receives a prompt report summarizing the findings from a given mailout. Each report consists of approximately a page of introductory text and summary, and then a repeat of all the items in the questionnaire with the percentage of students answering in the keyed direction of "True" or "Very True," with the sex differences where appropriate.

The first mailing included the questionnaire and a long explanatory letter describing the nature of the project and outlining the participation hoped for. Slightly more than 50 percent of those contacted responded. Questionnaires were not anonymous—each bore a label with the name and student number of the respondent, a technique adopted to permit matching a student's responses to all subsequent rounds of the study.

All who responded to the first questionnaire constituted the study group used for the second and subsequent mailouts; those who did not respond to the first questionnaire were removed from the study group. Response rates to later distributions—by those who had committed themselves by returning the first questionnaire—were above 90 percent (with the exception of the fourth round, mailed after the start of the second semester, when a significant number of students moved to different dormitories, moved off campus, or withdrew from school). While the initial design for the study had envisioned six questionnaires, three each semester, it now seems possible to reduce this number to five. The fifth and final questionnaire will be distributed immediately after spring recess.

The Cohort '76 Project design, as implemented, seems to be satisfying its general goals—the development of a body of reasonably accurate data about various issues which do or do not trouble students and the duration of these problems and worries. Through successive comparisons of the experimental group with the control group, an assessment will be made of the efficacy of the feedback guidance technique in reducing the intensity of the worries and uncertainties that are being investigated. Service-linked ("providing membership in a group which had psychological, if not physical reality," "giving group members some reference facts with which to compare themselves," "providing an avenue for them to express their reactions to the university," and "providing formalized opportunities to think through their own beliefs [Bloom, 1971]") and recipient-linked (freshman) strategies are exemplified by the Cohort project.

Implications for Training and Research

Counseling centers that have moved into campus community work are sometimes faced with a dilemma similar to that of community mental health agencies (Bloom, 1969) where poor conceptualization and definition of territory and professional activities have been prevalent. Those who pursue the role of psychologist-generalist that tends to be associated with community psychology often end up exhausted and ineffective by trying to be all things to all people in a community. Bloom's call for conceptual clarity, research on effectiveness and methodological rigor are important considerations. Each center also needs to determine for its own campus what skills it needs, how they can be effectively put into practice, and to decide where it will and will not put them to work, as well as to establish means for getting feedback on the effectiveness of its interventions.

The Directors of College and University Counseling Centers Conference participants (Southworth, 1972) were asked to indicate the skills they hope to find in new professional counselors and the availability of these desired skills. Desirable, but in short supply, are skills in organizational development, behavior modification, facility in consultation, change agentry, creativity, research, conceptualizing problems (and model building), administrative skills, crisis intervention, and institutional diagnosis. There is also a shortage of candidates who know how to train paraprofessionals. Readily available and desirable are the traditional skills of individual and group counseling and psychotherapy and ability for individual diagnosis and academic teaching.

The conclusion from this survey is similar to that of Banning's (1972a), which was based on an earlier form of the directors' survey. Traditional training continues to dominate the preparation of graduate students. Banning's review of inservice training programs in Western states revealed that inservice training programs tend to provide more of the same. It is easy to conclude that we are perpetuating outmoded models of training and service. It is not that traditional skills are no longer desirable. Our shortcoming is that we are not moving ahead rapidly toward extending the range of competencies needed in practical settings.

Warnath (1971) has stressed the need for counseling centers to extend their influence through sharing their skills, to influence on a large scale the teacher-learner processes on their campuses, to familiarize themselves with the concerns of special interest groups, such as ethnic minorities and women, and in general to address themselves to the quality of learning and the social issues where they work. His goal is to improve the experiences of all students, not a 5-15 percent minority who might seek out a counselor in his office for individual counseling.

It follows that training programs must prepare graduate students for new functions by updating academic programs and by providing field experiences relevant to new kinds of application. The traditional internship in a medical setting or a college counseling center is a limited and limiting preparation. Students need to train in counseling centers and other settings where the focus is truly on sharing counseling knowhow widely, on quality teaching, and on generally providing growth-producing experiences for students.

A number of forces are working to change the education of counseling psychologists in the directions that we have indicated as desirable. At a conference sponsored by the Western Interstate Commission on Higher Education in October 1972 (Banning, 1972e), a number of these were discussed. They include the identification of relevant skills for work in community psychology (skills in training paraprofessionals, skills in diagnosing campuses, skills in change agentry, skills in assessing experience-based competencies, skills acquired from the human potential movement, and so on). Awareness that the campus *is* a social system that can be assessed (diagnosed) and understood helps to define entry points for those who wish to influence the campus widely. We can address ourselves to students' need for meaning in their college experience. Our heightened sensitivity to students as resource people support the kind of interventions (for example, peer counselor training) in counseling centers that can affect students on a broad scale.

There is a need to give up the notion that traditional coun-

seling skills—those for professionals only—are all that matter. As we
begin to contemplate the relatedness of Eastern religious experience,
altered states of conciousness, novel life styles, the needs of women
and minorities to human development and happiness, we may need
to turn to students for new approaches. We can learn from our students.

The time to make radical changes in the delivery of human
services is clearly on us. The question is not whether we should
change, but what we change and how we can change to provide
the trained manpower to do what clearly needs to be done on our
campuses. The following section deals with some promising directions for changes in intervention strategies.

Future Directions

Some approaches to outreach interventions which we consider worthy of increased attention and further development are
those of planned change, ecological/transactional and educational.
These points of view are interrelated and overlap one another, but
we want to focus briefly on the unique contribution of each perspective. Perhaps the most direct utilization and application of
the principles, concepts and theory of planned change (Bennis,
Benne, and Chin, 1969; Lippitt, Watson, and Westley, 1958) to
the problems of higher education and the campus community is the
manual of Sikes, Schlesinger, and Seashore (1972) which "draws
heavily on our four years of experience with a project, 'Training
Teams for Campus Change' . . . (as well as) our own and others'
work with teams from scores of institutions during NTL Institute's
summer Higher Education Laboratories over the past twelve years."
The purpose of the manual is to aid "persons who wish to improve
higher education institutions. The particular focus is on the use of
groups as change agents but many of the ideas and methods which
are presented are also relevant to other kinds of renewal efforts."
It discusses "selected issues which we consider to be most critical
for the effective functioning of change groups . . . a model for
planned change . . . team building, selection of change goals . . .
ideas about the uses and misuses of consultants . . . suggestions
about activities to enhance group development and self-assessment."

The University of Massachusetts is one of the sites of campus change efforts referred to above (Sikes and others, 1972). Our firsthand experience with this approach has demonstrated its potential usefulness and relevance. It is difficult to evaluate the total impact of our current efforts since they have been underway for only a few months. A number of specific change projects are in the process of being developed both in academic departments as well as in student affairs. We are building a data bank on the resources and skills available in our change network which is known as the "Applied Behavioral Science Alliance." The Alliance members represent a variety of disciplines and human service agencies (for example, Business Administration, Education, Nursing, Psychology, Counseling Center, Mental Health, Community Development and Human Relations, International Students, residential areas). The university administration has provided financial support and faculty appointments for four off-campus consultants. We look forward to the further development of the Alliance and increased innovation in the campus community. However, we are also aware of the obstacles and resistances dealt with in order to bring meaningful change such as those presented by Hurst and others (1973). The contributions of Bennis (1973) and Sarason (1972) on the subject are also particularly illuminating.

The ecological/transactional perspective is acknowledged by some professionals (Banning, 1972a; Bloom, 1971a; Kaiser, 1971; Kelly, 1971; Warnath, 1971) to have great promise as an approach to analyzing and dealing with campus stress. "The ecological approach . . . is concerned with the creation of campus environments which potentiate students as physical, mental and social and spiritual beings (Kaiser, 1971)." The focus is on "the transaction between the student and the University environment" and "how best to design the University community to meet the needs of its members." The Western Interstate Commission for Higher Education has provided significant support for the ecological point of view. The Commission has been concerned with improving mental health services on Western campuses for several years. Recent task force reports prepared by Program Director James Banning (1972c,d), are excellent sources of creative ideas, approaches, and insights in the area of the campus community psychology. The report entitled *New Designs: Prevent Educational Casualties, Promote Educational Growth* is particularly relevant. "The new designs imply that mental health delivery systems on campus will have to become more open and involved with community programming and participation. Task force members offer a brief questionnaire by which services can judge how responsive they are to community involvement and how prepared they are to adjust programming efforts to new designs. The new designs suggested by the task force are offered not only as a means to prevent stress and conflict on campus, but also as a means to increase the quality of educational life for each member of the campus community (Banning, 1972d)." Warnath's ideas regarding the future role of counseling centers also make a great deal of sense. "Although it may sound strange, the counseling center must turn itself into a human resources center for the welfare of the institution as a whole. . . . Interest and concern will be concentrated on methods by which the center can humanize the educational experiences of students through existing agents rather than on better or more efficient ways of injecting special humanizing experiences into a decreasingly human environment."

The final strategy or perspective which we feel provides considerable opportunity for innovation in outreach programming is that of the educational model. The primary focus of educational interventions is to "enhance the functioning of individuals (Morrill *et al.* 1972)," to educate people to function in such a way as to lead them to increased feelings of personal and interpersonal competence and satisfaction (Guerney, Stollak, and Guerney, 1970), and to give the individual "insight into how our system works, and how it poses threats to individual freedom (Sanford, 1966)" and growth.

In other words, education should help individuals learn what kind of people they are, what are their aptitudes, what they are good for and not good for, what can be built upon, what are their good raw materials and potentials? The rationale for educational model is based on the thinking of Bandura (1967, 1969), Miller (1969), and Guerney and others (1970). The following brief quotes from their contributions illustrate some of the underlying assumptions of an educative model for outreach. "The day may not be far off when psychological disorders will be treated not in hospitals or mental hygiene clinics" or counseling centers "but in comprehensive 'learning centers' where clients will be considered not patients suffering from hidden psychic pathologies but responsible people who participate actively in developing their own potentialities (Bandura, 1967)." "There simply are not enough psychologists even including nonprofessionals, to meet every need for psychological services . . . our responsibility is less to assume the role of experts and try to apply psychology ourselves than to give it away to the people who really need it—and that includes everyone. . . . The people at large will have to be their own psychologists and make their own applications of the principles that we establish (Miller, 1969)." "We would define the role of the practicing psychologist following the educational model as 'teaching personal and interpersonal attitudes and skills which the student can apply to solve present and future psychological problems and to enhance his own and others' satisfaction with life.' . . . As far as clients or students are concerned, the main question is no longer who needs the instruction ('who is sick') but who wants to learn what (Guerney and others, 1970)." Service to more people with limited professional manpower is one of the advantages of the educational model. Additional presumed advantages include the following: greater public acceptance and utilization of services; a better conceptual and a more practical framework for problem prevention; reevaluation and clarification of the role which value judgments play in psychosocial services and a broadening of the research base for personality and behavior modification.

There are a number of examples of educative programs which have been implemented in the campus community. In addition to the Peer Sex Education Program and the Undergraduate Internship examined earlier, the following outreach programs appear to be based on an educative model (although Morrill and others [1972] prefer to classify them as developmental programs): Couples' workshop designed to enhance the growth and enjoyment of a marriage relationship (Hinkle and Moore, 1971) and career development programs aimed at providing individuals with skills to influence their own development (Morrill and Forrest, 1970).

A very significant aspect of the educational model is "the investigation of and the communication to the campus community about the process of higher education, student development, and

the learning and motivation of young adults (Warnath, 1971)."
Sharing our knowledge in the areas of human development, personality theory, behavior and institutional change, interpersonal
communications and particularly principles of learning is one of the
most important contributions we can and must make to the campus
community. Ohmer Milton (1972) points out that "although extensive research about learning has been documented in innumer-
able publications, many faculty do not have the time and familiarity
with its specialized language or the inclination to avail themselves
of the literature."

　　We need to find as many creative ways of intervening as we
can in order "to modify the procedures of the institution to conserve
(and develop) human resources and humanize the institution's
impact on students (Warnath, 1971)."

IX

Counseling Blacks: Abstraction and Reality

Richard A. Brown

🙶🙶🙶🙶🙶🙶🙶🙶🙶🙶🙶🙶🙶🙶🙶🙶🙶🙶🙶🙶🙶🙶🙶🙶🙶🙶🙶🙶🙶🙶🙶🙶🙶🙶🙶🙶🙶
🙶🙶🙶🙶🙶🙶🙶🙶🙶🙶🙶🙶🙶🙶🙶🙶🙶🙶🙶🙶🙶🙶🙶🙶🙶🙶🙶🙶🙶🙶🙶🙶🙶🙶🙶🙶

The black student presence on white campuses, small as it is, poses a variety of new problems for higher education. One of those problems relates to the effective counseling of ethnic minority students. From the perspective of black students, especially the great majority who do not come from middle-class homes, the typical white American college is completely unprepared to deal with their special needs, especially in the area of counseling.

In 1965 Congress passed the Higher Education Act to provide millions of dollars for the education of so-called disadvantaged students. With this new money available, colleges began to actively recruit ethnic minority students who were judged to show promise of academic success by standards developed by the individual colleges. The competition for those students who could meet normal admission requirements became heated among the more prestigious private and public colleges. Many colleges, however, using letters of reference and other nontraditional admission requirements, found themselves admitting authentic ghetto blacks. Whether admitted through regular or altered admission standards, the blacks who enrolled have been a different type of student from those colleges have been familiar with. The socialization processes which black students have experienced have given them an entirely different view of almost everything in the campus community from that of the traditional white middle-class student. However, these differences may be expressed so subtly in counseling by the black client that most traditionally trained counselors may not even be aware of them.

The counselor of the professional literature is someone who is accepting, who is able to establish an empathic relationship with another individual, and who can give insights and clarifications to another person based on his understanding of the other person's experiences and thought processes. For instance, Vontress (1971) has indicated that a well-trained counselor should be able to function in any environment. By well-trained he means that the counselor is not only trained in the academic content of his profession but also that he is a sensitive, understanding, and accepting human being who continues to take stock of himself. Those around him sense his sincerity, honesty, and acceptance of others. The color of the counselor's skin, like a bald head or speech impediment, may result in the client's initially reacting to him negatively and constitute a temporary barrier between them but once the counselor has shown his genuine interest and his ability to help, these feelings will usually give way to acceptance by the client.

I disagree in part with Vontress. On the basis of my recent experience as student and as counselor for black students in a college Educational Opportunities Program, I believe that no matter how honest and sincere the white counselor may be, he can never be truly sensitive to the special needs and unique perceptions of ethnic minority students. Moreover, this is currently an academic question for it is my impression that very few ethnic minority college students believe that white counselors can be sensitive to their special problems and their different life styles. Black students, and I am certain chicano and native American students as well, have every reason to be suspicious of white counselors.

Blacks have almost uniformly had poor experiences with guidance people in the secondary schools. Almost every black graduate and undergraduate student with whom I have talked has told me about his frustrations with a white high school counselor who had advised him to take trade courses rather than courses which would give him an opportunity to apply for college admission. My personal experience supports these reports in that the white counselor who talked to me about my vocational goals advised me to prepare for a trade.

The black student recognizes that his counselor has based his advice primarily on his assumptions about appropriate goals for blacks rather than on individual considerations. This has planted the seed of distrust of white counselors in those students who do enter college. It should not be surprising that most black students want nothing to do with the college counseling center. Since federal funds have become available to support the college education of ethnic minority students, these students are now being encouraged by their white counselors to go on to college. On the surface this appears to be an improvement but the same insensitivity to individual differences among members of ethnic minority students is still involved. The point is that counselors continue to respond to ethnic minority students as members of a group rather than as individuals. Thus, there has really been no fundamental change in counselor attitudes. There are black students who could complete college if encouraged; there are also black students who are not interested in or capable of doing college-level work and are most appropriately advised to prepare for some trade or other occupation which does not require a college degree. In advising both types of students, the counselor must be sensitive to them as individuals and their unique needs and potentials. No racial yardstick can be applied uniformly to measure their potentials and no one level of occupation can be assumed to satisfy all.

Another problem which I have with the Vontress statement is that I believe that it is impossible for whites to feel the weight of being black no matter how many blacks they may know or how many racial ghettos they have lived in. The counselor can feel and express sympathy, but gut-level empathy and sensitivity are dependent on similarity of experiences and whites are not participants in the black experience or culture. A person may have many contacts with different people and situations but he can never totally experience something until he experiences that feeling of knowing that there is no way out of the situation and that no escape option is available to him.

There is a related but separate issue involved. When a person is a member of the dominant American white culture, it is very difficult, if not impossible, for him to be sensitive to a subculture such as that comprising the black experience which functions within the dominant white culture. A member of a subculture must be familiar with the dominant culture if he is to function in any capacity within the total society; however, a member of the dominant culture is required to know nothing of a powerless subculture in order to function within the society.

In order to perform his role adequately, the counselor has not been required to be interested in or informed about subcultural groups other than those which may exist as an integral part of the institutional setting within which he works as, for instance, the fraternity and drug culture groups on campus, both of which are primarily composed of members of the dominant white culture. It is my feeling that counselors have tended to deny the existence of groups which differ in fundamental ways from the dominant white culture by rationalizing that we are all human beings and thus have similar experiences and can be counseled in similar ways. Through their counselor training programs, counselors have been encouraged to perceive of themselves as omniscient. This prevents them from recognizing that they do not know very much about people from subcultures outside the institutional setting. Their training has also led them to view sensitivity as an abstraction: a total characteristic that one either has or does not have. This type of thinking itself prevents the counselor from being aware that his sensitivity is limited to discrete types of people and situations. As a result he is blind to the fact that he is not sensitive to the special problems of subcultural groups and that, in fact, he may have very little usable information about groups which he considers less significant than his own dominant cultural group. To test this contention in a less threatening situation than a racial confrontation, the white counselor need only quiz a Canadian friend on what he knows about the United States and then compare the variety and completeness of the responses which he gets with what he knows about Canada. I am certain that the American counselor would find that his Canadian friend is much more likely to be familiar with a wider range of information about the United States than he is about Canada.

I do agree with Vontress when he states that few well-trained counselors are available to work with ethnic minority students and that college administrators would be well-advised to be careful in their selection of counselors. Skin color should not be the only criterion. A poorly trained black counselor should not be employed to work with black students simply because he is a black for he renders them a disservice if he has nothing but his blackness to offer them. The adequate black counselor is first and foremost secure as a black person. The black counselor secure with his black identity can offer students not only sensitivity and empathy but also the opportunity to evaluate their potentials from a baseline of pride rather than the encouragement to change themselves to conform to white expectations based on self-hate and shame of their racial heritage.

Frazier (1962) vividly describes the effects of self-hate on black people in the higher socioeconomic levels of the black population. He presents examples of activities engaged in and organizations joined by blacks for the sole purpose of elevating themselves in the eyes of the white society. This obsession to conform affects all parts of their lives as they become totally involved in demonstrating to whites that they are personally better than blacks generally are perceived by whites. Stated simply, this member of the black bourgeoisie wants to be accepted by whites as better than the stereotypical black. He wants to avoid the connotation of being black in this country which leads him to despise what he perceives as the cause of his inability to get ahead: his being black. This leads him to a crippling and destructive self-hate.

The majority of black college students with whom I have had contact are not willing to adopt the facade for whites which will gain them acceptance but will lead to self-hate. Counselors of black students must take this new attitude into consideration. Although they may be helpful in establishing initial rapport with black students, skin color and an Afro hairstyle alone are not sufficient for being an effective counselor for black students.

Another major barrier stands between the black student and the counseling services offered by the college: the formal structured system of delivering the services. Warnath (1971) points out that college services are supported to the extent that students and their parents feel comfortable with the type of services offered. Although his references relate to the use of psychiatric services in colleges drawing students primarily from upper-middle-class and upper-class homes and vocationally oriented counseling in colleges whose students are primarily from working class families, I would extend his concept even further. Taking a problem to someone sitting in an office whose sole purpose is talking to people about their problems is itself a white middle-class invention. It is basically a system that can be supported only by an affluent group which can afford non-productive professional helpers. Blacks have experienced this system primarily in their contacts with school guidance personnel, welfare clerks, and social workers; and, in each case, something was generally being done to them. They have not been exposed to a socialization process which includes going to a professional person sitting in an office and talking about a personal problem. The assumption by college administrators that black students should use the established counseling center of the institution is, it seems to me, a perfect example of the inability or unwillingness of whites to recognize that many of the things which they take for granted are unknown to or have been experienced in quite a different way by subcultural groups. On a basic level, blacks have learned to be suspicious of any help offered by whites.

The typical counseling center, staffed primarily by whites, is generally perceived as a potentially hostile agency whose structure and office atmosphere projects to the black student a sense of "going to see the Man." But tradition in higher education often blocks the modification of programs and structures even when adult members of ethnic minority groups are involved in establishing the program or designing the structure. I have been astonished by the fact that the programs set up on college campuses specifically for ethnic minority students have more often than not been structured in almost identical ways to similar programs offered by the institution for the general student body. The counseling services particularly are offered in the traditional way with counselors being assigned office space, given a desk, and expected to maintain regular posted office hours. I have not been surprised that many students will not come for assistance under these conditions even when they are in serious academic or personal difficulty, but I have been bewildered that nonwhite administrators would expect ethnic minority students to feel comfortable and to relate to counselors under these conditions.

Black students will not use services which imply that they are going to see the Man; therefore, they do not use the services offered. Alternative methods of counseling blacks need to be employed. From my experience, I am convinced that counseling must be offered with much less structure and in surroundings familiar to the students. The first step in establishing this form of counseling service is the hiring of ethnic minority counselors who are secure enough as persons and as professionals that they can relate to students in places where the students feel comfortable rather than only in a counseling room which bolsters their own feelings of status and control.

Moreover, I feel that it is of critical importance that the counselor participate in the social interactions of the black students with whom he is dealing. He must be considered by the students as flexible enough to be able to relate to them socially as well as professionally. He must take the initiative of being in the places where students gather. The counselor should not consider his office as the only place in which counseling can take place. On the other hand, the students should not be put in the position of thinking of him as a peer involved with the usual student cliques but as someone whom they can all respect as a person who will, in turn, respect them and maintain confidentiality about anything they discuss with him. The counselor must convey to the students that he is available to discuss matters of concern to them at any time and in any place; but he must guard against becoming involved in gossip if students are to confide in him. This role is taxing physically and psychologically. Based on my own experience, I feel that the black counselor must have more inner strength than his white counterpart who offers his services within the traditional counseling center delivery system.

Even if he is an older student, the counselor must always remember that he can never be accepted as a peer because he is in a professional role with responsibilities not only to himself and the students but also the office for which he is working. This means that the black counselor runs the risk that students may initially see him as a Tom who has been coopted by the white institution. However, in the final analysis, his success will be determined by his ability to communicate his concern with and interest in the students, and more importantly his ability to counsel wisely.

Bernstein (1964) has pointed out the inappropriateness of the traditional counseling approach when used with black students, noting that, because the helping relationship implies some admission of inadequacy on the part of the student, counseling represents a further threat to the black student who may already have feelings of inadequacy in his relations to the white institution. Both he and Bond (1972) have indicated that the situation is aggravated by the use of client-centered techniques which are unsatisfactory for black students, since their ambiguity increases the feelings of threat to the students and does not meet the need for assistance with specific concrete problems. Haettenschwiller (1971) states that the counselor must be open and direct at all times and provide the student with unequivocal feedback regarding the nature of the relationship. He believes that it is far more important that the counselor level with the student and be willing to use the high impact words of the student's normal conversation.

A more direct counseling style, it seems to me, would be much more effective within the context of a less structured system. Cultural characteristics have been downplayed or ignored in the training of counselors. The typical counseling approach has been structured to meet the needs of members of the white middle class and is being applied thoughtlessly to black students. The counseling approach to black students must fit into the cultural expectations and needs of blacks. I should point out that this difficulty in relating to the traditional counseling system is a problem not only for blacks but for other ethnic minorities and lower-class whites as well.

In conjunction with less structure in a counseling program, I have found that the use of peer counselors offers advantages not available if professionals alone are employed. Peer counseling has proved to be effective in various school settings (Jackson, 1972). It has helped ethnic minority students at a community college adjust to their new environment (Pyle and Snyder, 1971). It has also helped college students develop social skills and overcome loneliness (McCarthy and Michaud, 1971). Counseling with his fellow students can be demanding on the peer counselor because he must cope not only with the demands placed on him by the students but also with the demands of his regular class work. If he is to be effective as a counselor, he must be selected carefully on the basis of his ability to meet the academic demands of his courses as well as his acceptance by other students. He must receive training in interpersonal relationships prior to his becoming a counselor. And, finally, he requires close supervision and support from the professional staff.

Unless the objectives and the rationale for the use of peer counselors has been worked out in advance, the peer counselor has a title but no direction or real responsibilities. Peer counselors can be a valuable asset to a program for ethnic minority students since they are the first to hear of problems that students within the program are facing. However, how the peer counselor should use information he receives must be worked out carefully by the staff since the peer counselor must still maintain normal interactions with the other students. The peer counselor is a student with emotional needs and anxieties similar to those of the students he is counseling. He is not a full-time member of the staff and, thus, cannot leave the school setting and interact with a different social group. In short, the peer counselor must remain on good terms with his fellow students. Hiring peer counselors as informers simply widens the communication gap between the students and the staff and discredits the peer counselors in the eyes of the other students. The responsibilities of the peer counselor should be restricted to those tasks which can be performed without disrupting the personal relationships between the counselors and their fellow students, such as disseminating information, giving assistance with immediate situational problems, interpreting student problems to the staff, academic advising, and helping with orientation. In this way, the peer counselors can relieve the professional staff of many of the day-to-day minor problems which make life difficult for ethnic minority students on a white campus.

Conclusion

I have written this chapter from my own experiences and observations because little in the current counseling literature has relevance for black students. That literature has been written almost exclusively by whites for white counselors working with white middle-class clients. Even some of the writing that is directed toward those who counsel ethnic minority students tends to reflect the basic assumptions and orientations of the dominant white culture.

I am convinced that if counseling is to be effective for blacks it has to reflect the socialization and cultural values of blacks. Counselors of blacks should be well trained; however, their training must reflect perceptions of the counseling process other than those which are now being instilled in graduate students by counselor-training programs. Until now, the counseling of blacks has proved largely ineffective. New, flexible models of counseling must be developed which encourage counselors to work with clients outside their counseling rooms with an informal personal approach. In addition, the profession has to become more accepting of the legitimacy of the counseling of those below the doctoral level; it is unlikely that enough minority people can be trained to this level to meet the needs of their groups and, more importantly, the counselor with the doctorate is likely to be less sensitive to the problems of minority students than someone with less academic status. Minority students are much less impressed by academic status than they are with the counselor's sensitivity to and understanding of their day-to-day problems of survival in a white society. Counseling for black students must be based on the realities of life for black students. It can no longer remain merely an abstraction of the textbooks and their white professor-authors.

X

Women: Clients and Counselors

Jane B. Berry

❀❀❀❀❀❀❀❀❀❀❀❀❀❀❀❀❀❀❀❀❀❀❀❀❀❀❀❀❀❀❀❀❀❀❀
❀❀❀❀❀❀❀❀❀❀❀❀❀❀❀❀❀❀❀❀❀❀❀❀❀❀❀❀❀❀❀❀❀

Women students are complaining about counselors. They feel that counselors have messed them up or let them down by failing to understand what is going on with women today. Many counselors continue to operate from a framework which promotes traditional role patterns for female clients. They seem concerned with the status quo for women, counseling in terms of their own socialization experiences and the time-honored traditions of their institutional managers. They fail to tune in or take account of the new dynamics which surround the aspirations, role expectations, career development, and life perspectives of girls and women involved in the contemporary educational enterprise. In other words, counselors are still sitting at their desks in campus counseling centers while the action is elsewhere. Women are turning to rap groups and quasi-community organizations for support in exploring life options and alternatives.

Even female counselors have few links to the new woman—the now woman—the girl student who daily comes under social, political, or peer influences directly or indirectly related to the women's movement.

The campus action for women started in the early sixties—in a gentle advising and programmatic approach for the housewife who was returning to campus for refresher courses or to find some meaningful activity after the children left home. These early beginnings have blossomed beyond anyone's expectations. Continuing Education for Women programs have been adopted by most institutions of higher education and are viewed by many as major forces in getting women to focus on themselves and society. Increasingly, social and political scientists say the women's movement is the revolution of our time. There is every indication that the impact will be profound and farreaching because the demands of our urban industrial society will no longer permit significant differences between men and women in many societal roles. Indeed the women's movement is the one substantial movement of the sixties still very much alive.

Stereotype Counseling

Women everywhere are learning about male-oriented economic values and are embracing new values which reject doubts about their abilities and personal potential. Women want more options and role choices. They want to explore and project life patterns which will accommodate new combinations of personal and work experience. Counselors need to understand these new realities and to utilize this understanding but are hampered by societal expectations, including their own familiar, traditional, middle-class life patterns. This may create a problem of empathy, a communication clog, or even generate a verbal or nonverbal counselor disapproval.

An example of stereotype counseling is discussed in the Thomas and Stewart (1971)' study of counselor response to high school girls who selected vocational goals considered traditionally masculine. Female counselors appeared to be more accepting than their male counterparts both of women's nontraditional career choices such as engineer, chemist, or business executive and their conforming career choices such as teacher, nurse, and social worker. However, counselors regardless of sex rated the conforming goals as more appropriate. Both male and female counselors rated female clients with so-called deviate career goals as in greater need of personal counseling than those with traditional and conforming aspirations.

The researchers' use of the term *deviant* for nontraditional goals is itself an indication of the subtle influences which affect perceptions of women's aspirations, abilities, and activities. Deciding on a career in which men predominate is termed by Almquist and Angrist (1970) an unconventional career choice.

Another example of sex-role stereotyping by clinicians was indicated in a research by Broverman (1970) which ascertained that clinicians believed "healthy" women compared with "healthy" men were more dependent, suggestible, excitable, emotional, passive, submissive, and sensitive. However, the more positive and aggressive male traits were highly correlated with the most socially desirable traits. Obviously, then, a conflict is created for the woman who is expected to "adjust" to and accept those norms for her sex that are nevertheless not as socially desirable as the male norms.

Many counselors are not comfortable encouraging young women to consider a full range of vocational options and continuous career involvement, or an eventual top management, administrative, or leadership position. It is a long way from women as handmaidens, secretaries, or possibly administrative assistants to executive vice-presidents. Yet many women today see these higher horizons, along with the steep and rocky incline which leads upward to them. They are not afraid or discouraged by the obstacles. They are more likely to be exhilarated and motivated by them, and they need counselor support. Many counselors still tend to see themselves as the guardians of institutional control. They identify with the traditions and values which they feel are in their own self-interest. In this era of diminishing budgets, they rationalize that it is necessary to follow the party line to stay in business. Unfortunately, this shortsighted approach will catch up with them as clients and potential clients are bound to reject them. Reduced intake and client dissatisfaction will surface. Students are increasingly involved in evaluation of personnel services and even in recommending budgetary priorities which involve the curtailment and reorganization of such student services. It does not seem too far afield to suggest that women clients involved in such evaluation will be particularly sensitive to sexist counseling that moralizes about values and subtly supports life plans which fail to take account of a new era for women. Women may be liberating themselves at a faster rate than society is ready to accept, but counselors deceive themselves if they think they can impede the process.

Counselor Bias. Although awareness is the first step in the counselor's reversal of his sexist bias, awareness alone is not enough. It is essential that counselors also examine their own prejudices and biases with respect to women's roles.

Male counselors need a better understanding of the origin of the bias. They need to recall that their own socialization experience has been for traditional roles for men and women. Both men and women counselors are hampered in their relationships with young people who have had their concerns raised to the point of understanding sexual politics. Younger people, and particularly younger women, are becoming aware of how male privilege has been perpetuated. The system has kept women as secondary citizens under a guise of values and traditions. This antique perspective is dear to the hearts of legislators, administrators, and, as has been mentioned, many faculty members.

Women versus Women. Women counselors are also guilty. Many of them fail to appreciate the movement or see it as connected with liberal attitudes or lesbians, which they find unacceptable. As a group they tend to be turned off by the sisterhood concept, and have a backlog of personal experiences which tend to inhibit meaningful counseling relationships with today's young women clients. Their own difficulties in moving upward in a sexist system have often left them with a perspective that seems to say to young women, "I made it the hard way, so can you."

Many women counselors operate within a framework which adheres to traditional life styles and preservation of outmoded societal values. They like to be tidy and to subscribe to the historical view that prescribed role patterns are better for society at large.

Some have feelings about the incompatibility of motherhood and a serious career, and have even been known to drop hints about the incongruity of achievement and femininity.

Thus, women counselors need to become more aware of themselves as professional role models for young women, and to explore their own personal "women vs. women" index. Professional women are not always aware that they lack regard and respect for other women. This attitude is exemplified by their expressed preference for a male boss; by their shunning of increased work responsibility; and their avoiding opportunities for promotions. They may also discover that their own socialization and the climate of an institution dedicated to traditional values affect their ability to relate to the needs and problems of young women. They may even discover a subtle tendency within themselves to resent the many and varied avenues open to girls today. Many women who have reached positions of responsibility have discovered that they tend to covet the options more readily available to today's educated women.

New Directions

Counselors should become more informed about the impact of the women's movement in general and on their particular campus. They need to tune into and become more involved in the campus action and curriculum developments discussed in the following section. The counselor must be familiar with the feelings, aspirations, and hostility which account for these developments. Some women clients and potential clients may be passing up the counseling center and seeking rap groups because they find or hear through the grapevine that counselors are too insulated and isolated from what is really important to women today.

The new definition for women and new dimensions of opportunity for education and employment, the appeal of a greater variety of life styles, and other related developments suggest the need for a critical look at what is going on with counseling services for women. How is this new woman perceived by counselors? She has new attitudes, aspirations, and life expectations which have been generated and reinforced by what is going on in the larger society. These developments trace from legislation which prohibits discrimination in employment. Such legislation is forcing new attitudes about both hiring and promotion for women. Even previously immune institutions are being forced to account for their ancient attitudes and personnel policies.

The manifestations of the women's movement are everywhere—certainly on the majority of campuses. Every campus has some student activity. From the newly established community colleges to the venerable graduate and professional schools, there is a growing concern for women's altered educational and vocational aspirations. Government contract regulations with penalties for noncompliance are stimulating administrative development of affirmative action plans to increase opportunity for women and minorities. Even state legislatures have entered the arena as they debate the Equal Rights Amendment. Nationally, the picture is one of massive change.

Consciousness Raising. Women's rap groups, commonly referred to as consciousness-raising sessions, are an important aspect of the movement. These groups serve an important function because they provide a vehicle through which women students can explore together their roles and options as female persons. Among other things, consciousness-raising groups provide an opportunity to share the meaning and at times the burden of being a female in a sexist-society by talking, listening, counseling, and being counseled. There is an atmosphere of both teaching and learning. These groups are an example of what Warnath (1971) refers to as the self-initiated arrangement. For many women students of all ages, they are more satisfactory than one-to-one sessions with a counselor at the campus counseling center. The Free School movement has fostered such groups.

In the Communiversity Bulletin for the University of Missouri-Kansas City (Summer, 1972), the course description under *Women's Rap Group* reads: "Just talk, clean wholesome talk, talk talk, dirty, sordid, uppity talk, just talk. No formal readings. Come and talk with us. We want to hear you. Let us lay it on you about the women's movement. Disagree. Praise us. Talk."

Women's Studies. Another campus manifestation of the women's movement is the rapid growth of women studies courses which may be departmental or interdisciplinary. These courses are where it's at for numbers of women. Generally they are taught by women for women. Their main purpose is to offer compensatory education to women and interested men because regular curricula has frequently ignored the history and life concerns of 50 percent of the population.

An examination of a typical feminist studies program offered at the Cambridge-Goddard Graduate School during 1972–1973 will be illuminating for the traditionally oriented faculty member, counselor, or administrator. The five seminars offered are *The Family, Forms of Female Expression, Women and Socialization, Women and Work,* and *Female Sexuality. The Family* studies the relationship of family structure to socioeconomic stages of history, to social relationships between men, women, and children, to sex role expectations, to productive relations outside and inside the home, to patterns of child-rearing and to class stratification. There will be an ongoing relationship with the community. *Forms of Female Expression* explores the various aspects of female creative expression and how it has been trivialized in the broader society. The possibility of the development of a definite female culture will be explored. There will be outreach into the community in an attempt to disseminate to other women the results of this course. *Women and Socialization* deals with the consciousness of women in terms of education, the media, politics, and religion. The primary objective is a synthesis between practical work and self-education. Again, there will be an outreach into the community. *Women and Work* reviews the economic history of the American woman as it applies to women's work in the home, women's work in the labor force, women and the welfare system, and women as consumers. The method of study will be oral history combined with analysis and research. *Female Sexuality* explores the new morality using an analytical and historical approach. There will be involvement with the community through projects with birth control and abortion clinics and high school girls, for example.

Subject matter for women studies courses touches major disciplines such as literature, psychology, history, sociology, political science, and so forth. A recent issue of the *Women Studies Newsletter* (Fall, 1972) indicates that there are now upwards of one thousand women studies courses offered throughout the country.

Counselors should be aware that a master's degree in Women
Studies can be obtained from these three institutions: Cambridge-
Goddard, University of California-San Francisco, and Sarah Law-
rence. A bachelor's degree in Women Studies is currently obtainable
from: Douglass College, University of California-San Francisco,
SUNY/College at Old Westbury, CUNY/Richmond College,
Roger Williams College, and University of Washington.

Other institutions offer Women Studies minors or courses
available on an elective basis. A sample of course titles are: *Female
Psychohistory in America: the Family; Role of Women in Child
and Family Life; Sexual Politics; Female Psychology; Visual Images
of the Female in the Western World; Black and White Women
Since the Civil War; Communism and Women: the Chinese Experience; Creativity and Women.*

Continuing Education for Mature Women. Special programs
for women beyond traditional college age are also a part of today's
campus scene. CEW women mingle with younger women in classes,
women's rap groups, and sometimes in special efforts related to
child-care programs or women's activist courses. They share their
anxieties and problems with their younger sisters on campus as well
as with each other. They speak of a personal confidence crisis as well
as their concerns about further education or employment after
the CEW educational program. They worry about child-care and
home-management arrangement. Financial assistance is often a
primary concern—no scholarships for parttime students are available, and age barriers for scholarships and fellowship programs are
still prevalent on many campuses. Historical sexist attitudes and
policies which have benefited their male counterparts down through
the years still exist at many institutions.

CEW women share something else. They recount the inadequacy and downright sexist quality of the counseling received in
their earlier college careers. They lament, report, and complain of
counseling for traditional roles and career limitations. Today's
mature woman student remembers subtle attitudes such as "a
woman's place is in the home . . . women don't think logically
. . . women are tender and emotional" which were communicated
by counselors and faculty members. Only a few can recall a counselor or teacher who had an understanding of what it is really like

to be a female in our society. These women, and the young women with whom they interact, tell us there is still scant appreciation or awareness that problems of girls and women are not only personal but political.

Although credit programs in women's studies are increasing, the typical CEW program consists of noncredit courses and workshops focused on the changing role of women in contemporary society and the options open to women at various stages in their lives. Group counseling and ability and interest testing are often included in these programs. Some colleges have opened centers devoted to this clientele. The nonthreatening atmosphere of these centers attract many who lack self-confidence and feel inadequate after limiting themselves to homemaking for several years.

One of the first institutions to establish a continuing education program for women was the University of Minnesota. The Minnesota Planning and Counseling Center was established in 1960. Since that time, special services for women have become a feature in universities and colleges across the country. The growth of such specialized programs for women has been documented by the Women's Bureau of the Department of Labor. In the 1963 edition of Pamphlet 10, "Continuing Education Programs and Services for Women," twenty programs were listed. In the 1966 edition, the number had grown to 100. The latest revised edition lists 450 programs which were in operation in 1971.

One interesting program has been designed by Jean Eason of the Continuing Education Guidance Center of the University of North Carolina at Greensboro for counseling mature women from the leisure class. Many older women return to school after responsibilities decrease only to discover that school and volunteer activities are meaningless in the ultimate sense of self-actualization. The project at Greensboro sought to counsel each woman in terms of an alternate lifestyle that would be self-fulfilling and integrating for her.

Eason (1972) says the term lifestyle means "how behaviors relate to basic values and purposes." Four lifestyles, each representing a basic value that was primary in the individual's background and pattern of living, were used in the project. Each woman worked in one of the four groups: the Theoretical Life Style group that dealt mainly with ideas, writing, and reading, the Influential Life Style group that was political in nature and attuned to problem-solving, the Aesthetic Life Style group that engaged in activities involving the arts and athletics, the Social Life Style group that was highly social in nature, deemphasizing education and introspection.

Workers on this project believe that lifestyle planning provides a flexible and lifelong framework from which women may choose alternatives as these alternatives arise from within themselves.

Affirmative Action. In spite of much affirmative action, a survey on employment conducted in 1972 by the United Church of Christ indicated that employment for women and minorities had increased only a total of 1 percent for each group.

The women's movement is not a white middle-class phenomenon—minorities and women share many goals. A glaring example is that white males hold 97 percent of the jobs paying over $15,000. This leaves only 3 percent minorities and women.

The National Center for Educational Statistics has for the first time published college and university salary figures according to sex. Reports from 2480 institutions in fifty states and the District of Columbia showed that on the average, women faculty members are paid 17 percent less than men.

However, new federal legislation and compliance policies on behalf of women and minorities are affecting the climate in educational institutions as well as business and industry. Title VII of the Equal Rights Act of 1964 established the Equal Employment Opportunity Commission. The Commission's responsibilities are to investigate complaints of discrimination in hiring and promotion and to help with programs of voluntary compliance by employers, unions, and community organizations.

Compliance with the Civil Rights Act is mandatory for employers who receive federal contracts. Affirmative Action programs must be designed and implemented by such employers to show positive steps taken to employ and promote women and minority applicants and to give equal pay for equal work.

On campus, there is political and practical administrative maneuvering to comply and save the vital federal money without shaking things up too much. EEO committees and token female and black jobs are the order of the day. Lean budgets provide an out and liberal white male professors speak of preserving quality and of interference with sacred academic freedom.

The administrative machinations and busy work associated with the Affirmative Action mandate are still to be evaluated. Some fallout appears beneficial. Ancient and honored private club hiring practices have more public exposure. Counselors and counselor educators have certainly followed the pack in this regard. Professional meetings, publications, Ph.D. selection committees, and so on have perpetuated white male privilege. Women and minorities have encountered a rough road to the top in the counseling profession. Practically every investigation by the Department of Health, Education and Welfare has uncovered cases of women who were paid less than male colleagues even though their qualifications were higher.

Affirmative Action for women students should mean equal admission policies, more access to professional schools, quota style. Sexist scholarship and fellowship manipulation will be more accessible to public view. Myths about women in academia are being dispelled—among them that education is wasted on women. A study of women doctorates by Helen Astin indicates that 91 percent of them were employed. A study entitled "Four Years After Entry" by the American Council on Education's office of research between 1967 and 1971 found that, almost without exception, college women in all types of institutions do better work, achieve higher grades, are more likely to complete the four-year academic program and are more highly motivated than their male counterparts.

Institutional responsibility for child-care facilities for female students and staff is taking hold and should make some difference in recruiting and retaining both. Information on child care and day care, including pending legislation and programs, theoretical position, and research results may be obtained by writing Day Care and Child Development Council of America, 1401 K Street, N.W., Washington, D.C. 20005.

Policies concerning leaves for child-bearing and child-rearing are being considered. These should mitigate against the penalties which academic women have faced in competing for staff benefits, promotion, tenure and income comparable to those of men in similar positions. Policies for parental leave may also educate campus faculty, staff, and administrators to male parental responsibilities and privileges. A statement adopted in November 1972 by the board of directors of the Association of American Colleges says in part: "Widespread adoption and implementation of such policies could indeed alter campus climate. The essence of nondiscrimination is treating each person not on the basis of group membership but on the basis of individual capacity to work. Women should not be penalized in their conditions of employment because they may require time away from work for pregnancy and childbirth, and parents should not be prevented from assuming appropriate responsibility for the needs of their families. All policies relating to insurance and leave should be applied without regard to sex."

The statement also says that an employee's right to benefits, promotions and tenure must not be threatened because she has requested an unpaid leave of absence for child-rearing purposes.

Professional Women Caucus. Approximately five years ago, academic women began to organize their own professional associations. They have organized caucuses, committees, and task forces to focus on the problem of women within their respective disciplines. These groups conduct special sessions at annual association meetings and carry on a variety of activities to promote communications about problems faced by women in academia. Efforts vary from group to group and it is too early to assess their effectiveness. Such caucuses are important in that they provide visibility for women scholars long submerged in professional associations completely dominated by male leadership. Young women aspiring to academic careers cannot help but benefit from efforts of these groups to combat the many myths associated with academic women. The spirit and solidarity provided by the women's caucus movement spills over into campus politics and constitutes another force for women in the contemporary campus milieu.

The American Association of University Women and five other national organizations have issued an 11-page "Joint Statement on Women in Higher Education." The four primary areas of consideration are: women's education, employment, involvement in decision-making, and the benefits and institutional services. One important recommendation also includes "upgrading counseling and advisory services to help women define all their academic options."

The New Challenge

Today's women students represent a new breed. They feel the new influence for women in society and on campus. They are experiencing new pressures and problems which accompany new challenges, choices, life options, and opportunities. They experience conflict as the growing solidarity of the sisterhood confronts the time-honored and traditional roles which have been prescribed for women. Counselors now see a changing woman in a changing society.

Sexual and Institutional Politics. Women clients of the seventies are aware that they have a lot of catching up to do. They are also becoming more aware of the male power structure which has controlled their education and life options. Academia has a long history of training males for leadership roles and generally ignoring women. As young women become involved in developing new horizons and life goals, they are beginning to understand how sex-role ideology acquired in childhood limited female personhood, as well as aspirations and ambition. They are also seeing how institutions of higher education have served to perpetuate society's traditional system of stereotyped sex roles and limited opportunities for women outside the home. Sexist attitudes and chauvinistic institutions are more readily identified by today's coeds. They are beginning to understand the systematic and insidious relationship between sexual and institutional politics that have conspired to preserve a male-dominated society. This conspiracy will prevail as long as institutional personnel and programmatic priorities are geared to the preservation of a system which does not make any waves.

Girls and women still view counseling as the same old status quo game which prescribes different tracks for men and women and, above all, ensures continuation of what counselors perceive society wants. Counseling approaches continue to emphasize the difficulties of breaking into a "man's" world and the conflicts and pressures which result from attempts to swim upstream.

Individual counselors are beginning to perceive women as

persons, but too many counselors are seen as persisting with sexist attitudes and traditional approaches.

Services. Women want babysitting and quality child-care services that are both complete and convenient. They feel that such services should be at least partially supported by campus budgets. The recommendations in the "Joint Statement on Women in Higher Education" indicate that many want these health services at no extra cost, including coverage for pregnancy and childbirth. They are less interested in traditional and social programs and club activities.

Women desire more adequate services in all areas of medicine—gynecology, psychiatry, and general medicine. Their concern for health services today has new dimensions. They seek recognition of their need to better understand the aspects of a woman's life in relation to her body. This includes her physiology, sexuality, and related health needs. Many young women feel that if they are to have control over their lives, it is imperative that they learn about their bodies. Counselors who take the trouble to understand will discover that younger women believe that sexual oppression and sexist attitudes are related to the woman's body—a belief which has been too little understood by helping professionals.

There is a movement toward community services and self-help clinics staffed by women for women who are fed up with inadequate campus attitudes and facilities. *Our Bodies, Ourselves,* recently prepared by The Boston Women's Health Book Collective, provides interesting insights. The Woman's Institute in Chicago, Illinois, was formed by a group of women psychiatrists, psychologists, educators, and students to provide women with alternatives to traditional sexist psychotherapy. "Identity groups" assist women in realizing their complete potential as human beings.

Another example of a community service is WOMAN— The Women's Organization to "Mash" Alcoholism and Narcotics. Located in downtown Detroit, the project assists women addicts and their children by offering a broad range of services, including vocational counseling, counseling and treatment, and skills development.

Life Planning. Finally, women students at all levels seek career planning worthy of the name. Many plan to stay in the labor market all their lives. They do not intend to follow their older sisters who, they discover, have returned to campus in an effort to find some meaning for their lives. Substantial numbers of young women have a perspective on child-bearing which differs radically from their own parents. They project small families and frequently intend to bear no children. A recent report on the national Zero Population Growth movement indicates that the birth rate has dropped to the lowest in twenty-seven years. It attributes this to an attitudinal affect which demographers credit to the women's movement and the parallel movement on behalf of the environment.

Singlehood is no longer viewed with the stigma attached by previous generations of college women who tended to panic if they did not have a ring by their senior year. Single women must work for a living, and not simply to escape boredom. The U. S. Bureau of the Census (1969) states that more than one third of the women who work are single, divorced or widowed, frequently supporting children or parents.

Positive Action for Counselors

Counselors should take a more active role with respect to women's campus groups. However, women students see too little evidence of counselor concern and seldom any visible support from individual counselors or from the conventional counseling center conglomerate.

A few counselors, mostly female, have become involved with women's campus committees and informal women's group concerns. Male counselors have shown little courage or sensitivity. Deserved or not, male counselors are perceived by many women students as sexist as male physicians.

This image can be altered, even reversed, if male counselors develop the interest and inclination to do so. This requires a sincere effort to seek first-hand information from women in all aspects of the movement. Counselors must also give attention to the new research on women and women's roles and to special publications which have been generated to convey the concerns of women today. In short, counselors need to check both the campus and national scene on a continuing basis.

Judith Lewis, writing in a special issue of the *Personnel and*

Guidance Journal devoted to women and counselors (1972), suggests that some counselors might wish to create a network of women's rap groups within counseling center settings. She mentions that the rap group concept could be utilized to encourage exploration of issues immediately important to women today. Career development, alternate lifestyle, coupling, and the Equal Rights Amendment are examples of such issues.

Betty Meador, Evelyn Solomon, and Maria Bowen of the Center for Studies of the Person (1972), have been conducting encounter groups for women for a year. They believe that a mixed encounter group is representative of society as a whole and only serves to reinforce stereotyped female models of behavior and attitudes. Discussing their fears and ambitions with only women present better enables women of all ages to overcome their feeling that they exist primarily as wife or lover. Women can begin to see themselves as unique individuals and not just as wife or mother.

Tainted Tools and Techniques. Textbooks, films, and other media presentations utilized by counselors for personal orientation and career planning are beginning to be carefully scrutinized at all educational levels. There is evidence that inventories such as the Strong Vocational Interest Blank and the Kuder, as well as other instruments of measurement standardized on male populations, do not accommodate the aspirations of today's women.

At this time, researchers are in the process of combining the male and female items on the SVIB forms into a single inventory. A man or woman will be scored on *all* of the male and female scales and one profile containing the profiles for both sexes will be provided.

Counselors must take note of standardization data, as well as the action-oriented efforts of respected professionals (Schlossberg and Goodman, 1972) to correct guidance procedures which perpetuate sex stereotyping. Efforts are underway to scrutinize a variety of materials employed by counselors. Male author bias is being investigated and new instruments are being developed which will provide better assessment of the potential of women.

Research. Studies are beginning to yield data about basic time-honored cultural attitudes that account for women's lower vocational aspirations. The recent work of Horner and Gornick and their associates at the University of Michigan (1969) have provided some important insights. These studies indicate that women are being socialized to fear success in terms of educational and career achievement. In a provocative article, Sunny Hansen (1972) states that women are conditioned to believe that marriage is a primary goal in their lives and that preparation for a career is advised only in the event that something might happen to the husband. Such negative terms as *old-maid schoolteacher* have been perpetuated, giving no thought to positive contributions she may have made in molding young lives. The career woman has been accused of being too aggressive, or worse, of being unusual or odd. A new understanding of women's predisposition to failure must be understood by all educators and counselors.

New behavioral science research represents yet another breakthrough which is already generating new and important research focused on women's roles, responsibilities, and activities. The University of Michigan and the Coalition for Research on Women's Educational Development have recently sponsored a symposium on new research on women.

Inservice Training. Traditional counselor education programs can incorporate seminars which provide the opportunity to explore new research on women, as well as the impact of changing male-female relationships, counter movement, and other topics which need to be understood in order to reduce the credibility gap between professional counselors and women clients.

Other inservice sessions pertaining to midcareer explorations for women, community resources for child care, and male response to the women's movement are also recommended. Counselors can consider sharing such sessions with student personnel workers, faculty, and administrators. Institutes and seminars designed to understand and counter sexist conditions would be a first step.

The Department of Educational Guidance and Counseling at Wayne State University is experimenting with a conference for teachers and counselors who have not been willing to become involved in the major social action programs such as the National Organization for Women. During the course of the conference, each participant must devise a new action strategy of his own utilizing materials or a type of program that he must test in his particular school and demonstrate before the conference.

Community Resources. Counselors should be familiar with community organizations and agencies which have been developed to assist women with educational and employment problems. The Catalyst program is an example of such an organization. A national nonprofit organization, the Catalyst's goals are to help college-educated women combine career and family responsibilities and to work with employers to assimilate women at responsible levels and to promote greater flexibility in employment patterns for those who choose to work less than fulltime during early child-rearing years.

Today's counselors need above all to get themselves and their own house in order with respect to the needs of contemporary women. They can no longer take refuge in outdated psychoanalytic concepts such as penis envy and related notions. Counselors may have progressed to the point where they are no longer doing a disservice to women, but they need to ask themselves and their clients if they are really doing a service.

Women of all ages are seeking the mainstream of American life. Counselors must understand the new aspirations, motivations, and opportunities which make this possible for increasing numbers of females. Male attitudes toward women must change and male counselors can lead if they develop and nurture the necessary insights. Female counselors must examine their own socialization experiences and biases which spill over into counseling relationships with today's women clients. Today's young women have new and different dreams. Counselors can no longer afford to be gatekeepers for a sexist-society.

XI

Use of Research

Harriett A. Rose

Even as early as 1961, voices were raised in warning that the counseling center would cease to exist in its current form and that other models would have to replace it. At least one program at the Denver convention of the American Personnel and Guidance Association, chaired by John Black, then Director of the Stanford University Counseling Service, was dedicated to this theme. Nygreen (1962) one year later cited as an ominous portent the characterization of counselors as the "nonacademic civil service" in *The Academic Marketplace* by Caplow and McGee (1958). He foresaw that counseling would receive a diminishing share of the available dollars, if indeed the counseling center continued in its role of pure service to students, neglecting the basic functions of the university— teaching and research. Although the warnings continued through the years, little heed was paid, and the research of the early sixties demonstrated the profession's resistance to such advice, as it maintained its preoccupation with the art or skill of counseling. Articles in both the *Annual Review of Psychology* and the *Review of Educational Research* were concerned with client characteristics, counselor characteristics, client-counselor interaction, counseling outcomes, group versus individual test interpretation, the old conflict between directive and nondirective counseling, and the new conflict between behavior modification and existential therapy. In short, our research reported efforts to become therapists and to develop excellent techniques of counseling or psychotherapy, but little or no attention was paid to the appropriateness of that skill in the context of higher education. Now and then new voices cried in the wilderness—usually in presidential addresses (Greenleaf, 1968; Berdie, 1966)—but we had a good thing going, we have to do our thing at the taxpayers' expense, and we could prove to many people's satisfaction that counseling is beneficial to students. The last statement may provoke dissent, but this is a book for counselors, and most of us share the conviction that *we help people.*

The ill wind of the student revolts perhaps blew counseling centers some good. Layton said in a speech to the Conference of College and University Counseling Center Directors in 1967 that the two most pressing concerns of college presidents during those years were student unrest and the growing concern about future sources of financial support. While the students were drawing most of the attention by making most of the noise and nobody seemed to know what to do about it, our contribution was needed for the peace and well-being of the campus. Even then, we were urged by some leaders of our profession to become more relevant, to have impact on the campuses and the environment of the students we served. Although the recommended steps differed depending on the orientation of the speaker, one recurring theme was the use of our skills as behavioral scientists to help achieve the goals and purposes of higher education (Berdie, 1966). The 1966 articles on counseling were indeed reviews, but by 1968 the chapter on counseling in the *Annual Review of Psychology* had become "Student Development and Counseling." In it, Segal (1968) expressed the hope (unrealized) that the 1970 chapter would warrant the title of "Counseling and Student Development." In 1966, there were separate chapters in the *Review of Educational Research* on "Higher Education" and "The Counseling Process and Function," but by

1968, the merged chapter had become "Higher Education Programs and Student Development." Still the message was ignored. Nowhere was it suggested that counseling centers give up their traditional roles of individual and group short-term and occasional long-term counseling, only that their capability was greater than that circumscribed role and that it was unlikely that a tax-burdened public would continue to support individual therapeutic service. In 1966, Koile, Harren, and Draeger suggested that we use our knowledge of the campus environment and its students to build effective student affairs programs; by 1968, Korn was suggesting that our behavioral science skills were needed to help in the day-to-day problems of the campus community as well as the crisis in higher education.

One of the most frequent suggestions to counseling centers was the use of outreach programs, designed to affect more students than were moved through their own unhappiness to seek the services of the center. Outreach services were perceived as preventive and developmental, but few counselors conceptualized research as a form of outreach. A second new role suggested for counseling center personnel was that of consultant to the campus (Oetting, Ivey, and Weigel, 1970).

It seems to me that before we can become consultants, we need to be consulted. And before anyone consults us, he needs to know that we can help solve his problem, and it is primarily through research that one's consultant status may be established. In much of our own literature, our unique qualifications are cited (Korn, 1966; Berdie, 1966; Korn, 1969). It remains for us to establish our qualifications with other colleagues.

The previously mentioned Layton speech reminded us that the faculty make and implement academic policy and that to make faculty cognizant of what we have to offer, we have to do acceptable scholarly work. We have demonstrated our research excellence to our own profession; we need now to turn that special talent and training to research in and for our institutional community.

To many practitioners research has been merely one of the hurdles to the degree which allowed us to counsel on the college level. To others, research became a challenge and a game. Now, research may become a lifeline to survival—the way to demonstrate our capacities for consultant and outreach functions—in other words, to our becoming an integral part of the mainstream of the college, not just a peripheral "nonacademic civil service."

Several kinds of research encompass what Meehl (1972) calls "first- and second-order applied psychology." First-order relevance, in Meehl's terms, refers to research directly on the firing line of a practical problem. Second-order relevance refers to research which does not deal directly with the help-seeking individual institution, but with a class of the applied problems. Meehl's distinctions between first- and second-order relevance in applied psychology seem especially cogent as a framework within which to discuss counseling center research. Let us borrow his concepts and extend them for our use.

As an example of first-order relevant research, a counseling center would do the bookkeeping for the annual report we all submit to the administration. The report proves that we saw so many people for so many hours of individual and group counseling on educational, vocational, and personal problems; therefore, our budgeted money was well spent. Another example of first-order relevance is an evaluation by clients of the service they received in the center. These studies are on the firing line, of interest only to the individual center staff and the administrators to whom they report. Yet the results are extremely important in terms of accountability and program budgeting, already recognized as the theme issues of higher education in the seventies.

A second approach to research which qualifies for first-order relevance concerns only the institution in which it is done, sometimes called inhouse research. This is one way a center staff can fulfill its obligation to its institutional community. Examples of this kind of research are comparison of the demographic and academic data of students enrolled in different colleges of the university or in different majors and evaluation of present probation and drop rules. On my own campus, this evaluation was followed by my appointment to the rules committee of the faculty senate, where we revised the probation and drop policy on the basis of our data. When the new policy had been in effect for two years, a comparison that showed survival rates for an entering class under both sets of rules was circulated by the Counseling and Testing Center to the faculty, so that they could see how many students increased their chances of graduation because of the rule change. Inhouse research also involves development of academic predictions for various curricula and for individual courses within those curricula and analysis, rearrangement, and distribution of data from national research programs such as American Council on Education and American College Testing Program, so that the information can be easily assimilated by the general university community. A useful compilation of such data on its freshman class of 1971 was circulated last year by the student affairs staff of Ball State University. Another inhouse research is the development of criteria on which to base admission to academic programs which have limited numbers of students and for which no national testing or criteria exist.

This kind of research does not usually appear in journals; the only way we know about it is by exchanging local publications with each other. Following are some examples of excellent local projects across the country.

Indiana University Counseling Center examined the university policy requiring the center to function in a truant officer role, investigating class absences. When they found that the procedure was considered an intrusion between faculty members and students, their request for elimination of the policy was granted. The center is currently investigating procedures dealing with withdrawal from the university, hoping to recommend a revision which will encourage the return of students who have withdrawn.

The counseling center at Western Michigan University learned through questionnaires that 85 percent of the faculty and administrators and 89 percent of students believed that counselors should advise administration and faculty on existing structures, and suggest new structures and procedures to promote the mental health of students.

West Virginia University Counseling Center began a program of growth-groups, in response to a master's thesis (Behar, 1971) which demonstrated that a factor labeled "Lack of Social Self-Acceptance" was the discriminating factor between persisters and nonpersisters at that institution. How many such findings have resulted in preventive measures being implemented? Not many, if we judge from the literature.

Iowa State University, Kansas State University, and the University of Nebraska circulate excellent brief reports of information concerning their students related to curriculum and academic survival. At the University of Kentucky, the dean of admissions abandoned the counseling center interview required for applicants with prediction of an academic failure. The purpose of the interview had been to suggest strongly some other school; followup data by the counseling center indicated that the interview did not deter the students' decision to enroll at the university (Rose, 1965).

Meehl's second-order relevance applies to the kind of research we were all enjoined to do in graduate school. Psychologists in training become familiar with the practitioner-scientist model and are reminded of their ethical duty to add to the knowledge of the profession. This sort of research appears in professional journals (for example, the *Journal of Counseling Psychology* and *Journal of College Student Personnel*) and serves to make its authors known across institutional boundaries, eligible for promotion to exalted academic rank in their own institutions and employable in others. Examples of second-order relevant research are vocational choice theoretical explorations, comparisons of counseling methodologies and effectiveness, the whole range of process and outcome studies, training methods, and the selection of trainees.

The most important counseling center research encompasses both first- and second-order relevance. That is, policy is affected in one's own institution and the effect is of interest to other institutions through publication. Here are some examples: For ten years, the University of Kentucky has routinely collected Omnibus Personality Inventory (OPI) scores from all entering freshmen. This data bank has enabled us to do a large amount of research of second-order relevance and some of first-order. Just as routinely we have notified freshmen by letter of the opportunity to have their test scores interpreted and about 20 percent responded. Notifications were sent out in batches, chosen at random, whenever we had time to see the students. Three years ago we developed a personal problem likelihood (PPL) factor score on the OPI, based on students who had come to the center with a problem they labeled personal. We tested the validity of our PPL score on a subsequent class in the following manner. Students who were sent the notification of availability of orientation test interpretation were selected at random from a stratified sample of those with high ($>$ +1 SD), low ($>$ −1 SD), and average (between $\pm$1 SD) PPL factor scores. The response for both males and females was significantly greater for those whose PPL score suggested that they would seek personal-problem counseling than for the other two groups (Rose and Elton, 1972). These results were confirmed for the second year on an unreported study. The freshmen from this high-likelihood group were also more likely to return as clients after the test interpretation. This is a form of outreach, of contact with troubled students before they are in difficulty. It has become part of our standard policy; certain faculty and administration seek our consultant services because they are aware of our capability in applied research. We have now used this same technique to develop a retention score, which identifies on a personality basis students who are likely still to be in school at the beginning of the fifth semester.

A second example was a study requested by a faculty member of the College of Engineering in an attempt to find out why so many qualified freshmen transfered out of Engineering at the end of the first year. The net result of the study was a partial revision of the introductory course required of all Engineering freshmen. This first-order relevant study was published in *Engineering Education* (Elton and Rose, 1971), a journal rarely seen by psychologists and reportedly had an effect on Engineering departments in other institutions. The faculty at the University of Kentucky who taught the new course asked counseling center personnel to serve in a consulting role in redesigning the course.

A prime example of research which combines research of first- and second-order relevance was the project to reduce dropouts at Penn State University, reported by Ford and Urban (1966). Although the Division of Counseling did not survive a subsequent change in university administration, it was an outstanding example of counseling center research. A systematic study of 2500 freshmen who entered the university in 1955 led to an evaluation of the university's operation. Consequently, Penn State developed a post-admission preregistration counseling program for students and their parents, with the objective of making the best possible match between what the university had to offer and what the student wanted. The dropout rate fell significantly, dismissals for academic reasons declined to almost nothing, and several thousand students have now graduated from Penn State who presumably would have flunked or dropped out, had this outreach counseling program not been in existence.

These three examples illustrate the kind of applied research by which we bring our competencies to the attention of the faculty, and faculty talk to each other across disciplines and institutions. As a result of such studies at the University of Kentucky, our services as research consultants and access to our data bank on student characteristics are increasingly sought, and the projects are almost invariably designed to confront a problem of first-order relevance to the department or person seeking the assistance.

This brings us to the sine qua non of the entire process, which is the existence of systematically obtained data on one's students. It is not easy to establish the desirability, even the necessity, of collecting data on other than academic ability. We began our data collection in 1962 long before the widespread demand for accountability began. In the summer of 1967 we relaxed the compulsory nature of the orientation testing, as an experiment, and tried persuasion instead. The result was the emergence of volunteer bias and more importantly the loss of data from 35 percent of the freshmen. If higher education is to establish any evaluation criteria other than the credit hour or contact hour now suggested by some program budgeting experts, we need to know where students stood in their development on entry and where they had arrived by the time they left. All that can be said of that "last" 35 percent is that most of them were not in school for the third semester; we can speculate about what their test profiles might have revealed, but we know nothing for sure. The message is loud and clear (Rose and Elton, 1971), that painful administrative decisions need to be made about requiring test data on admission to institutions of higher education. There is and will be resistance, but if students wish to travel abroad they submit to the inoculation requirement, whether or not they believe in the germ theory of disease. I admit to prejudice, but perhaps it is justifiable. If data are haphazardly collected, the distribution is perhaps skewed and institutional decisions based on skewed data are fraught with almost as many dangers as decisions made on no data at all.

Such research ventures as ours with Engineering, the Agriculture curriculum revisions at Kansas State University based on reports of student characteristics by Acker, Danskin, and Kennedy (1967), and the involvement with the history department in developing student participation in a freshman survey course at Stanford reported by Korn (1966) serve to strengthen our credibility with faculty, as Layton in his 1967 speech suggested we do. Our relations with top administrators benefit from good faculty relations and from our willingness to provide easily understood data. The data may at most become a basis for decision-making and planning, as suggested by Berdie (1972), or at the very least as a basis for speechmaking. Either way, we gain in recognition, and only by that recognition are we admitted to the decision-making councils where we can have impact on the climate of the institution as it affects students, our clients.

The findings of our studies need to be simplified before we circulate them on the campus. They cannot be assimilated in the form of the scholarly articles we take pride in. Colleagues have reported reactions similar to those I experienced when asked to comment on what I called simple-minded information from another school. My response was something like this, "Why, we've got much better data than this!" To which the administrative response was, "Then why do you sit on it?" What may seem of little significance to those of us accustomed to educational and psychological research is very meaningful to colleagues in other disciplines whose access to knowledge about institutions or students may be limited. We err seriously if we fail to realize their frame of reference, just as we err in counseling if we disregard the client's frame of reference. The answer to dissemination of the findings, it seems to me, is in frequent mailings which attack only one issue at a time. Some titles from the Iowa State Student Counseling Service Bulletins are: "Characteristics of Present Veterinary Medicine Students at the Time They Entered ISU as Freshmen," "Effects of Scholarships as Reported by ISU Graduates," and "A Preliminary Study of Grading Practices in Multi-Section Courses." Kansas State University Student Counseling

Center research reports include: "Student Attitudes, Motivations and Implications for KSU," "The Relationship of Socioeconomic Status and Living Unit to the Use of Campus Facilities," "KSU Entering Freshmen, Potential Ability (ACT) and Obtained Grades," and "Who Uses the Counseling Center?" University of Nebraska publicized, among other things, "Some Black Students' Perceptions of the University," and "How Selected Residence Units View the University." Hardly earthshaking studies in their significance, but perhaps they help account for the strong support the counseling services of the Middle West receive from their administrations.

In some institutions, the research role I am recommending may be in part occupied already by either the Institutional Research Office or the Registrar, or both. Rarely, however, are those offices staffed by people as qualified as counseling psychologists to interpret data. Also, the primary orientation of both offices is usually different. Institutional research is generally concerned with the nuts and bolts of running a business, in this case a college. The registrar is generally interested in counting enrollment, and sometimes in the demographic data—in-state, out-of-state, county from which enrolled, academic prediction—but not in individual students. It requires the psychologist's knowledge of tests and their meaning and of students and their individual differences to interpret meaningfully the numbers which are so frequently reported and so frequently misinterpreted. These two offices are valuable sources of data, however, and time spent cultivating cooperation with them will reap rare benefit, if the personalities involved permit.

In spite of a few large and well organized research efforts and many small nonsequential studies which bear on higher education, very little evidence of the impact of research has been observed in administrative and management decisions. During the frantic crisis-dominated sixties, perhaps it was too much to expect that the advanced thinking of the few (Sanford, 1962; Katz, 1968; Berdie, 1966) urging the use of research for decision-making could be absorbed by the besieged world of administration. Campus life now, however, is calmer, almost quiet, allowing attention to be directed long-range again, in other words, to the principal business of higher education to learning. With some variation as to role, counseling psychologists involved in student personnel work have been suggested as prime movers. Morrill and Hurst (1971) suggest that counseling psychologists' roles include: contribute to, support, and enhance the learning environment; facilitate maximum utilization of the learning environment; and study the student, the learning environment, and the interaction between them as a base for implementation. Berdie (1972) recommends the use of programs of research on students to identify problems in advance, to inform the university about students and students about the university, and to identify students who have potential to assume leadership in the government of the university. The most forceful of the recommendations for involvement of counseling psychologists in institutional self-renewal comes from Parker (1971), with his proposed restructuring of the student personnel endeavor. He recommends a different organizational arrangement which would eliminate the separation between academic and nonacademic programs by utilizing faculty from various disciplines along with student personnel workers. Parker divides personnel within his Center for Institutional Self-Renewal into: logocentrists, who would be behavioral scientists charged with assemblage of data, theoretical formulation, and research consultation; practicentrists, who would be charged with counseling and consulting with individuals, small groups, and organizations; and democentrists, who would be concerned with interpreting the research and disseminating the information to the university community.

What I have been urging in this chapter resembles Parker's plan, except that my concept includes only the counseling center personnel and presents a narrower version than Parker envisions of the tasks in all three divisions. All counseling centers are staffed with practicentrists; most centers have at least one behavioral scientist (counseling psychologist) whose training prepared him for the logocentrist role; only time and cooperative effort are required to develop the democentrists within our centers. Parker "thinks big" and finds the solution to the survival of both the student personnel movement and of higher education in his creative plan. I think less globally and find the solution to the survival of the counseling center and the enhancement of its contribution in the efforts reported here. Whether or not such efforts could reach the ultimate goal—the ideal proposed by Parker—they do represent a healthy step toward an immediate and intermediate set of goals—preserving the existence of counseling centers and enhancing their contributions in consulting and outreach activities through research efforts.

Counseling activities have become nonprofessional; everyone is considered capable of counseling, with or without appropriate education and with variable outcomes and unspecified goals. There are employment counselors, pastoral counselors, friendly loan counselors, counselors on how to lay away your loved ones who have gone beyond, counselors to fit all entrepreneurial, educational, social, and soul-saving endeavors to the degree that counseling has become —or perhaps it always was—a nonexclusive function. Synonyms for *to counsel* listed in Soule's *Dictionary of English Synonyms* are "to advise, to admonish, to give advice to." McCully (1962) lists characteristics of a profession and says the members perform a unique and definite social service and that society has delegated to qualified members of the profession *exclusive* authority to perform that specified social service. Counseling activities do not qualify as a unique social service and counseling psychologists do not possess exclusive authority to perform them. This may be a propitious time for counseling psychologists to heed and even extend the admonitions of the wise elders of our profession to become teachers, supervisors, and researchers. We need to change our nomenclature along with our role. Perhaps we could become educational ecologists, scientific researchers of the student and his environment. On all sides there is pressure: our leaders exhort us to forsake the practitioner role and to adopt the educational community role, just as Albee in an American Psychological Association presidential address in 1970 urged clinical psychologists out of the medical model and into the community mental health arena; we feel the none too gentle push from below—from those aspiring to our positions but unwilling to invest the time and effort in doctoral training. Even many of our counselor-trainers (Rioch, 1963; Gordon, 1965; Carkhuff, 1968) assure us that warm, accepting housewives can be trained in short order to be effective counselors—perhaps more effective than we cerebral types have ever been. And surely the public who pays the bill for higher education can add its own feeling that counseling done by doctoral level counselors is too expensive. As long as we educate counseling psychologists and emphasize their role as practicentrist, the practitioner model will continue to be their principal endeavor. Nevitt Sanford (1967) urged the development of a new specialty relating to individual development in the nexus of the educational environment. It may be that we can be the progenitors of that specialty by educating and employing educational ecologists who are, as is said in horse breeding circles, sired by Counseling Psychology out of Higher Education. Would we then turn out "horses of another color?"

XII

Innovative Group
Work

Sumner B. Morris

Historians and social critics of a humanistic bent often reflect an optimism about the evolution of a human spirit and the societies which nourish it. They have faith in the growth potential of man and belief that, as barriers to growth gradually dissolve or are reduced, man's goodness and creativity will emerge. Man needs only to "stand still in the light" is one of the humanistic tenets (Roszak, 1972). This posture feels good. But persons working with and committed to growth and change among people can experience considerable frustration, disappointment, and pain awaiting the emergence of such processes and their end product—a more decent social system.

   While it is believed that the works of men of goodwill and faith in the human spirit will triumph eventually, persons functioning as facilitators of change and growth must be sensitive to the realities of human behavior, including its frailties, fears, vagaries, and capriciousness. This applies especially to the interface of the desire for growth on one hand and the conventional order of things on the other—especially as the latter is anchored in the power system of institutions. In short, it is unwise for the counselor to take on the role of a change agent if he is insensitive to the forces for conservatism. People strongly rooted in the conventional order tend to see new ways and concepts that suggest change as threatening and, at times, downright offensive and subversive. The person hoping to improve society and its institutions in ways that permit an acceleration of human growth and actualization is thus faced with a dilemma. To assess whether his new idea or plan has merit there often must be a trying out, trial-and-error, or experimental venture. But in performing this preliminary test, he immediately becomes vulnerable and can stir up threat, hostility, and resistance. Nevertheless, some risk must be endured if change is to have any experiential base for constructive evaluation. Change simply for sake of change is deplorable and frequently motivated by tangential or base factors. Thus the change agent must deal as effectively and objectively as he can with the threat he may create.

The foregoing applies in higher education where change concepts and ideas find a climate of receptivity in keeping with the time-honored pursuit of truth and knowledge. Most goals of higher education aim at the development of the whole, fully functioning person. Colleges and universities aspire to graduate persons capable of vigorous inquiry into the nature and problems of their worlds and make constructive adaptations to their life circumstances. In short, higher education hopes to provide an experience for students in which they will grow intellectually and personally and where the antecedents of growth are established.

These goals are ambitious, but can be discerned in the charters and goal statements of most institutions of higher education. The charge is thus laid on the shoulders of college faculty and staff—to make student growth and development an increasing reality.

At the focal point are student affairs officers responsible for student growth and change processes. They are to be concerned with conditions that influence classroom performance and intellectual development. Such conditions inevitably include the student's affective-cognitive domains. To respond to the latter is to move into some highly charged, emotionally laden facets of human behavior and yet the charge to do this stems from the objectives and mission of the college or university itself. Not to do so would be a remission or avoidance of responsibility.

This chapter focuses on college counselors as they try to facilitate growth, deal with affective-cognitive domains, and occasionally suggest and attempt new ways and methods of helping the college achieve its goals. College counselors are usually psychologists and many hold a doctorate. Of all college and university faculty and staff, they should be best prepared to understand human learning and to intervene in educational processes—when appropriate— for the sake of the personal, social, and intellectual growth of students.

A relatively recent innovation in counseling programs is the use of sensitivity training, encounter groups, life goals workshops, and other group work. The utilization of such methods by a counseling center staff will confront the staff with all the problems faced by an innovator on the college campus.

And so the stage is set. The counselor's goals are generally synonymous with those of the college. Both are zealous about facilitating student growth and development and are committed to finding the most effective ways of realizing it. Occasionally this means change, and here lie potential problems. Perceptions of the ingredients of change may be different for nonpsychologists, and considerable dissonance can develop. What begins as a mutual move toward Camelot can become a morality drama of uncomfortable proportions.

Many persons, including academicians, see student growth as an integrated, steady unfolding of intellect and talent nurtured by knowledge in a climate of perspicacious teaching and quiet reflection. Such nurture and climate are vital, but are inadequate and even misleading in describing completely how people change. Change sometimes involves the kind of introspection that brings an individual to strong, vivid states of fear, anxiety, pain, doubt, anger, discouragement, inadequacy feelings, an occasional irresponsibility, joy, euphoria, exhaltation, and other mental-emotional realms. If he is to grow, a person must be able to experience fully, work through, and integrate the meaning and significance of these feelings and thoughts. His behavior may make others uneasy, for it may take the form of expressing anger and shouting rage (in role-simulated situation), retreating into quiet fuguelike meditation, sinking into despair, reaching out and figuratively or literally making contact with other people. These expressions or experiences usually are limited to the cloistered environment of a professional's office, but the idea of them phenomenologically and the conditions which facilitate them are not concepts which the uninitiated accept easily and which they may even find outrageous.

Other conditions for personality growth and change are freedom to risk and fail; opportunities to test experiences; interactions with mature adults—perhaps in a limited, microcosmic way —characterized by warmth, safety, and respect; honest confrontation and feedback; opportunities to query and examine ideas and concepts and be listened to without prejudice or rejection; and to search and find one's "center."

But do all concerned persons understand and perceive these ingredients in the same way? Sidney Jourard (1963) has stated that sexuality, hostility, and dependency longings account for many emotional-social problems in our culture. Given responsibility for assisting people with these emotionally charged and complex matters and given the dynamics and conditions of personality change, the counselor finds himself involved in processes that may be inharmonious with conventional society. This is especially true if he has the freedom to use his expertise fully, as best he sees fit within the boundaries of ethical and professional judgment. His responsibility and charge lead him directly into the intrinsic nature of humans involved in change. The dissonance manifests itself in terms of people not wanting to acknowledge the affective domains of student change at its deeper, authentic levels—as in the case of the faculty adviser who reported that he leaves the room when a student becomes upset and weeps. Academicians and administrators are human and some forget too soon the pain of their own struggles for identity, adequacy, and security. Occasionally their memories, and consequently their sensitivity and empathy, are refreshed by their own children's educational experiences. Generally speaking, however, peaceful, orderly processes and benign, rational behavior are preferred as the modality of growth and change by those who are responsible for it—such as campus faculties and staff.

Encountering dissonance from those around him, the professional counselor has an additional charge. He must deal with the differences in the way growth and change are perceived. And he must respond to the accountability that will be demanded of him as he functions professionally as a facilitator of growth and change. Something that has the potential to be as disturbing as the human learning process and the ways of expediting it is not easily understood and accepted by the layman. The counselor cannot expect to hide behind principles of academic freedom and the professional autonomy of his discipline. Unless he is to play it safe, with only conventional methods and traditional frames of reference, he is in for considerable self-defining about what he is doing. If he innovates he may even receive barbed criticism with a jocular facade from wary colleagues, as in the instance of the "touchy-feely" label applied to those attempting sensitivity training on the campus.

What one may experience as he innovates in higher education—some pitfalls and suggestions—is our focus here. A concrete example is apropos. The innovative process is the utilization of group methods. The agency is a college counseling center with commitment to direct service to the bulk of the student body and to a proactive stance to the college in general. In a sense, the college is seen as the client with the staff assisting it to achieve its goals as effectively as possible, within the purview of their expertise and resources. The staff attempts to do more than wait in its offices for students to request counseling help. It concerns itself with the total viability, efficacy, and ecological soundness of the system from the viewpoint of student fulfillment, achievement, and growth.

The counseling program with which the writer is associated is at the University of California, Davis. To understand the setting and the goals and commitments of this particular program, it would be well to review its objectives. The following was submitted to the administration in the Fall Quarter, 1972, for inclusion in the campus' Administrative Supplement to the Academic Plan.

STATEMENT OF OBJECTIVES: Within the framework of Student Development Services the Counseling Center seeks to:

A. Counseling
  1. facilitate the self-understanding and personal growth of students
  2. assist students in effective decision-making in understanding and coping effectively with environmental forces that affect them
  3. provide psychological testing, information about occupations, and other technical services of use to students and staff
  4. assist students to prepare themselves for an optimum learning experience in the classroom
  5. provide immediate counseling and support to students experiencing emotional crises in their lives (crisis counseling)

B. Training and Supervision
  1. catalyze and assist in the development of student peer counseling and paraprofessional counseling programs
  2. offer training to faculty and staff and student advisers in counseling and communication skills as it applies to academic advising and the interface of student affairs and academic purviews
  3. offer supervised counseling experience through the Counseling Center to selected and qualified persons with graduate work in counseling who want experience counseling university students

C. Consultation
  1. lend professional skills, as appropriate and needed, as consultants to special programs and various educational innovation projects
  2. facilitate, within our professional scope, the kind of climate that enhances learning and the personal fulfillment of all members of the university and surrounding campus community
  3. identify and seek to deal constructively with sources of excessive student stress and promote student satisfaction with the college experience
  4. offer programs that will support and supplement the faculty advising system and innovative emphases in undergraduate education

D. Research
  1. research the characteristics of students and the university environment and other matters affecting student growth and development

In attempting to meet and achieve these objectives, a variety of operational techniques were used—one was group work, which ranged from life goals workshops to couples groups to personal growth and short-term therapy groups. Each group was a response to a particular pattern of student needs as viewed by the staff. Some focused on vocational counseling and decision-making, while others explored interrelationship problems, such as those experienced by couples. All had an intrapsychic flavor, such as one experiences and feels in his introspective, inner life. The leadership styles varied but generally had a noncharismatic, participant-responsible characteristic.

The staff used group process because it has merits not possessed by one-to-one interviewing. It is social and capitalizes on the capacity of one person to help another. It catalyzes and legitimizes making personal and social connections with other persons, immediate feedback, the experience of more direct and authentic communication with others in a relatively safe environment. In many cases, it provides a sharing and caring that is in contrast to much of the alienation and aloneness that a young adult can experience. And some persons learn by the example and experience of others, even if their own participation is minimal.

Another reason for group work is the economy of having professional contact with more people during a given period of time. More students are worked with per unit of time. However, this is a secondary reason; groups, properly led by well-trained and experienced leaders with appropriately motivated participants, stand on their own unique merits. The economy of time is somewhat illusory anyway, as few group leaders can maintain a steady diet of group work compared with equivalent time in individual interviewing.

In our situation, group work appeared to be a vital operational means by which the staff could pursue its objectives. What we hoped to accomplish in the groups seemed congruent with the objectives of the university—that participants would grow in self-understanding and awareness of themselves, their feelings, strengths, and weaknesses. It was felt that the capacity to take a more proactive stance toward their university life would be catalyzed. We believed that the participants would move in some degree toward the type of person alluded to in many of the college and university goal statements as the polished "product" they graduate.

The staff members normally met together at the beginning of each quarter and commited themselves to lead a group or groups depending on perceptions of student need and interest and their own capability and interest. The modal method of publicizing the groups was by responding to student interest and request at the receptionist desk, although usually the groups were announced, sometimes piecemeal and briefly, in the student newspaper. The information was also spread to other student affairs agencies.

As an antidote for the hit-or-miss announcement of the group program, it was decided to determine the group program early and produce a brochure describing the groups to be offered in the quarter ahead for widespread campus distribution. Enthusiasm mounted as the staff saw the configuration of the entire group program in one document. It was also decided to list the staff leaders of each group in the brochure. The highest academic degree and in some instances, functional titles were included. Rather than list further credentials, qualifications, and so forth that conformed to the traditional ways of academe, each staff member wrote a personal statement about himself or herself. This was done in the hope of reflecting something about the leader as a person. The statements were direct, authentic, and quite personal. A staff member with unusual artistic talent sketched an attractive brochure cover that pictured a mixture of the heterogeneous faces that characterize a college student body.

Of special significance is the fact that vernacular language and slang of the contemporary campus scene was sprinkled through the brochure. It was written to and for students. For example, "Bread Making for Seniors" described a life goals workshop for seniors. "Open Rap Group" announced a "crisis-oriented group designed for students who want help for a specific concern at the moment." "How to Survive the 20th Century Without Even Trying" was another which generally dealt with "learnings and techniques from Gestalt, Psychosynthesis, and Meditation" areas in which one staff member was particularly qualified. Some titles were simply very direct and authentic, such as, "Close Yet Free in Intimate Relationships" and "Survival Course for Parents." Some titles could have been considered "far out" by many members of the academic community as they dealt with highly personal, sensitive topics. "Body Awareness and Sexuality" and "Yoga Postures, Self-Awareness, and Gestalt—Advanced Group" are examples. All groups were to meet on the average of two hours a week for the duration of the quarter—with the exception of the life goals group which met just four times over a four week period for two hours on the average. Nineteen groups were offered. The completed brochure was mailed to all academic and student affairs departments, distributed to the residence halls, and made available in places where students flocked.

It is difficult to be objective about something with which I was so heavily involved and generalizations should be drawn with caution. With a year's perspective from the time the brochure was issued, I can summarize what happened as follows. The students, most student affairs officers, and some faculty who commented on the brochure and what we were doing were positive and supportive. However, it was soon apparent that we had created some problems for the university administration. Not all members of the campus community shared our excitement and enthusiasm. The top administrative officers, particularly those with student affairs responsibilities, were criticized for what we were doing as portrayed in the brochure. A few persons were critical and hostile.

What semed to be criticized most were the groups concerned with meditation, Yoga, and body awareness and sexuality. These were the groups that filled most quickly to maximum enrolment, and this says considerable about student interest. But the feeling that we were doing "crazy" stuff seemed to prevail among our critics. One faculty member even perceived something sexual in the cover sketch of people crowded together, although the writer is uncertain to this day whether the critic was being facetious or serious. Not all the groups filled—notably the life goals workshops, a group on procrastination and study skills, and the two that dealt with minority student exeprience. In retrospect, nineteen groups were too many. All told, 229 students enrolled in the program.

While considerable concern was expressed by the administration, the total picture of criticisms and reactions to criticisms will never be fully known. Some private thoughts are privileged to remain just that—private thoughts. However, two very significant points emerged. One was that the administration took an active stance in responding to criticisms. The director of the counseling center submitted workload data that would give a broader picture of what the counseling center was doing. Also, a letter was drafted as a response to criticisms and made available to the administration, as were other statements and descriptions of the center's raison d'etre. These documents were to assist in the explanation and defense of our program, but they also had residual value in providing further opportunity for self-definition for everybody concerned—counselors and administration. The necessity and responsibility "to respond to the introspective processes of the scholar" was the central theme.

The second point emerges in time as highly significant and reassuring. No administrative officer ever told us to stop what we were doing. The principle of academic freedom and the professional right to pursue our objectives (and the truth), as the staff saw fit, was never encroached on and was sustained.

Followup opportunities brought further clarification and self-definition. A face-to-face session with one of the chief antagonists was most beneficial, maintained with dignity and a spirit of honest inquiry. Looking back, I consider us fortunate. Some aspects of the brochure could have meant dire trouble on other campuses, but the generally favorable attitude toward innovation on this campus and respect for endeavors which respond to student needs probably had a cushioning effect.

Nevertheless there are certain lessons in the experience and the feedback received that apply to the initiation of innovative programs in higher education. In our situation the pitfalls refer more to how innovative programs are presented—rather than to their actual content. From our experience with the brochure the following are to be avoided:

Be certain to describe adequately the context of the total program in which the innovation is being developed. For programs that deal with personality growth and change, it is risky to presume lay understanding. Make certain that patrons, critics, and consumers can see your perspective clearly. While our brochure stated that we continued to offer individual, one-to-one counseling and educational-vocational counseling, many readers did not notice this and got the impression we did only far-out group work. Make certain that everyone sees your program in total and in perspective—the tried and true ways, as well as the new ones. Use whatever works—large, bold print, more space, and occasional redundancy for emphasis.

Minimize contemporary slang in statements about your program. Persons who have little direct, informal contact with students may not understand and be irritated with what sounds like ingratiating attempts to patronize students.

Words that transcend the alleged generation gap are clear to all. The message (Coladarci, 1972), "He who would marry the spirit of the age soon finds himself a widower," has relevance to this point.

Innovations should have a solid conceptual base, and this base should be described to those especially responsible for your program so that a clear understanding exists about the innovation. Trust does not develop in a vacuum; it is more apt to develop with familiarity, open communication, and a discussion of mutual goals. Warren Bennis (1972) aptly makes this point in describing his experience with institutional change at the State University of New York at Buffalo. How your program fits with the university's mission should be clear.

Statements of group leaders' identity and qualifications should be appropriately modest and traditional in form. In the brochure, the "who are we" entries of each of the staff were warm, personal, honest, and authentic. They reflected the enthusiasm and openness of the staff to each other and their students. But one suspects that the statements were too idiosyncratic and showed too much of the affective, phenomenological life of the leader for a faculty tuned in to the rigors of publication manuals and the circumscription of professional modesty. While no one voiced this directly, I sense the statements were taken as somewhat brash by some members of the faculty. No matter how sincere the intentions, it is the perceptions by others that become significant.

A final hazard that should be borne in mind, although one who is honest and open about what he is doing, cannot do much about it. In innovative programs, one deals much with the affective domain of persons. In the community of scholars, some will always tend to view students only as intellectual entities. Feeling and affect are often ignored. The idea of a person gaining something of a growth nature from doing Yoga postures, meditation, and releasing feelings tends to be antithetical to the traditional ways of academe. It is an occupational hazard in a sense. The only solution at this point is to pay great attention to defining and describing these processes as best one can in common, nonpsychological language. The law of parsimony borrowed from psychological diagnostic process, which seeks to first describe behavior in its simplest and most obvious terms, applies here.

Other, more general, points are axiomatic. More research needs to be done on what happens to people who participate in groups and the extent of transfer of gains to one's real life. More work on conceptualizing and an anchoring in sound theory systems are needed. While no one is perfect, the leader himself is going to have a high profile, along with the group processes he espouses. If he comes across as a dilettante who has not reflected deeply about what he's doing and who is on his own trip (Dreyfus and Kremenliev, 1970), he may be in for trouble. He must become accustomed to self-defining processes in higher education as they are certainly here to stay under closer scrutiny from all sides. A certain integrity and honesty about what he believes and a high self-disclosure quotient will serve him well in most instances.

XIII

A Student Development Center

Charles E. Larsen

I am the director of a student development center. I have often been asked by directors of traditional counseling centers how I feel our center at South Dakota State differs from the typical counseling center. I would like to use this chapter to present some of my responses.

In my judgment, a student development center and a counseling center are similar in that both provide individual and group counseling services to students. However, they differ in at least two fundamental ways. First, development center staff limit the number of individual counseling appointments to about half those which might be considered a normal load in a counseling center so that significant blocks of time can be scheduled with groups in the campus community for preventative and developmental programs. Second, the staff of a development center make every effort to eliminate all aspects of the medical model of service from their activities. The reasons for the former will become clear through my discussion of consulting activities later in the chapter; the reasons for the latter require some explanation at this point since the model of service is, perhaps, the fundamental difference between the developmental center and the traditional center.

My feeling is that the philosophical implications of the medical model will undermine any attempt to implement the preventative and developmental programs which are the highest priority service of a developmental center. Placing one human being in the care of another fosters the kind of dependence which cripples human capacity for self-direction and retards personal and social growth. The medical model encourages the dependence of the client. Its use by physicians is understandable. Its use by counselors can be harmful. Any part of an educational program which encourages students to place themselves in the care of some authority such as instructor, administrator, or counselor reduces their ability to learn self-direction and stunts their personal and social development.

Educational institutions have almost uniformly rewarded students for being docile and following directions; they have punished those who have fought against a dependent relationship. Students have responded by becoming physical and mental dropouts because forced dependence runs counter to their normal desire for independence. Independence requires self-direction and self-direction requires the learning of skills which schools have failed to teach. When a school discourages independence in its students, it creates the problems which bring students to counseling centers.

Ratner (1972) wrote: "Despair is the absence of hope. It is a feeling of helplessness, of impotence—a giving up of one's existence. It is a feeling that nothing can be improved or even changed. It is a capitulation to adversity." It is obvious to me that the sources of despair for students within educational institutions must be eliminated. And this is the reason that I believe the medical model with its emphasis on dependence must be rejected by the counselors of a student development center.

Student development counselors encourage those students
with whom they work toward self-direction and independence.
They teach students to cope with their life situations, not by adjusting but by overcoming obstacles and frustrations. They give priority
to working with identifiable groups of students who need assistance
in reaching positive goals. They do not, like the traditional remedial
counselors, wait for problems to be brought to them by students
frustrated by the rigidities of the system. They tend to work more
with the so-called normal students than with those whose problems
have already grown to the point where they seek psychotherapy.
Basically, the student development counselor and traditional counselor draw on much the same counseling skills; however, they differ
in the application of those skills and the attitudes with which they
approach their clientele.

In the delivery of services, the student development model
requires that counselor time be divided as equally as possible between prevention and necessary remedial activities. As with the
typical counseling program, the knowledge, skills, and techniques of
the behavioral sciences determine the means of intervention; but
the balance between prevention and remediation is a critical differentiation. Overemphasis on remedial services can seriously un-
balance a student development program. Preventative programs are
those which are directed to the normal developmental tasks of college-aged students. These might include such things as human
sexuality, career development, understanding of ethnic minorities,
marriage interactions, and drug usage. The particular problems in
which a developmental center becomes involved would be chosen
on the basis of their potential for decreasing the number and sever-
ity of the type of problems most prevalent on campus. The methods
by which the programs which the center will offer are chosen also
differentiate the student development center from the traditional
counseling center.

Setting Objectives

The objectives of traditional counseling centers are developed
from within the center and evaluated by administrative criteria.
Within these centers, the primary objective has been to treat as

many people as possible because to obtain financial support, the numbers of completed cases must impress the administration. Justification for additional staff has been made on the basis of increased caseload. Adding new services like relaxation therapy, establishing satellite counseling centers, or engaging in research have generally resulted from staff meeting decisions that a particular activity will look impressive on the annual report. If the staff is sensitive to campus needs, there may be a reasonable fit between those needs and the functions of the center. Unfortunately, in my opinion, most center objectives are more likely to reflect the needs of the staff than those of the campus clientele. Moreover, it has been my experience that when staff have attempted to establish overall goals for the center, the most painful meetings of the year usually occur. I suspect that most counselors have been trained to see themselves as independent practitioners who should be free to do their own thing rather than as members of a service agency with comprehensive goals and purposes.

The goals of a student development center are not set by the director and his staff talking to each other. They are developed through input from sources of potential clientele on campus. As I made the transition from the role of a director of a traditional center to the role of facilitator of a developmental center, one of my most difficult problems was developing a system for setting goals which involved not only the center staff but also students, faculty, and administrators. I did it because I felt I had to, not because I wanted to. That is, I did it because neither the institution nor any of its subgroups exhibited any commitment to the center while internal methods of goal-setting had been employed.

Through the use of a campus survey, we were able to construct two lists of potential development center functions ranked in order of importance to our campus constituency. One list described how we *are* perceived and the other described the service directions we *should* take. We followed up our survey with the establishment of an advisory board to our center composed of members of the campus community. The purpose of the board was to give us direct and personal input in our goal-setting. In one of its early meetings, a proposal was made for the center to coordinate an interdisciplinary pilot study of student developmental needs. In addition to these

inputs, I asked each staff member to prepare a set of center objectives for the year, together with strategies for meeting those
objectives. I suggested that they use Harvey's model for Administration by Objectives (1972) as a guide with the addition of personal
objectives for each counselor. I discovered that, although there are
advantages to going through this process with staff informally in a
series of individual conferences, a more formal process involving the
entire staff has the special advantage of permitting comparisons of
staff objectives with the objectives obtained from campus inputs.
This encourages discussion of how to fit our services and our personal needs to the needs of the campus.

Consultation with Groups

It should be apparent that when staff invite inputs from the
campus community as they set their objectives, the variety of involvements for developmental counselors on the campus is likely to
be much more extensive than those of traditional counselors. The
success or failure of these involvements is dependent on the skills
they have already learned from their preparation as counselors but
we have discovered that their effectiveness is improved as they gain
experience in organizational consultation.

As an aside, I should mention that we have gained some
support for our move onto campus through the results of a survey
which we sent to all administrators and a random sample of students
and faculty. We asked them how important consultation services
by our center should be. We discovered that students rated consultation services as more important than the traditional testing and study
skills services. The faculty and administrators did not agree, with
the faculty especially indicating that we should maintain our traditional services. Although this poses a dilemma for us, we feel that
our main concern should be student welfare and that we should
move in directions which will meet their primary needs with the
hope that our success will convince faculty and administrators of
the value of our consultation work.

In consulting with a group, I have developed a pattern of
activities which starts with assessment of the problem and is followed
by setting the goals which the group hopes to accomplish, outlining

a strategy for reaching those goals, implementing the program and, finally, evaluating the results. I have discovered that one essential rule for successful consultation is to involve all of the participants at all stages of the program from the planning through the evaluation. For example, if you are assisting with the establishment of a selection-retention program for a department which requires a test instrument, not only students but also the faculty and administrators should be tested. Moreover, students should be involved in the planning phase and should have significant roles in the interpretation of the results and the implementation of the screening process. The critical point is that no one group should ever be perceived as doing something to another. All participants should gain something from the experience.

This same guideline is particularly important when conflict between students, faculty, and administrators within a department results in a request for consultation. In such a situation it is very difficult to avoid being used by the students, faculty, or administrators as a lever to gain an advantage. This is reasonable because most participants in academia are familiar with argumentation and debate, but they are not familiar with the effective use of a nonpolitical consultant. When a dispute becomes bitter, it requires special effort on the part of the consultant to help the participants learn that if he were to permit himself to be used as a political force by any of them, it would destroy his effectiveness in helping the entire group reach an equitable solution. We have been accused by students of not supporting them, by administrators for being student advocates, and by faculty as meddling in departmental concerns. That we have been accused by all groups of partiality to the others convinces me that we are performing our role in an appropriate manner. Another guideline which we have learned to follow is that we do not enter consultation unless all participants have made it clear that they want student development personnel to work with them.

Some student personnel workers feel that students need a special advocate when their problems involve confrontation with faculty or administrators (Penney, 1972). That is, as student development staff, we should be student advocates. I disagree with this position because I feel that it tends to reinforce the in loco parentis role and would certainly destroy a student development staff member's ability to serve in the consultant role which I feel is a critical need on the college campus. At times we have to work with students to prepare them for their encounter with faculty and administrators; however, we provide the same service to all groups. Our central role is to help any individual or group, whether students, faculty, or administrators, with the analysis of the problem they wish to solve, the decision-making process, and a strategy for solving the problem. We are willing to facilitate an encounter between groups, but we avoid taking sides.

In order to perform this type of consultation effectively, the consultant should have learned the skills of a facilitator of basic encounter groups. I have observed that consultation by those who are more comfortable with counseling than with the facilitation of encounter groups often slips into group and individual counseling. In my opinion, this is a form of deception by the consultant. A professional who is requested to assist as a consultant has an ethical responsibility to remain in that role. Group or individual counseling may be appropriate parts of some meetings but should not become the central focus. Experience in counseling can be a valuable asset to the consultant as long as the consultant does not confuse the purpose of consultation with that of counseling.

Another skill much needed by a consultant is designing instruments for data collection. Without data, the consultant runs the risk of falling into emotional traps set by participants because he must depend on their biased perceptions of relationships and events which are probably self-serving rather than factual. Each participant has his own interpretation of any situation and tends to present himself, often quite erroneously, as representative of the group from which he comes. Few people are free from this need. For this reason, one of the most helpful functions a consultant can perform it to assist participants to design instruments which will provide objective information needed to solve their problem.

The staff of the South Dakota State Student Development Center has been engaged in consultation activities for a comparatively short time. We do not consider ourselves experts and I may be considered presumptious in having presented the guidelines which we have developed for our consultation activities. However, my impression is that traditional counselors have had little experience in working as consultants to the college community. What we have learned has had to be learned through trial and error and my hope is that those centers which are moving toward a student development model and are considering the possibility of consulting with campus groups may, by reading about the guidelines which we have developed through experience, avoid some of the failures we have experienced.

To conclude this section, it might be appropriate to present two very short examples of successful consultation in which our staff has been involved in order to clarify the role of consultant as we see it. Due to budget cuts, a college was sending out a considerable amount of information about the seriousness of the financial situation. In addition, some faculty had been notified that their positions might not be funded for the following year. One attempted suicide resulted and precipitated our being asked by the college administration to assist in developing a process for keeping the faculty informed which would not increase their anxieties but would still meet the needs of the administration. Another request came from a dean who found himself on the horns of a dilemma over whether he would have to discharge one of his brightest and most energetic faculty members who was having difficulty communicating with his students. We proceeded to work with the students to help them express their frustrations openly and with the faculty member to improve his communication with the students. Our success relieved the dean, the students, and the faculty member of their problems.

When the student development model is applied to groups on a college campus, the outreach program can come to life and gain added significance. Before long, the center staff may find itself helping the drama club discover what art forms the students can relate to; helping the building and grounds committee accept its responsibility for the environment; helping students and residence halls staff deal openly with racial prejudice; helping a fraternity system confront the bigotry of its selection procedures; helping develop a course in human sexuality that is more than the usual biology or health science; helping student government set goals and assume new responsibilities; or helping departments initiate interdisciplinary programs.

In all its consulting activities, the student development center staff is attempting to facilitate the normal functioning of parts of the campus community. The ultimate goal is to create conditions which will lead to greater growth and development possibilities for all students which, in turn, should reduce the need for some of them to seek remedial counseling.

Vocational Decisions

A student development center staff, although giving priority to consulting activities on campus, continues to offer individual counseling. As with other college counseling centers, educational and vocational decision-making comprises a substantial proportion of the problems presented to counselors for assistance. In this type of counseling, the differences in approach to client problems between the student development counselor and the traditional counselor are clearly evident.

As Warnath (1971) has pointed out, traditional vocational counseling of college students is no longer appropriate. Vocational choice theories are inapplicable to many students. Tests are of little value (Goldman, 1972). From a practical standpoint, many counselors have routinized their work with vocational clients to the point where it is repititious and boring for the counselors and frustrating for the clients. All in all, traditional vocational counseling has little to commend it as a useful activity.

The central problem with vocational counseling, as I see it, is the fact that counselors have concentrated on the cognitive aspects of the process while ignoring the affective. The assumption has been that the counselor's job was to provide the client with information. The feelings of the clients, their motivation for and their involvement in the process, has been almost completely avoided. The developmental counselor approaches his clients with a different orientation. In simplest terms, counseling is not categorized as educational, vocational, or personal. A client, no matter what his problem, is encouraged to relate himself to all aspects of his development as a person. He is not separated into who he is in his social relations, who he is in school, or who he is in his home community. Rather he is responded to as a complete person who may have some specific problem which can, for purposes of convenience, be classified but which is related to all other parts of his development. A vocational problem is simply one part of the student's total development which has been going on since childhood. The student development counselor does not concentrate on the specific decision-making process as does the traditional counselor but rather helps the client understand the relationships of his specific problem to other aspects of his life. He assists the client in placing his vocational problem in the context of his total developmental experience as a person and teaches him the skills he needs to make decisions about his life in general.

The fact that most people will have to work at two or three different occupations during the course of their lives can demoralize the thoughtful counselor whose orientation is helping a client make a specific vocational choice. From a student development counselor's point of view, nothing he does can be more than tentative. The client is seen as being at one point in a continuing process of developing his skills and attitudes and faced at the moment of counseling with opportunities for moving toward increasingly rewarding goals, not simply in a vocational field but in his total life.

Conclusion

Most colleges and universities give little attention to affective learning. They have been cultivators of the intellect. The use of admission standards, autocratic teaching methods, grades and failures has reflected the emphasis given to the training of the intellect. In my judgment, there is a need for more attention to the normal affective development of college students.

I am proposing that a student development center can serve this need. It can fill this need by giving first priority to services for the general student body rather than remedial services for a relatively few students who come to the center with problems. Choices must be made by the staff of any center in regard to where it will invest its energies and, in my opinion, the returns to the students and the college will be much greater in working with larger numbers of students in facilitating their normal development than in trying to salvage a few with more serious problems.

The student development center with a well-trained professional staff should take the lead on campus in providing learning experiences to students through programs designed to assist them with the normal developmental tasks of the college-aged group such as interpersonal relations, human sexuality, and drug and alcohol usage. Every program should have an intrinsic interest and value to a broad range of students on campus rather than a narrow interest to a small minority. Decisions about what programs meet these requirements should involve active participation by members of the campus community.

Crucial to the establishment of a student development center are the attitudes of the staff toward their own development. If each counselor sees himself in the process of development and the center itself as developing and changing to meet the needs of the campus community, then, a base exists for the establishment of a student development center. Those directors who have had to cope with the rigidity of the "finished product" syndrome in a new staff member who has just received his degree and rejects any suggestion that further personal or professional growth is possible will recognize that our training programs do not prepare counselors for positions in a student development center. The director and his staff must create the climate of change through their own open interactions and their recognition of the need to change themselves if they are to make any significant contributions to the students on their campus.

It is, perhaps, appropriate to end this chapter with a short quotation of unknown origin which was called to my attention by my wife and, to me, seems to sum up in three brief lines the basic premise which the student development counselor accepts as a guiding principle in all of his work: "We see things/Not as they are/ But as we are."

XIV

A Small Center
in the Bind

David A. Hills

Like all counseling centers, our small shop was caught up in the currents of change of the late sixties. The waves of campus unrest rippling from the epicenters at Berkeley, Columbia, Wisconsin, Stanford, Jackson State, and Kent State took a little time to reach us, but our campus was profoundly affected. Like most centers we were already struggling to adapt to the call for a "restructuring of the services of college counseling center staff to improve their versatility and make their presence on campus significant to greater numbers of students (Warnath, 1971)." We were attempting to engage in outreach, use paraprofessionals, and petition for the student viewpoint in the committees dealing with programs and budgets. At the same time we were discovering that the student demand for direct counseling services was increasing. The students did not appear to be fussy about whether the counseling was delivered by

227

near-peer dormitory counselors, experimental videotape feed-back behavior therapy sessions, marathon encounter groups, or traditional one-to-one, face-to-face counseling. In retrospect, it seems that whatever the mode of delivery, our students needed contact with someone who would respond in a plausible fashion and with personal commitment that they apparently were not finding elsewhere. Thus, while we were trying to divert time away from direct services, the students were queuing up outside our door in longer lines. In the first decade of operation we had come to expect about 6 percent of the students to seek our services in a year. The typical client used to be a sophomore male concerned about an educational-vocational matter such as choice of major. By 1971, 9 percent of an expanded student body was banging on our door. The typical client was now likely to be a senior or a graduate student, a man or a woman, and concerned with a personal-emotional problem, such as acute depression with fear of suicidal impulses. To summarize, this change in student request for services amounted to nearly 80 percent more people asking for help and a shift from younger students with specific educational or career-related problems to older students with what sometimes was a life-or-death personal crisis.

We had no explanation for the change. Some other counseling centers in the region were reporting similar trends, but apparently not all. In order to find some basis for what we were observing, we hypothesized that one cause lay with the death of the counterculture as exemplified by the pathetic mouthings and misdirected bombings by the once noble-sounding militant left wing, the patently over-thirtyish spokesmen of the wilted flower children, and the failure of the hallucinogens to bring peace to their consumers. As long as the counterculture appeared alive and well, national guilt rested on the shoulders of the bumbling adults on the other side of the chasm called the Generation Gap. The hope for the future and the format for making choices was firmly vested in every sophomore who had recently read Hesse, Thoreau, or the Tibetan Book of the Dead. When the counterculture died, anger out became anger in and the hope for a quickly won world of love died with it. Our clients included people who were suddenly rootless after having had a clear purpose only a few months earlier. Yet our clients also included a large number for whom this explanation made no sense at all. But, we felt this "death of hope and loss of individual choice guidelines" hypothesis was as plausible as alternatives offered elsewhere such as long hair drives you crazy, rock music corrupts your will, or Dr. Spock is an agent of the communist conspiracy. Our explanation did not suggest any remedy other than to help students find reasons to hope and ways to make choices.

Wake Forest is a small residential institution of about 4000 students including law, medicine, management, and graduate school students. The medical school is a few miles across town so that the medical and allied health students are not ordinarily among the counseling center clientele. Although we occasionally feel it a delusion of grandeur to call ourselves a counseling "center" because of our small size, our center staff consisted of two and one-third fulltime equivalent counselors. Translated into flesh, blood, and anxiety, this meant two men, two women, a psychiatric consultant one half a day a week for a semester, and occasionally as many as four graduate students. All of us were parttime and had other responsibilities elsewhere, chiefly teaching in the psychology department. Two clerical employees—one a homegrown psychometrist—staffed the front office on a fulltime basis.

We were frankly unprepared to deal with the combination of changes in our roles, in our clients, and in other student services on campus. The student personnel people were revamping the residence hall counseling programs. We teetered between the hope that improved residence hall counseling would reduce our loads and the fear that referrals from the residence halls would overflow our already bulging waiting room. Neither our hope nor our fear was realized. Better services were made available to the students but referrals to the counseling center did not increase dramatically. We were not able to launch a large-scale paraprofessional training program, but were consulting with the student personnel deans and the counselor educators for ways to supplement their efforts. The community ministers and campus chaplains had opened a coffeehouse. Students and former students had organized a drug crisis and walkin counseling center with a 24-hour telephone hotline. We were represented on their advisory board, helped with their training program, provided backup consultation and assistance in hospitalization, hauled in food for hungry street people, and learned how to

say "smack," "grass," and "rap" (instead of "heroin," "marijuana,"
and "discuss"). Another change was the effort of the faculty and
campus ministry people to create helping people communities
through their sensitivity, encounter, and growth groups. Would
they pick up large numbers of potential clients and safely wrap
them in a protective circle of concern or would they create more
customers for us? After all, we had self-consciously taken off our
ties and shoes, grown hair all over our face and down our collars, sat
on the floor, and tried to be participant-consultants to some of these
groups. Once again the group movement, like the other changes, did
not alter the rate at which students sought counseling. It was almost
as if the groups were tapping an entirely different subpopulation.

Thus, there were now more people helpers of one description
or another than ever before. Why were the students still coming to
us in increasing numbers?

Some faculty critics suggested that there was a self-fulfilling
prophecy implicitly at work. The more counselors and helping
people popped into view, the more students came to feel that they
were expected to have problems. The programs themselves were
programing the students into imagining problems where none
existed. Other critics insisted that it was fashionable to have psychological difficulties. Our experience was that there is nothing fashionable or popular about being plagued with hallucinations or a
compulsion to vomit when people come close to you. There may be
secondary gains associated with these behaviors, but neither Dale
Carnegie nor Timothy Leary recommended hearing mocking voices
or throwing up as ways of advancing in the esteem of one's peers.

The administration was sympathetic to requests for more
staff to meet our demonstrable manpower needs, although the budget officers were beginning to peer anxiously at what appeared to
them to be the growing army of professional counselors, deans and
their assistants, chaplains and volunteer ministers, faculty engaged
in groups and in training student counselors, and dozens of paid
student residence-hall counselors. Beginning in 1967 they had allowed us gradually to employ the time equivalent of one additional
fulltime-equivalent staff member to bring us from one and one-third
to our two and one-third senior staff equivalents. When it became
clear—to us, at least—that now a staff twice as big as ours would

scarcely be too many, the administration shrugged its shoulders. We were given an opportunity to talk to an alumni policy group and the University Board of Visitors in an effort to alter priorities from that direction. We emphasized to these groups the increasing number of students with serious problems applying directly to the center, the impact of this onslaught in terms of reduced time to spend with student development goals, and the steps we were taking as stopgap measures. We offered our explanations for the increasing rate of student distress and urged support for additional staff. It was never clear exactly what our appeal was supposed to accomplish, beyond the slight hope that the alumni might be moved to help find new sources of funding or that a recommendation to divert money from the instructional budget to the counseling center might emerge. We tried to portray the counseling center as part of the general instructional scheme and to suggest that additional funds did not represent a departure from educational goals. The alumni and the Board of Visitors thought we presented some interesting ideas but reached no consensus on how they might usefully react. We were discouraged.

Being unwilling to reduce activities in either outreach or in-house counseling and finding the university unable to grant us additional staff, we adpoted an emergency measure. Each student was seen for an intake interview on a half-hour schedule. Those presenting an acute problem with which we could deal quickly were scheduled for followup sessions. Those whose severe difficulties looked like a long-term problem were referred elsewhere if possible. (Sometimes it was not possible because of the student's lack of money, in which case we tried to cope on a holding-action basis.) Students with educational-vocational problems or personal difficulties of a chronic, quiet-stew variety were put on the waiting list. Warnath (1971) points out that "counselors in their training receive little encouragement to evaluate quickly and make prompt concise decisions about the appropriate disposition of a case." Whether or not we were competent to make quick decisions, we did not always feel comfortable doing so. When possible, we tried to assign two people to intake interviewing during active intake periods so that we could use both counselors in the intake interview if students came in one at a time. While this may appear to be an expensive

use of staff time, it helped staff morale and provided a better feel
for the client. Also, clients seemed to accept referral or delay well
when two counselors had participated in the decision. Having
geared outselves to respond as best we could to immediate student
requests, we then returned to the question, how could we either
get more staff or multiply our effectiveness without sacrificing other
areas of involvement? We had already all but completely abandoned
our modest research efforts. If one counted all contact hours, we
were close to 20 hours per fulltime counselor in a week. (I know
that some counseling centers can point to an average of more than
25 hours per week, but we have difficulty remembering our own
names after running on a schedule of 20 consummated contact
hours per week.) In desperation we dusted off all the unused ideas
sitting on the shelves and looked to see if any answers could be found
among them. As of this date, none of these ideas have been implemented. They are offered as examples of the ways our center and
others attempted to relieve the crunch between rising needs, changing and expanding goals, and dwindling economic resources.

Floating Psychometrists

Counseling centers existed or were being established in three
of the five other small colleges and universities in the city. One
institution which was historically a black teachers college had been
upgraded to university status and, in the process, had developed an
active counseling center; another one, a residential college predominantly for students interested in careers in the performing arts
was creating a residence-hall counseling corps with the student
personnel dean's office serving as administrative and organizational
center. We proposed centralizing all test ordering, administration,
scoring, and profiling in our center to take advantage of volume
discounts and production-line methods. A testing team consisting of
our home-trained psychometrist and one graduate student would be
dispatched to each participating center on a regular schedule. A
standard packet of most-used tests (such as the Kuder tests, the
Strong Vocational Interest Blank, the Edwards Personal Preference
Inventory, the Minnesota Multiphasic Personality Inventory, and

the Differential Aptitude Tests with local norms)' would be supplied to each center for emergency use. By spreading costs, we estimated that our center initially would gain access to part of the time of one additional administrative-psychometrist and have a large pool of scores for local norm development while providing all centers with a better testing service. We also thought that eventually we could gain an additional half-time counselor. Unfortunately for our plans, our client load problems were not focused in the areas where testing was of primary concern. And two newer staff members were raising questions about the value of testing for any reason—in keeping with a notion then current in other training centers. Further, we had tentatively explored the plan earlier with staff members at both the formerly black teachers college and the performing arts college, and both had agreed that while the idea had merit, their agencies felt compelled either to continue their own testing programs or to develop testing capabilities for themselves. The director of the new center at the women's college echoed their sentiments. In view of these negative reactions and our own lukewarm feelings, the scheme was abandoned. One counselor did consult the new center on new programs and agreed that our center would offer certain tests such as Miller Analogies Tests for them.

A related version of the floating psychometrist plan thus was judged to be worth further consideration—an institutional research office for all the colleges and universities in the immediate vicinity. The participants would need to agree on at least one measure appropriate for cross-campus comparisons and one for the special needs of a particular campus. Data-gathering would be confined largely to testing incoming freshmen and graduating seniors. We believe that our center would gain, as would all participating institutions, from having more and presumably better data than possible from one institutional research office on one campus.

One of the most obvious and traditional outreach efforts is that of describing and interpreting the students to the faculty, administration, and student personnel people. The faculty may see the students as a dull sea of vacuous faces brighened by an occasional eager soul who shows the uncommon wisdom to want to follow in the footsteps of the faculty to their respective graduate schools. The administration and student personnel offices are apt to encounter either the straight-arrow junior executive type student who serves on student-faculty joint committees or the grumblers and malcontents. While these are indubitably part of every student generation, the almost invisible majority bear little resemblance to any of these groups. A number of years ago a member of the counseling center was assigned to select and coach a team of students to compete on a television program called the "G. E. College Bowl." To assemble the squad, he asked for student and faculty nominees. Of approximately sixty faculty candidates, only one survived the selection process—tests and ratings in a game simulation situation—to end up on the final team. Seven of the eight team members were from what faculty would regard as the "unwashed barbarian" ranks. Yet seven went on to graduate school; one received a Woodrow Wilson grant, although at the time of his selection for the television team his grades were modest, and he was not considered prime graduate school material. The point is that the faculty may not even necessarily know who the good students are. Any input beyond the SAT, ACT, and grade-point scores which can be fed to the faculty curriculum development committee and the student personnel living-learning programing can potentially have considerable impact. Whatever the inadequacies of mass testing data from biographical inventories and group interest schedules, the information is likely to be more reliable and relevant than the collection of anecdotes and small sample observations faculty often have to depend on.

In our situation, our earliest attempts at interpreting the students were received with interest. But, we also discovered that our reports on student characteristics and attitudes could be considered answers to questions no one was asking. As in therapy, descriptions and interpretations must be properly timed if they are to be accepted and acted upon. We then began to look for ways to get people to ask the questions. Individual conferences with deans and department chairmen set the stage. Now we are concerned with promoting the idea that questions about the impact of curriculum change or altering procedures should be asked at the time the change is contemplated, so that the answers are available after the alteration is accomplished. This proactive attitude toward research is difficult to sell; we forget it ourselves.

The student profile data often raises the question, "Are other institutions finding the same trends, or is it a local phenomenon?" The institutional research consortium would be a vehicle for answering that question. The immediate payoff for an overworked counseling center staff is probably small, but the long-range returns should benefit all sectors of the university.

Community Career Center

In comparing our counseling services with standard service agencies in town, we concluded that the thing we do best that is relatively unique is educational-vocational counseling—although the state employment office services are probably superior to ours at the skilled labor and trades level. By trying to contract for all the educational-vocational counseling in town, we thought that we could generate enough income to pay one additional senior staff member and one administrative or clerical level person. Since off-campus counseling would tend to be relatively evenly demanded in comparison with the seasonal ups and downs of college counseling, we could envision obtaining up to half the time of the additional personnel for student service. It was a tempting notion—but we have currently abandoned it. After our experience with the floating psychometrist, we concluded that we were woefully naive about the administrative time necessary to implement a service involving other agencies. Also, we began to scare ourselves with the idea that we might be too successful: if the administration found we could be partly self-sufficient, we might eventually be invited to raise all our own budget! Finally, our small school-small center staff has some institutional identification, and private practice is relatively low on the staff's need hierarchy. And, the newest counseling center in town—The Salem College Life Span Counseling Center—has just initiated a long-range career development counseling program open both to their own students and to people in the community. While the Salem program is currently restricted to women, little would be gained by opening a service partly in competition with a developing program.

Student Hospital

The university health service is proposing an expansion and reorganization in an attempt to bring back some of the convenience and continuity of the old family doctor. In some communities emergency open-heart surgery is almost easier to get than an appointment for a routine physical. As a part of the proposed reorganziation, we are considering providing the hospital with several specialty clinics, for example, obesity and diet control, anxiety management, and—surprise!—a career clinic. Since educational and occupational unhappiness often results in the physical condition known to physicians by the technical term of "feeling crummy" and since the reorganized health service would have a strong whole-person emphasis, it makes as much sense for us to locate all traditional services within the health service as it does to remain in our current, overcrowded quarters.

We have a close working relationship with the campus health service, and see an opportunity to help enlarge its image and responsibilities without it becoming a captive agency and subordinate to a medical master. Until insurance laws are changed to cover nonmedical service personnel, it can be an advantage for financially beleaguered counseling centers to gain funding under a general health care umbrella. Also, since we are the de facto primary mental health agency on campus, it makes sense to help integrate the student clinical services. However, as of this date, money for medical services is almost as scarce as student services funds.

Counseling Center Consortium

In this plan we would approach both the public and academic-based personal services agencies in town who deal with a similar age group and invite each to ante up a quarter-time equivalent of one person to a professional talent pool. Without trying to predetermine how this pool will be splashed around, members of the consortium can use up to half of the talent pool time to decide what to do, and where and when to do it, and the remainder of the time doing it. The time would inevitably tend to go to particular projects and to concerns peripheral to direct service. But, our center would gain by having access to expertise not on our payroll without paying a consultant's fee. Interagency cooperation should be a natural byproduct. Referral routes could be solidified. Clients involved with several agencies at the same time might benefit from possible program coordination. If we did not do anything more than consult with each other on an exchange basis, we could gain in staff morale and perspective. We have already taken one step which could help. The center's regular weekly training staff meeting has been expanded to include representatives from several other college-based counseling centers and student personnel deans in the community. Matters of common concern, local and journal research, and strategems for improving service delivery systems are discussed. Representatives from other campuses thus far have appeared to welcome the chance to share in a little professional renewal without having to bend their individual schedules much.

Other Steps

"Innovative proposal" can be another term for "active fantasy"; and while we all know that exercise of the imagination is supposed to be good for those of us still working at becoming actualized, dreams do not transmute automatically into programs. What the world may need now is more management and less creativity. In any event we concluded that our scheming required more managing than we could muster and more development lead time than we could spare. The university administration then offered to buy half the time of one senior staff member as a student personnel consultant for a year. The time thus created was to be used for inventorying and reviewing all the university's existing remedial and student development services, seeking ways to facilitate communication and coordination among the services, and, perhaps most important, helping to generate goals and directions for a thoughtful, purposeful student development program for the university.

One example of our procedure is The University Game. After an evening trying to help a residence-hall counselor facilitate cooperation among the residents through a *Psychology Today* bargaining and communication exercise called The Cities Game, the residence-hall counselor, a faculty member, and the counseling center representative jointly hit on the idea of a university simulation exercise. Working with the student personnel staff and a campus minister who had learned about simulation games in seminary, the counseling center helped create the University Game in which trustees, administration, faculty, and students bargain over the fate of a hypothetical university. To our surprise and delight, several trustees agreed to join with a university vice-president, several faculty members, and a group of students in the first run of The Game, as it was quickly labeled. Roles were switched, with some trustees taking a student role, some faculty playing administrators, some students acting as faculty, and so forth. While playing simulation games scarcely solves all problems, we viewed it as a useful device for stimulating discussion of goals and purposes. One immediately useful outcome was that a trustee was taken on a quick tour of a coeducational dormitory in the middle of the game when the hypothetical issue at stake dealt with expanded coeducational living arrangements and the trustee had expressed concern that coeducational dorms meant an image of institutionalized cohabitation.

For the time being at least, the counseling center is trying to meet further increases in direct counseling demands by becoming experts at referral. In the words of a colleague, "We will try to help others to do whatever it is we have done that others can do." Effective referral does not just happen; it is an art that must be practiced. In some instances, this colleague has directed the staff to literally walk through the referral paths to see what a student might encounter. With increased referral avenues the center hopefully can continue to function as a primary care facility or mental health first aid station for acute emotional crises and still provide the current level of outreach and development programming.

With respect to generating goals, directions, and a philosophical framework for a comprehensive student development program, we are focusing on the most commonplace notion—alma mater, the university as parent. It is the contention of many that the court decision challenging the in loco parentis role of colleges and universities was *not* the end of alma matering, but simply an updat-

ing of institutional mothering patterns to fit more closely the contemporary middle-class parental practices. Parents permit children
to own cars, come and go after dark without accounting for their
time, wear their hair in novel configurations, and confront a wider-
than-previous range of personal and sexual decisions and experiences. Colleges and universities cannot be legally allowed to enforce
a hoopskirt-and-handlebar-moustache parental supervision of a
color-television and moonwalking generation. Neither college administrators nor faculty had a readymade set of alternatives to replace
in loco parentis as it was overturned. With the rapid growth of
college population in the post-Korean War years, many deans and
faculty quietly abdicated, and the stage was set for the *Lord of the
Flies* atmosphere that appeared on some campuses. It is oversimpli-
fied, of course, but the parallel between the issue that ignited Berkeley in the days of the Free Speech Movement and the problem of
the parents who do not know what to do when their child learns
his first four-letter word is striking. The answer was simple for the
Victorian parents: wash the little fellow's mouth out with soap and
send him to bed without his supper. On empirical grounds, we
can now say that this style will not work at the college level.

The catchphrase of the early seventies has been accountability. At one level it simply calls attention to and summarizes the
need for tighter budget practices. Industrial budgeters have long
recognized the advantages of linking clear, concrete statements of
objectives with systematic allocation of resources. In other words,
you are more apt to get someplace if you have selected a goal and
examined in detail what will take you there. Since our campus
had been engaged in some of the same program expansion that
characterized higher education everywhere in the post-World War
II era, our Model-T budget planning procedures were inadequate.
Accountability translated out of sloganese meant "improve budget
planning operations." But, at another level, the word called attention
to the lack of consistent models for institutional interaction with
students. As one student said, "The University seems like a big,
nebulous It. I want to kick it to see if it feels anything." The concept
of universities as immense sausage factories which grind students
into little pieces pleases no one, and was perhaps the picture produced by the absence of accountable student personnel policies

rather than resulting from careful implementation of policies of
planned demoralization concocted by mad scientist deans and
sadistic presidents. Acountability thus translates into the question
"Who's in charge?"

Katz (1972), commenting on student-teacher interaction,
suggests that there is value in the traditional apprentice-master
relationship even if much of learning actually takes place among
peers. Sanford (1966) and others associated with a developmental
approach to the college experience argue for the growth potential
of the creative rebellion in which an *individual* student completes a
part of his or her identity through a direct, personal challenge to
the establishment. The creative rebellion is going to have considerably greater personal significance for a student if that confrontation
can occur with an acountable professor or dean rather than a distant
committee manifesting itself through multilithed handouts. In the
same vein, Erikson (1963) says, "Adolescents have to refight many
of the battles of earlier years, even though to do so they must
artificially appoint perfectly well-meaning people to play the roles
of adversaries." If faculty and deans are expected to act in this
manner, perhaps the counseling center can help them understand
how to play their role without hurt feelings. Learning has been
associated more positively with a parental model than a military,
bureaucratic, industrial, or anarchistic model. Uncomfortable as
academic people may be with the humane exercise of authority
which lurks beneath the parental model, counseling center people
may have to help them find ways to manifest a quasiparent attitude
of accountability for the individual student. Silberman (1970) contends, "Our most pressing educational problem . . . is how to
create and maintain a humane society. A society whose schools are
inhumane is not likely to be humane itself." To contribute to this
"most pressing problem" and to ultimately shift all but the most
specialized kinds of personal crisis intervention and educational-
vocational planning from the counseling center to the faculty
would appear to demand that the counseling center change from
an exclusively student-centered focus to an equal concern for the
morale, functioning, and life goals of the faculty. It is interesting
that in 1971 and 1972 the number of faculty seeking referral assistance and direct counseling service at our center more than doubled.

The absolute number remains small but a trend may be developing.

The view of the college or university as an institutionalized, idealized model of the enlightened parent to which flesh-and-blood parents entrust their offspring for completion of the socialization process, for better or worse, is not defunct. The question then becomes: What styles of enlightened parenting can a college promote? Some faculty and administrators immediately borrow from their own experience as parents to create an effective surrogate-parent style. Others choose to function as older brothers and sisters to the students, serving as role models and letting their younger siblings occasionally tag along (but not always). Janitors, nighttime campus security personnel, adult dormitory supervisors, and friendly bookstore salespeople are often seen by students as temporarily filling the shoes of an aunt or uncle on a temporary basis. Individual faculty members automatically elect differing parental roles, including even that of the absent parent. Even though there is an automatic and natural process at work, the college or university must officially recognize and seek to support the process through conscious student development programs and endorsement in its hiring and promotion policies. Otherwise, university and college people, like rats and pigeons, tend to go where the reinforcements are being dispensed. A vehicle for recognizing and rewarding student advising by faculty must be sought. While not all faculty and staff need to function actively as idealized parent or older sibling to the students, for those who are interested, perhaps counseling center personnel can prepare role guidelines in the form of pamphlets, workshops, and adaptations of Gordon's (1970) parent effectiveness training along the lines of "How to be an effective, enlightened parent surrogate and still retain your research grant."

One demonstration of the receptivity of the faculty to the idea of serving as effective change and growth agents was seen on our campus in 1972 at the height of student requests for counseling services. A staff member with a joint faculty appointment announced at a faculty meeting that the counseling center could no longer guarantee acceptance of faculty-referred students. The counselor assured the faculty that teaching practices and classroom management techniques were not the primary cause for the increased student distress and encouraged faculty to persist in, even increase their availability to students, not as amateur psychotherapists, but simply as people. The concepts of parental surrogate and effective person role model were briefly discussed. Half expecting to hear a chorus of protest about babying the students or losing valuable research time, the counselor was surprised that a majority seemed relieved to hear that their presence and efforts at relating to the students still served a useful function. Some seemed to feel that psychologists had banded together with student radicals in labeling them personally, along with higher education in general, as irrelevant or perhaps even positively poisonous. The simple act of re-endorsing their importance appeared to encourage them. While nothing very dramatic followed, several faculty members subsequently commented spontaneously that they were spending more time than ever in helping students with personal problems, and that it seemed that more of their colleagues were making an increased effort, too. Whether or not the comments of the counselor in the faculty meeting were instrumental in this development cannot be determined. The important point is that few faculty were actively negative to, and many seemed genuinely interested in, assuming some responsibility for student growth and problem alleviation.

All this armchair speculation about alma mater and parenting may seem a bit unreal or antiquated in cold print, but from our experience it provides a common ground for discussion around which faculty, administration, and student personnel staff can develop organizing principles and explanatory fictions for programs in student development. Brown (1972) urges higher education to design a curriculum which has "an impact on the affective life of students as well as their cognitive styles" and to "work more aggressively to personalize and individualize the student's educational experience." While to me Brown is promoting the enlightened alma mater concept in intelligent and thoughtful terms, some trustees, state legislators, and faculty reflexively raise their hackles at such language. These same people may have trouble attacking Dear Old Mom.

Apart from the language and independent of the various parenting styles or particular people, curricula, and projects which implement these styles, the underlying theme is one of deliberately reassuming and reaffirming responsibility for students as almost-adults and young adults in an extended-family network. The accompanying assumption is that the college and university—even the gargantuan multiversities—have something to contribute to the continuing personal development of the student. Stated differently, the entering freshman does not already represent the highest flowering of human adult development. And, in addition to such marvels as how many electrons are in orbit on the head of a pin, the college or university houses people who can teach something about courage, justice, wisdom, and tolerance of ambiguity, not only through study of the classics, but also through personal contact and example. Difficult as it may be to define the enlightened parental surrogate model, it is even more difficult to discover a social institution which brings more expertise and equipment to the task than the colleges and universities.

We are still in the stage of discussing philosophy and cataloguing resources on our campus. One unlikely result would be that virtually every employee of the university becomes a parttime brother, sister, father, mother, or uncle to every student with whom they have consistent contact. A more probable outcome will be that, in various small ways, we will discover motivation to bring the university a step or two toward student development goals and ideals.

XV

A Center Survives
a Crisis

Thomas K. Hocking

Austerity. Retrenchment. Reallocation. Accountability. Enrollment shortfalls. Economy. Nonretention. Words, events, policies, and practices like these lately are causing increasing pressure and uneasiness in college counseling centers. In his address at the annual conference of the Directors of College and University Counseling Centers, James Bond, president of California State University at Sacramento, said, "As most of you know and are experiencing, counseling centers are under attack across the nation. I have been in any number of situations where the budget crunch is not only hitting the total university, but is hitting specifically in the counseling areas" (1972). Bond and others (Stubbins, 1970; Warnath, 1971, 1972) have been raising serious questions about the value of current counseling services, the new directions in which counselors should be moving, and the political and economic considerations involved. Thus, trained as they may be in crisis intervention, college counselors now find themselves facing a crisis and wish fervently that someone or something would intervene to help them. Most college counselors have probably always felt a certain amount of tension in the academic settings because they are service personnel instead of teaching faculty—the "applied" people, not quite academically respectable faculty members who do not generate credit hours of student contact in lectures or discussion sections. In some colleges and universities, counseling center personnel are not even given faculty rank. Recently, however, additional tensions and pressures have been generated by enrollment shortfalls and a host of political and economic difficulties. One result has been that college counselors are being increasingly pressured to demonstrate that they are integral parts of the college community and that they are worth what they cost. As an illustration of the problems which confront professional counselors today, the Counseling Center at the University of Wisconsin-Oshkosh has recently experienced, and survived, a crisis situation and continues to struggle with another.

The University of Wisconsin-Oshkosh is a coeducational state university in East Central Wisconsin. In the fall of 1971, it had a student enrollment of 11,800 and a faculty of more than 600. While the university offers a number of master's degree programs, most notably in education and business, it is primarily an undergraduate institution. The university has been preparing teachers since 1871, and the School of Education still enrolls about 36 percent of the student body; however, about 43 percent of the students are now enrolled in the School of Letters and Science, and the remaining 21 percent are enrolled in rapidly growing Nursing, Business, and Graduate Schools. The student body is fairly homogeneous, made up largely of state residents, predominantly from the local Fox River Valley area, the second most densely populated region in the state. The university offers, in addition to its on-campus programs, fairly diverse continuing education, cultural development, and resource and research services to business, industry, professions, and government. The university maintains an essentially open admissions policy. In November 1971, UW-Oshkosh and eight other universities which had formerly comprised the Wisconsin State University

System merged with the University of Wisconsin to form the fourth largest educational system in the nation. Control of the system was assigned to a single state Board of Regents, and an administrative head with the title of president. Each campus is administered by a chancellor. In the fall of 1972, for the first time in many years, UW-Oshkosh experienced a drop in enrolment of about 500 students, an experience shared by every other institution in the newly merged UW System except UW-Madison. While UW-Oshkosh remained the third largest university in the system, and the largest of the former state universities, this enrolment shortfall triggered a crisis situation of farreaching consequences.

The effects of the general crisis began to be felt in the Counseling Center in the spring of 1971, when the vice-president for student affairs announced his retirement, effective at the end of the 1971 summer session. At that time, the Division of Student Affairs was composed of the Counseling Center, Testing Center, Reading-Study Skills Center, Health Center, Placement Office, Financial Aids Office, Dean of Students Office, Housing Office, and the Student Union. The division was administered by a council of directors presided over by the vice-president for student affairs. During the spring and summer of 1971, a series of meetings were held which involved the Council of Directors, student government leaders, and the President and his Administrative Council of Vice-Presidents (Business, Academic Affairs, Student Affairs) concerning the reorganization of the Division of Student Affairs. At the end of July 1971, over the vigorous objections of several directors and the student government president, the university administration officially eliminated the division and with it the office of vice-president of student affairs. A new position of vice-president for executive functions was created, and the former student services were split up among the three vice-presidents. Counseling, Testing, and Reading were placed under the Vice-President for Academic Affairs; the Health Center, Financial Aids, Housing, and the Union were placed under the Vice-President for Business Affairs; the Placement Office and the Dean of Students Office were placed under the new Vice-President for Executive Functions.

This reorganization had three major implications for the Counseling Center: First, organizationally the director of the Counseling Center now reported to the vice-president for academic affairs, a man who did not possess a student personnel point of view or an understanding of counseling services. He was, however, now in control of staff, budget, and facility allocations for the Counseling Center, Testing Center, and Reading-Study Skills Center. Second, no one at the highest organizational level could speak exclusively for students and student services or relay student viewpoints to the administration for decision-making and policy formulation. Third, the nine student services were now fragmented and divided among three organizational units. Despite efforts to maintain communication among these agencies, close working relationships were gradually diminished and, in some cases, lost.

While this reorganization of the Division of Student Affairs was in progress, the Counseling Center coordinator of research and I were attending an outreach research workshop in Colorado. On my return, I was informed by the assistant director that four members of our staff had received letters, dated June 28, 1971, which read as follows: "I am sorry to inform you that Wisconsin State University-Oshkosh is not in a position to offer you reappointment for a fourth year of service for the academic year 1972–73. Your employment will be terminated no later than at the conclusion of your third year of service. We regret that this notice to you is necessary. We hope that your service here next year will be personally rewarding, and we wish you well as you pursue your professional career in the years beyond 1971–72." The letter was signed by the President of the University. I later learned that forty-eight faculty members had received such letters, and that fifteen (31 percent) held positions in the Division of Student Affairs.

Needless to say, the Counseling Center was in a state of shock. I had been permitted no part in the decision-making; as a matter of fact, I had not even been informed. The letters were sent to each staff member's home by registered mail. Each person must have wondered, at least momentarily, whether I knew of this action and whether I had betrayed the trust between us, even if he did not want to believe that. The letters were cryptic, brutally so—on the advice of the state attorney general's office, I was told—and no reasons for termination were given. We were soon informed, however, largely via the grapevine, that the forty-eight faculty members represented "the class of '69." They had been hired in 1969, were in their third year of employment at the university, and were eligible for consideration for tenure, which was earned after four years of employment under the law existing at that time.

As nearly as we could determine, the intention of our administration was to provide itself with some flexibility in personnel matters during 1971–1972 if any of the following happened: First, if the university experienced a drastic enrolment shortfall in September 1971; second, if the university's budget was considerably less than requested and needed; and third, if the national economy took a drastic plunge, making money for education scarce. There apparently was nothing personal in giving forty-eight people notice of nonretention, but the effect on faculty morale in the Counseling Center and across the campus was appalling.

If the loss of our vice-president and our organizational identity and the threatened loss of nearly half of our staff were not enough to make us wonder who in administration did not like us, another shock was due just before the university opened for the fall 1972 semester. The Counseling Center, Testing Center, and Reading-Study Skills Center are located in three separate buildings which were once private residences and were purchased by the university primarily for the land on which they stand. The buildings are not perfect for our purposes, but they are warm-looking and comfortable places, are near each other, and are at the center of the major campus "traffic pattern." One morning, several maintenance personnel came in and asked if we were aware that demolition orders had been written for our three buildings. They said they had been told by other personnel who had reputedly seen the orders at the Administration Building. At first the idea that our buildings would be ordered demolished without so much as a word to the directors seemed too ludicrous for us to get very upset or excited about. However, in view of the events of the preceding three or four months, we did some hasty checking. The Vice-President for Academic Affairs, our immediate superior, referred us to the Business Affairs office where the Assistant to the Vice-President for Business Affairs confirmed that the rumors were indeed true and promised to send over the Executive Director of Physical Facilities to discuss the matter with us.

The Executive Director of Physical Facilities appeared in my office the following afternoon, replete with drawings and floor plans which roughly translated the total square feet of space being occupied in the Counseling Center building to space available on the third floor of the Administration Building. He had been authorized to prepare these plans weeks before, and the space available in the Center was estimated while the staff had been on vacation after the summer session. He explained that the property on which our buildings stood was purchased to acquire the land, not the structures. Since several new buildings had been completed on campus in the past three years, classroom and faculty office space were no longer a critical problem, and nearly the entire third floor of the Administration Building was now empty. Why, then, should the university continue to provide heat, light, and maintenance service to several separate buildings when the programs which they housed could be moved to a site where these services were already provided? In addition, the university had the money immediately available to tear down the buildings and it might not be available in the future. Funds were also available to renovate parts of the Administration Building, including the third floor. It was a simple matter of economics. Neither he nor his superiors had any understanding of the effect of such orders and plans upon our services, nor could they see the incongruity in a budget category system that could provide funds for razing buildings and remodeling others while forty-eight faculty members were being dismissed. The Executive Director of Physical Facilities confirmed that our buildings would be demolished "on or before February 1, 1972," that we would be moved to temporary quarters on the third floor of the Administration Building, that remodeling to meet our needs would begin when funds were available, and that these orders and plans were irrevocable. He showed no concern about our lack of input into, or even information about, these decisions.

Our vehement protests brought no response from either the president or the vice-president for academic affairs. Aside from the ethics of the decision-making process, we were concerned with being taken out of the mainstream of campus activity and having our "visibility" reduced to zero and with being located directly over the administrative offices of the university where students might associate us with the record-keeping, policy-making, disciplinary processes of the university. Our feedback from centers across the country indicated that such a physical arrangement was anathema to effective counseling services. Our frustration was heightened by the lack of understanding demonstrated by the administration, and by its tendency to perceive us as merely resistant to moving.

By the time classes began, however, students and faculty were taking some interest in what was going on in the university generally and in our situation specifically. Articles critical of various administrative decisions and actions began to appear in the student newspaper. On September 8, the President sent me a letter in reaction to a student newspaper article in which I said that the university was beginning to make decisions based more on financial and economic considerations than on consideration of people and programs to meet the needs of people. In more informal communications with the president and other administration officials, we were being assured that counseling, testing, and reading programs were still valued as they had been previously and that no one was "out to get us or student services generally." However, these assurances, coupled with events of the summer and early fall, seemed to constitute a double message which did nothing to allay our depression. In my reply to the President's letter, I concluded as directly and honestly as possible: "To say that I, and my staff, are 'disappointed' in actions taken this summer is a gross understatement. We see counseling services on this campus, and perhaps other services also, being systematically killed and buried. It is a terrible blow to me to see programs which have previously been valued, supported, appreciated, suddenly seen as peripheral, expendable, and perhaps superfluous. My morale, and that of my staff, is at an all-time low."

Thus, as classes began in September 1971, a very definite crisis situation existed for the Counseling Center and its staff. To our dismay, our protests seemed to fall on deaf ears where decisions were being made. Shortly after our four staff members had received their letters, we solicited support from two sources outside the state, reasoning that an outside, objective, authoritative viewpoint might help our administrators to see our point of view. Both sources were men respected in the fields of psychology and counseling, with whom we had made contact through a nationwide research project. They had studied our Center, its staff and programs, during 1970–1971, and they were professionally involved with us during 1971–1972. One of them, in a letter to our President, attempted to explain where the UW-O Counseling Center stood professionally, "hoping that the situation will eventually allow you to be more flexible, and that they can be offered greater support." The writer commented on the high level of training, drive, and enthusiasm of our staff, and on our relationship with faculty, especially in the School of Education. He concluded with the opinion that UW-O "has an exceptional counseling service, well run, very practical, and creative in the right ways. I want to add that this judgment is a professional one and not based on friendship . . . I have surveyed and evaluated counseling services across the country beginning in 1962. I would rate your Counseling Center as one of the top 15 percent in the country, and would deeply regret it if the staff cuts hurt them in essential ways." The second source wrote in much the same vein, stating that "my major reason for writing is to offer some outside and hopefully objective evidence about the quality of the Counseling Center at Wisconsin State." Neither of these letters drew a response from anyone in our administration.

In addition to this support, which we solicited, we began to get unsolicited support from sources closer to home. A member of the United Campus Ministry at UW-O wrote to the President expressing dismay that fifteen of the forty-eight letters of nonretention were in the area of Student Affairs: "Particularly alarming to me was the nonretention of four men from the Counseling Center . . . I find it unbelievable that as this university grows it sees fit to cut the Counseling Center staff almost in half." He went on to express the opinion that the university was dismissing four well-trained counselors. "Surely there are other ways and places to economize within this university than arbitrarily truncating the Counseling Center . . . I write asking you to do all in your leadership and power to reverse this decision of non-retention in the case of the aforementioned people!" The university psychiatric consultant at the Student Health Center also communicated with the President, concluding his letter with the opinion that the university should not assume the role of mental hospital or clinic in offering long-term treatment to students with major mental disturbances, but that it could offer much to enhance the social and intrapersonal development of students. "At this point in time I know of no other group at WSU-O so effective and so dedicated toward that end as our Counseling Center. To decrease staff and subsequently their services would most certainly have an ill effect on the emotional well-being of our student body. It is my hope that every possible alternative would be explored prior to making such a decision final."

In addition to these reactions, letters to the editor and articles began to appear in the student newspaper. Concerned students and faculty members called or visited the Center to ask questions which we answered as directly and honestly as we could. Some of these people then directed questions to the administration, both publicly and privately. What our own entreaties and the letters of support from concerned colleagues could not accomplish, student and faculty pressure began to achieve.

The first breakthrough came with regard to the impending irrevocable plan to demolish the Counseling Center and five other so-called temporary buildings. Some student leaders and others with campus political experience communicated their displeasure with this action, and the manner in which it was being taken, directly to the President and several of his chief administrative officers. They pointed out that 1971–1972 was the university's centennial year, and that disruption and discontent should probably be avoided in view of the public attention which would undoubtedly be focused on the university campus. Their logic and concern apparently had an effect on members of the administration. because on September 10, only two weeks after classes began, the President wrote an urgent letter to the Director of the State University System at Madison strongly recommending that the Counseling Center building and a building housing a journalism laboratory, the student newspaper, and the student yearbook be saved. The President indicated that the Center building was regarded by students and faculty as superior in many ways to any facility which could be created in space available elsewhere. He further indicated that students and faculty failed to see the logic of tearing down the buildings and that their convictions were "beginning to carry strong emotional overtones." He advised the System Director that "a quick reaction" might ease a lot of tension on the campus and help convince students that "the 'brass' really does care." Only a few days later, the President appeared in person at the Student Government Office, and then at the Counseling Center, to inform us that the buildings would be saved. In fact, five of the six buildings earmarked for demolition were eventually saved and designated semipermanent.

The second breakthrough was a little longer in coming, requiring all of the first semester to accomplish. Student and faculty criticism of policies which permitted extensive maintenance and renovation projects while forty-eight professors were being dismissed continued and intensified. The four Counseling Center positions became one of the focal points because the four were all extremely well trained and qualified, had performed their responsibilities competently and ethically for three years, and were different from many others who were being dismissed because they did not have doctorates or were not fully qualified for their positions. The administration asserted that the Counseling Center situation was a special case because issuing contracts to the four counselors for 1972–1973 would be tantamount to granting them tenure and then the entire staff of eight counselors would hold tenure. Thus, the administration would lose its option of retaining or dismissing personnel in the Center. Only two academic departments in the university were fully tenured at that time, and one of these had an intramural conflict going which was embarrassing to the administration and to the entire university. Coupled with this consideration seemed to be the fact that despite their advanced degrees and faculty academic rank, Center personnel were service rather than teaching faculty.

Student newspaper articles, editorials, and letters to the editor continued, and a group of student formed an organization called the Ad Hoc Committee of Concerned Students for the Counseling Center. The Center staff did not promote or solicit the support of this group, but we did provide information honestly and directly when requested. Eight students drew up and signed a petition calling for immediate retention of the four counselors, exploration of the possibility of hiring four additional counselors representing minority groups, implementation of a study of resources to support the additional staff, and preparation of a study of the potential of other services for relieving the demands on the Counseling Center. They concluded by recommending without any reservation support by the President and the Vice-President for Academic Affairs. The petitioners collected the signatures of over a thousand students and also received formal support from both the Student Senate and the Student Assembly. During November, the Faculty Senate unanimously approved the following resolution: "that the Faculty Senate supports the efforts of the Concerned Students for the Counseling Center (an Ad Hoc Committee) to maintain and improve the vital services of the Counseling Center."

On December 2, I requested a decision at the earliest possible moment from the President regarding our four faculty members because, "the ambiguity and strain under which these four men have labored this semester is beginning to take its toll on staff morale, and I feel that it is now an urgent matter to resolve this state of affairs as soon as possible." Shortly thereafter the vice-president for academic affairs visited me. He informed me candidly and without rancor that he would not support retention of the four counselors because he saw classroom teaching as the primary mission of the university and any "learning" accomplished at the Counseling Center as peripheral and extraneous. He indicated that in his opinion counseling and other student services were fringe benefits—nice to have in affluent times, but a luxury when budget trimming is necessary. He recalled that counselors were not available when he was an undergraduate and concluded that perhaps survival of the fittest is not such a bad idea.

Several days after this disheartening conversation, I was summoned to a meeting of the President's Administrative Council, knowing that my immediate superior would not support me. No final decision had been made, however, and the whole situation still hung in the balance. I was heartened to find that I did have some friends at court, notably the President himself. It was clear that they were trying to find an acceptable way out of this situation which would not alienate students and faculty and with which the administration could live. The discussion came around to the academic credentials of the four counselors and their competence as teachers. The members of the cabinet inquired whether the four would be willing to accept a six-credit academic teaching load if they were granted tenure. I replied that if it should become necessary, I thought they would. Following this meeting, each of the four received a letter from the president stating that if he would agree to teach, "in case it should become necessary," six credits a semester "of courses of your own selection" in the School of Education or in the School of Letters and Science or in both, then "it would seem that the university's major concern which led to the necessity of forwarding to you a notice of nonretention for 1972–1973 would be ameliorated to the point where your retention and appointment to tenure status could now be reconsidered." Each of our four counselors subsequently accepted the terms and was retained and, in essence, tenured. Although we realized that if it should become necessary for our people to pay off on that commitment we would lose the equivalent of two positions, we felt this was a reasonable price to pay to retain our four colleagues.

Thus, by the middle of the academic year, we had resolved two of the three crises which confronted us when the school year began. Problems resulting from the dissolution of the Student Affairs Division and the loss of our vice-president will probably take much longer to solve. We have found it much more difficult to function effectively without a spokesman at the highest decision-making level of the university who is committed to the continuing development of student services and without an organizational structure to coordinate them. The effects of this situation have already been felt by the Counseling Center. We were not permitted to replace our highest-ranking staff member, who was on a leave of absence during the past year and resigned at the end of the year. A doctoral internship funded during her absence with a portion of her academic year salary was not renewed.

I am convinced that our surviving the two crisis situations was due in large part to the intervention of students and faculty members. The question is: Why did we get that kind of support? I feel that the following factors supply a partial answer.

The mission of our Counseling Center is student service, and thus our staff is involved primarily in counseling contacts with relatively large numbers of students, individually and in small groups. Counseling is what we do best, better than anyone else on the campus. While individual and group counseling is no longer a central activity for many counseling centers, it remains the primary reason for our existence. Last year, through individual counseling alone, we were in contact with nearly 15 percent of our students. Our crisis increased the demand for counseling services because the Center was more visible to students and faculty than at any time in the past and because it seemed clear to students that we were not part of the administration. For the past five years, the Center has staffed satellite offices in the residence halls and in the Multicultural Center, where counselors have had informal contacts with students and staff.

Our counselors have also had contacts with students as instructors of courses at both the undergraduate and graduate levels. They have consulted with residence hall assistants; taught in the Free University; facilitated various small groups whose members have come from all schools of the university; served as consultants and backup personnel for the university-community hotline; co-operated with the Student Government and the United Campus Ministry to provide draft information and abortion information and referral services. We have maintained good working relationships with the Student Government and its officers.

Although we perceive counseling as our primary role, we do spend considerable time and energy in outreach activities. Many of our outreach activities on the campus have brought us in close contact with individual faculty members and administrators. We have taught in the Department of Counselor Education; led personal development seminars as part of the introductory course in the School of Education; conducted a year-long affective education research project with School of Education faculty; and facilitated human relations groups for majors in the helping professions. Our staff has consulted with individual faculty members, worked with their referrals, and trained advisors for undecided majors in the School of Letters and Science. Staff members have been active on a dozen university committees. We have had at least one representative on the Faculty Senate for the past seven years. We have a close working relationship with the members of the United Campus Ministry and with our colleagues in what was the Division of Student Services. Our staff frequently interact socially with other faculty members both on and off the campus.

Our extensive involvement with both students and faculty, both professionally and personally, over a period of years probably had a great deal to do with their coming to our aid in our year of crisis. The fact that we have consistently hired only well-trained, professional counseling and clinical psychologists who devote a great deal of time and energy to their work must also have been a factor.

I wish I could conclude this case study by indicating that our troubles have subsided and that we are now devoting our energy to getting about our business. Unfortunately this is not the case because the current school year has brought a new crisis. The drastic enrollment shortfall which the administration feared in 1971–1972, did in fact occur at the beginning of the 1972–1973 academic year resulting in a severe budget reduction. The Board of Regents projected that fall 1972 enrolment at UW-O would be 12,300 students, an expected increase of 500 students over the 1971–1972 enrolment. The actual registration fell 1000 below this projected figure. Because state financial support is based on per-student funding, the university was required to return to the state nearly a million dollars. Phase I in meeting this new crisis was accomplished in early December 1972, when the university identified some $382,000 in nonpersonnel monies to be returned. Phase II came on December 15, when forty nontenured faculty members in their second year of service received letters advising that their positions would be phased out at the end of the academic year, in May 1973. Some $400,000 was returned as a result of this action. In March another twenty nontenured faculty members were sent letters of nonretention, but some of these people and some of the forty people notified of nonretention in December were later rehired. Thus, as the school year ended, a total of thirty-nine nontenured faculty members had been dismissed. In addition, in May, twenty-two tenured faculty members were notified that they would not be retained. This number included one tenured member of the Counseling Center staff.

Obviously these are difficult economic and political times for higher education in Wisconsin and in many other parts of the country. Consequently, the times are also difficult for counseling center and other student services professionals. Fortunately for our Counseling Center, this present crisis at our university did not occur when we had four members of our staff on nonretention status for almost six months. We have now cut our operating budget nearly in half, but our eight staff members are all tenured. While tenure is being threatened in the University of Wisconsin system as a guarantee of job security, it is some measure of protection, and the legality of dismissing tenured faculty appears certain to be tested in the courts soon. As distressing as the relative insecurity of these times may be for us personally, we can feel equally ditressed about the anxiety and upset of our faculty colleagues, tenured and untenured alike, which unavoidably is being transferred to the student body. As a result of our experience, we are now aware that no matter how well we serve students and the university community by our own criteria, we are still susceptible to administrative evaluation based on institutional standards dictated by circumstances, resources, and recurring crises. However, our decision has been to continue to do what we do best and to function as well as we can, given the present economic and political circumstances. If students and faculty continue to approve of and support what we do, then perhaps they will continue to come to our assistance during times of crisis.

XVI

Student Services
in Britain

Audrey Newsome

ᗰᗰᗰᗰᗰᗰᗰᗰᗰᗰᗰᗰᗰᗰᗰᗰᗰᗰᗰᗰᗰᗰᗰᗰᗰᗰᗰᗰᗰᗰᗰᗰᗰᗰᗰ
ᗰᗰᗰᗰᗰᗰᗰᗰᗰᗰᗰᗰᗰᗰᗰᗰᗰᗰᗰᗰᗰᗰᗰᗰᗰᗰᗰᗰᗰᗰᗰᗰᗰ

The history of higher education in Britain is long and distinguished; its development has been steady and reasonably uneventful until recent years. For centuries no other institutions challenged the traditions and privileges of the Oxford and Cambridge colleges. When some slight expansion of educational facilities did occur (in Durham and London) these served as the model as well as for the establishment in the late nineteenth century of facilities in civic centers like Leeds, Manchester, and Birmingham. Following the World War II, a flurry of activity in the creation of new universities and in the retreading of some existing establishments of teacher and technical education changed the entire profile of higher education in Britain. The picture which has emerged is complex and confusing, especially to those who are a part of it. To make sense of it

259

takes as much imagination and trust in its creators as does most contemporary paintings and sculptures. The shape of *our* contemporary work of art is as impressive as a work of Henry Moore, but the holes in the middle are attributable not so much to the design as to the lack of adequate planning and an unwillingness, or incapacity, to recognize the basic needs of students in a learning situation. The British deserve their reputation for caring for the extremes in society, the sick, delinquent, and difficult, but until such problems hit them in the eye they do little to prevent the distress and misery of social alienation.

Britain is in the middle of an unprecedented educational revolution. The kind of educational experience that before World War II was regarded a privilege of a largely middle-class elite is now considered a right for all who demonstrate they have the ability to benefit from it. Secondary education is now compulsory until the age of sixteen and an increasing percentage of students are choosing to remain beyond the age of sixteen in order to acquire the qualifications to compete for places in institutions of higher education. Financial assistance, depending on parental income, is automatic for those who are successful in gaining places in higher education; therefore, those from low-income families receive maximum grants. Since the employment situation for the young worker has become more difficult, an increasing percentage of the most able students are availing themselves of higher education and delaying their entry to the labor market. Most arrive in institutions of higher education not as a result of mature decisions which they have made for themselves, but on the persuasive advice of parents and staff or merely to make the best of a poor situation. An increasing proportion of students find their values in conflict with the values of staff in higher education and their expectations of the experience unfulfilled.

The approximate number of students in our universities in 1972 was 240,000. By 1976–1977 the University Grants Committee, which allocates the budget for higher education in universities, proposes a total of 304,000 places for fulltime and fulltime equivalent students to be split between arts-based and science-based students of 45 percent to 55 percent. This represents a similar distribution to that in 1972 but a 30 percent increase in the total. These projections are subject to alteration with little notice, depending on governmental decisions on how the total educational budget is to be distributed. Allocation decisions will be made not only on the various stages of education from nursery to adult, but also on the sections of education at the tertiary level, more especially on the universities and the polytechnics.

The University Grants Committee advocates the expansion of more broadly based curricula in both arts and science-based subject areas. This recommendation results from the difficulties our manpower planners have experienced in planning for manpower needs in a rapidly changing technological society as well as the problems related to the educational and vocational retreading of narrowly qualified specialists. Those who claim to know something about the world of work and the vocational maturity of young people welcome the proposed developments, but doubt whether the advocates have given even cursory attention to the implications of their recommendation. Until recently students have been required to choose their major field of study before leaving school. Most of them have already narrowed their possible range of choice by deciding in their fourth year of secondary education on their subjects for the ordinary level examination in the General Certificate of Education, which (usually taken at the age of sixteen) is the first step to a university place. The two oldest universities, Oxford and Cambridge, and some of the newest postwar universities, in which Keele has taken the lead, have been exceptions in this otherwise rigid system, where it has been, and still is, possible for a young person to study no more than three subjects in the sixth form and only one for three years at the university.

Who will assist students with the choices and commitments which they will have to make after they have embarked on their university lives and who will help them with the kind of wheel-wobble which often accompanies such decision-making? The percentage of students in universities who, for one reason or another, fail to complete their degrees is currently only 14 percent. In such an elitist and narrowly tracked system the stigma attached to being a dropout is considerable. It takes courage in the face of such stigma to decide to discontinue an education which is so competitive and so highly prized. It takes understanding and skill to encourage such young people to capitalize on their potential in another enterprise without loss of self-esteem or status.

Instead of looking more carefully at the nature of the so-called dropout, the British pride themselves on its low level compared with a similar statistic in the United States or Europe. We dismiss those who leave before completion of their courses with the comment "They were clearly not up to it and it's as well they've found out now rather than wasting their and our time and money!" We expect our young people to make up their minds early; if they do not we do it for them and then dismiss them if we were wrong. Small wonder then that in loco parentis has become a grossly disparaged term for young Britains today in a society where many adults have abdicated mature responsibility for them in a world of changing values and greater insecurity. Employers who only three or four years ago complained that they did not get their fair share of the graduate market now declare vocationally redundant the fathers of some of our students. This resulted in family hardships and caused a growing number of students to reject the values of our manpower planners and to seek to create what they now call an alternative society. At a time when a number of University Appointments Services changed their names to Careers Advisory Services to win greater approval, careers became for some a dirty word, associated with traditional values of a reactionary generation, and the staffs of such services run the risk of being rejected by those students who are most confused and need the most sensitive help.

Never have British universities come under greater scrutiny than they have now. The ivory towers have been attacked and found vulnerable, and those who worked in them developed a curious defensiveness, particularly the administrators. They seem to feel compelled to justify the academic system in terms of its value to society in specific occupational ways and, in particular, to answer publicly for the disturbances in staff-student relationships which have left few campuses untouched, least of all those more progressive institutions which have attracted some of the more passionate demonstrators. University education is, theoretically, available to all who evidence the ability to benefit from it. Many of those who have not had university education, through no fault of their own or because they failed in the competition for a place, feel that the universities should be accountable to them for the percentage of the national income that the universities consume. Even those who have had the benefit of a university education in less confusing times than now seem to feel entitled to attack the universities for failing to put their houses in order or to control those dissident members of their communities who command the attention of the national press, radio, and television. University administrators cannot win: on the one hand, they must respond to the demands of the University Grants Committee to increase their intake of students or run the risk of having their budgets reduced, and on the other, they must strive to cater to the needs of an increasingly heterogeneous student body in a larger and more impersonal community or run the risk of continuing disruption from those students and a minority of staff who feel alienated. The combined roles of discipline and welfare which were embodied in the positions of wardens of residence halls or tutors and advisers to men and women students are no longer acceptable to some of our more militant students. Furthermore, developments in the field of mental health led to a greater social consciousness of the problems underlying some of the behavior of those students who bring themselves forcibly to public attention. Those staff who previously felt equipped to cope with student concerns by their combined qualities of caring and common sense are somewhat undermined by this confusion and are no longer as confident. On their part, students are less willing to entrust their problems to the enlightened amateur unless that amateur is within the peer group.

Throughout the centuries British students, at least a significant minority of them, have demonstrated their social consciousness and idealism in a variety of ways: some fought against oppression in Spain; some demonstrated against nuclear warfare; others took to the streets against the victimization of blacks in South Africa and Rhodesia. More recently they have turned their attentions inwards, campaigning for more rights and responsibilties for themselves, for greater recognition of their adult status and the contributions which they ought to be making to the shaping of educational institutions, and for greater assistance to the less privileged within their own student communities. The National Union of Students grew in size and power with the increase of the total student population. It became a force to be reckoned with and its officers, people to be consulted in any major development affecting its members. In a very direct way, the lowering of the age of majority, which enables young people to vote at the age of eighteen, affected governmental attitudes to this powerful body of students who began to develop a greater awareness of their power and a stronger desire to use it.

The National Union of Students was a powerful force in the demand for the establishment of counseling services in universities and colleges. Its requests have been listened to by staff with varying degrees of enthusiasm. Could it be that the appointment of a counselor might damp the fires of revolution and appease those difficult students who do not seem amenable to logical reasoning? The recognition that such an appointment might become necessary would be an admission that the services which already exist in universities and colleges are inadequate, even though the British have always prided themselves on their pastoral care embodied in the moral tutors, advisers, medical consultants, and welfare staff who have been long established in most colleges. For the students to allow the university or college to appoint counseling personnel as an integral part of their staff implies a trust in the administration they do not always show. Rumor trickled across the Atlantic that counselors are not always impartial, that some use their position with confused students to help them to adjust to a society and system for which change would be more appropriate. Whether or not this is true, it is understandable that such rumors feed the students' suspicion and lead them to suspect the motives of those who accede to their requests for the establishment of counseling services, as well as those who might be appointed by the administration. A small but highly vocal minority of students would rather sacrifice some of their contemporaries in the intersts of changing the existing order. Counselors, they argue, would get in the way. There is another small minority who would rather see counseling services established within student unions in colleges and universities than as a part of the establishment. Both points of view are understandable but fail to take into account what I perceive to be the principal objectives of counseling in higher education: assisting staff and students to be more effective in their joint enterprise. The students appear to view counseling in a peripheral enterprise concerned principally with the sick, disturbed, and delinquent.

Another interesting development in the past two years was the setting up of courses in teaching methods for new faculty members. Written into the contract of some universities is the statement "new members of staff will be required to attend a course on teaching methods to be organized by the university"—one of the few demands of institutions traditionally loathe to impose regulations on academic staff. Such courses last between three and ten days and are usually concerned with methodology, but at some stage usually give consideration to understanding students, even if only at the last session. Who are the people who understand students? It may reflect changing attitudes of the organizers that at the first course of its kind in one of our universities, it was a physician who took the session; at the second session, it was a student counselor. For me the most significant implication in this new development is that those whose job is to understand human behavior are now seen to have some contribution to make to the teaching of staff. To begin to recognize that academics have something to gain from being introduced to professional training constitutes a significant advance in universities; to see that counselors have a special contribution to make in the learning process is revolutionary. What I sincerely hope is that the counselors who are appointed to positions in higher education recognize the importance of their contribution to education rather than to therapy, to human development rather than to personality reconstruction or the curing of disorders. So much depends on the orientation of counselors; their perceptions of their roles and the ways in which students and staff perceive them, as well as the size of their budget. How can one counselor in an institution of 11,000 students where suicide has been a sizeable problem fulfill the expectations of students and staff even to a limited extent and survive the strain of such a position? When only one post is to be financed, what sort of person is sought to fill it? If the Archangel Gabriel were to be appointed, it is doubtful whether even he would emerge triumphant.

Today there are only some thirty or forty people who bear the title of counselor in the institutions of higher education in Britain. Their backgrounds are many and varied; only a handful emerged from programs specifically established to prepare counselors, for such programs have existed in Britain for only seven years and most of them concentrated on preparing counselors in secondary education. If you ask who does the counseling in many institutions, you will be told either that all the tutors counsel or that doctors undertake whatever counseling is necessary and that all problems are referred to them. While there may be an element of truth in both statements, obviously neither tutors nor doctors are equipped as counselors. On the whole, academic staff are selected to their positions on their merits in research, publication, and sometimes teaching expertise. Few have received any training in the understanding of learning, let alone any other aspects of human behavior. Physicians, too, have been trained in ways which make a counseling relationship with patients difficult. They are experts at diagnosis and treatment, but would consider it professional incompetence if they share power with their patients in identifying the problem and share responsibility for its resolution. A number in university and college health services do have qualifications in psychiatric medicine, but the nature of their training and the expectations of students and staff make it difficult for them to be seen as anything other than experts in the treatment of the sick. Many are frankly worried by the proposal to introduce counseling into their institutions outside the medical setting. They argue that only training which includes an understanding of the entire human being (including his physical makeup)' equips a person to counsel. Except for those specifically designated as counselors, the logical conclusion of this argument would seem to require prior qualification as a physician for most staff in the academic enterprise. But so far, the physicians are not prepared to consider logical conclusions.

In the absence of a precise definition of counseling and adequate professional courses, and in response to the obvious needs which psychotic breakdowns and delinquent behavior demonstrate, it is not surprising that a number of people appointed to new counseling posts have been working in the field of social work, more especially in psychiatric or medical social work, or that others who have received a training analysis or analytical treatment have been attracted to apply for these new positions. Without considerable modification their preparation is as inadequate to assist the learning process of students and the effectiveness of staff as a knowledge of Freud alone would be to the professional preparation of teachers.

Others working within higher education who might also lay claim to being counselors are the wardens of residence halls whose title, though unfortunate in the American context, is better understood in Britain. Traditionally, they have assumed responsibility for discipline and welfare within the residence halls; some are full-time in their appointments, others combine academic appointments with their duties as wardens. Increasingly they are required to redefine their roles, either because the lowering of the age of majority has affected their responsibilities or because of an increasing reluctance on the part of students to take their problems, particularly those related to questions of authority, to those who have a disciplinary responsibility. At the same time, students often demand that wardens assume responsibility for discipline in situations where they themselves prove to be impotent in controlling their peers. In their eagerness to establish themselves as growing adults, many students find difficulty in asserting their own rights with their contemporaries and ask staff to intercede. In these situations wardens find themselves dealing with a wide range of problems and feel that they too are acting as counselors.

Chaplains are another group of staff in universities and colleges who assist students in a variety of ways. Their pastoral role is traditional but used only by a minority of students who would feel it appropriate to seek help from those whose values are obvious. Few have received any preparation in counseling, but they enjoy an unusual position in higher education which might be used to even better advantage. Similarly, appointments officers who assist students to find jobs and postgraduate training increasingly view their role as a counselor, at least in relation to that limited but important function of vocational choice, but are still frightened by the word counseling. Some prefer to see themselves as administrators; few appointments offices would be sufficiently well-staffed or their personnel professionally equipped to extend themselves beyond the vocational counseling of students who seek their help in the final or prefinal year of their university education.

So the dilemma is obvious. Universities are growing in size and complexity. Students will be required to make choices and commitments to subjects of study after they enter higher education; the world of work is more complex and many students demonstrate different values from those traditionally held by staff in terms of the life styles both inside and outside the institutions. Many more young people demand higher education, but are dissatisfied with what they get. Staff are confused about the purposes of higher education and about how to relate to a student body which contains both a more aggressive minority and a more apathetic majority. Some problems become all too obvious, but their solution far from clear. In their eagerness to plug the gap, both staff and students seek to create counseling services, but fail to recognize that unless they consider carefully what it is they seek to do and what kinds of services and personnel will best achieve meaningful goals, they will succeed in gaining only temporary respite from a problem which will continue to grow.

A vast amount of wasted talent exists in universities, both of students and staff. If we concentrate on treating the sick and delinquent and neglect the needs of the vast majority of students, we shall never grasp the nettle and achieve something constructive in higher education. But it costs money. With a zero sums budget, one more counselor means one fewer on the academic staff and already institutions of higher education are under considerable financial pressure in competition with claims for more assistance for nursery education, more assistance for the underprivileged in primary and secondary education, as well as for such social improvements as higher pensions for a growing number of senior citizens. Technologically, we are better equipped and much of what we know can assist us to make better use of existing resources. Where people behave like computers, storing and regurgitating information on demand, that part of their activities can obviously be replaced by more effective methods of storage and retrieval. Where positions in higher education have become outmoded, for example, Tutors to Women Students that have existed in some of our older institutions, those aspects of the role which are still useful should be redistributed among other staff, releasing money for new-style appointments. Modifications clearly can be made, but they take time and careful planning.

Basically, what is required is a reappraisal of the purposes of today's higher education and an evaluation of the extent to which the institutions need to be committed to a more global view of the education of their students. It seems to me a gross misapplication of resources to allocate a disproportionate amount of energy and expertise to the rescue of the deeply disturbed while failing to recognize that investment in the rest of the student population will at least prevent some of the waste which currently occurs from breakdown and at best contribute significantly to the enormous potential of a most gifted section of our population. To say this is not to withdraw compassion and care from those who apparently most need it, but to recognize that not all can be helped while still in an educational setting. They need specialized therapeutic help which educational institutions should not be expected to provide. Institutions of higher education are, after all, principally concerned with learning and not with dispensing therapy to a small minority who are unfortunate enough to need it. It is estimated that something of the order of 1 percent of the student population will be in need of special psychiatric treatment some time during their university lives. Such people may ultimately graduate, but at the time of their disturbance, will need a kind of help which cannot be provided within higher education. The other 99 percent contains students with a wide spectrum of needs. The estimates of the percentage who at some time during their university lives are sufficiently disturbed for their academic work and their personal lives to be seriously affected vary from 5 percent to 25 percent. They obviously need help, but many more can benefit greatly from achieving a clear sense of direction for themselves. All stand to gain if the climate of the institution is improved by better teaching and better staff-student communication.

As I see it, counselors in institutions of higher education in Britain have a unique contribution to make if the planners are prepared to take a broader overall view of the needs of people within them. If they do, they may be prepared to wait until they can appoint people with the skill, vision, and level of professional preparation to enable counselors to behave as educators in the broadest sense and command the respect of both staff and students. The pressure to plug the obvious gaps is so great that many institutions are unlikely to stand back long enough to get the needs into perspective and make provision for them in constructive ways which will affect the whole educational community. Counselors are not gods— they can only make a contribution to the total educational enterprise in collaboration with administrators, academics, students, and other personnel associated with higher education. If they have a contribution to make, it is their understanding human behavior, particularly in relation to those in the academic exercise. They must be people with a thorough understanding of the purposes of higher education and of the motivations, values, and needs of both staff and students. In particular, they must be sensitive to the developmental stage of students in their colleges; they must have an appreciation of how best to assist these students with decision-making, with study difficulties, with those affective aspects of their development which have an impact on their academic and personal achievement, and with the varied concerns which revolve around their search for identity. Counselors in higher education must be concerned with helping individuals to recognize and utilize their total potential. They must be available to help students through the transitional period from school to university, at periods in students' university lives when they need help and in preparation for their postuniversity lives. Their knowledge must be used with both individuals and groups of students in a relationship of mutual trust which can only be fully achieved if counselors operate from a position devoid of disciplinary responsibility and in which confidentiality can be strictly maintained. The knowledge they gain from the practice of counseling will continue to add to their professional competence. This knowledge and skill must, at the same time, be made available to other significant members of the academic community if they are to be helped to be as effective as possible in their own roles. Although confidentiality can be used as a weapon for the defensive counselor to protect himself, it can also be used constructively to help individuals in ways which would otherwise be impossible. Only if students are given a normally acceptable reason for consulting counselors will the knowledge counselors acquire about students come from a cross-section of the student community rather than that 10 percent sufficiently distressed or disorganized to seek the help of a counselor.

In the small postwar University of Keele, which introduced a new approach to higher education in Britain and to some extent influenced developments in curriculum in other newer universities, it was possible to establish a counseling service currently operating in both a normal professional way with students and at a community level with other staff and student representatives and services. From a university of 800 students it has been possible to maintain a counseling service on a staff-student ratio of one counselor to 400 students until its current size of 2000 students. It has never faced the problem of attempting to graft on to an established university of several thousand students a new service where there are other services purporting to undertake some of the functions which a professional counseling service of an educational kind would perform. So far in Keele it has been possible to work with a complete cross-section of the student population, to offer a service which helps students over the transitional period from school to university, with subject choices which have to be made at the end of the first year, with study difficulties and with the personal and emotional difficulties of becoming adult, and with vocational exploration and decision-making.

By the time they graduate, the counseling service will have had individual contact with 95 percent of the students. In any one year its staff see almost 40 percent of the students an average of three contacts each, ranging from once to thirty-eight times. It meets with student representatives to obtain their reactions in the shaping of the service and collaborates with the Senior Tutor, academics, staff in residence halls, the Medical Officer, and administrators, while at the same time bringing them together in a seminar to discuss topics which affect all of them. The informal collaboration which has been achieved between the counseling service, academics, students, and welfare staff has developed partly as a result of planning, of the recognition of the Vice-Chancellor that counseling can only be effective in collaboration with all others in the community, and partly because other staff and students were aware of their own needs to improve their capacity to perform more effectively. Its neutral position outside, but alongside, the academic staff, independent of the administration and the medical and other services, has encouraged students to feel confident in using its services. Although much has been achieved, much remains to be done. Since the counseling service is concerned with transitional problems and with occupational choice, its staff have the advantage of contact with outside agencies, schools, and employers. To improve its capacity to help with particular problems it has contacts with marriage counselors, community counseling services, psychiatric clinics, and units concerned with helping in cases of drug dependency. This contact outside the university is vital in assisting counselors maintain a balanced perspective on the institution.

Many of those who are working as counselors in British higher education today are concerned about their roles. They can see some needs to be achieved, but are ill-equipped in staffing, lack adequate recognition, or lack the budgets to do more than behave as firemen in a conflagration which might well erupt out of control. They are beginning to join forces in informal gatherings of counselors working in various branches of higher education, but nothing other than self-help assist those who are anxious to improve their qualifications. Recently an association of student counselors was formed but professional standards still have to be determined. Is the welfare officer working in a polytechnic and dealing with student problems a counselor? If not, what constitutes acceptable training?

Today some ten or so institutions are concerned with the preparation of counselors, only two of which specifically set out to prepare counselors for work in higher education. One of these is the University of Aston, whose one-year fulltime course for counselors is now in its second year and is in process of preparing eleven students for higher education. The other is the Extra-Mural Department of the University of London, which has this year begun a two-year parttime course (one day a week) for students who are already engaged in some form of counseling work in an institution of higher education. Like the other programs which prepare counselors for work in secondary education, they are staffed largely by educational or clinical psychologists who have not themselves worked as counselors in a British institution of higher education. Their orientations depend heavily on the experiences of the staff. So far, insufficient attention has been given to counseling practicum, to the study of issues in counseling, or to assisting students develop their educational functions in the institutions in which they will practice. As for the upgrading of counselors who enter higher education with either limited qualifications or from some allied professional experience, there is no special provision. Courses on Community Mental Health at the Tavistock Clinic, courses in group dynamics run at great expense by the Tavistock or Grubb Institute, or one-day institute conferences are all that are available.

What appears to be needed is some sort of stimulus such as the National Defense Education Act provided in the United States to make the University Grants Committee and the Department of Education and Science take a careful look at the gap which exists in the provision of professional preparation. Social work training has developed over the years into a quite sophisticated professional preparation, but in the field of education the British are still past masters at the use of enlightened amateurs. Perhaps the light is dawning. We are beginning to recognize that academics might gain from short professional courses in teaching methods for which the University Grants Committee is providing stimulation. The Committee of Vice-Chancellors and Principals are beginning to develop courses to improve the qualifications of administrative staff in universities. Such provision is laudable but inappropriate for counselors, wardens, chaplains, and appointments officers, and others principally concerned with the helping relationship. It is conceivable that in a few years resources might be allocated to a central institute concerned with developing an understanding of human behavior in education in which the limited professional resources for staffing now scattered over the country might be concentrated for better effect.

Before adequate provision can be made for the preparation of counselors for higher education, however, we need proper preparation for counselor educators, for which no provision has yet been made. We also need to provide ongoing opportunities for practising counselors to add to their qualifications, as well as for appointments officers, staff in residence halls, and others to develop the professional aspects of their work. A central institute would give staff performing different functions a chance to meet and to develop a common respect for one another's work. Hopefully, we shall not continue to apply makeshift arrangements, to paper over the obvious cracks, and allow the gaps to become bigger.

The British are good at applying the telescope to the blind eye, at salving their consciences by surveying a glorious past without looking sufficiently forward to be able to avoid some of the mistakes which others have made across the Atlantic. Unless we move quickly we may still have the reputation for caring effectively for the sick, but doing little to develop the healthy education of some of our most talented youth. As British society has become more aware of the value of higher education, the numbers seeking it have grown and the individual institutions have become bigger. Problems of communication between staff and students have become greater and there are an increasing minority of students who feel alienated from the goals of the institutions they competed to enter. Many feel reduced to the size of a hole in a computer card and resent this growing impersonalization. It will take the combined effort of all those employed in higher education to prevent the escalation of this kind of feeling; it will take planning and the allocation of financial and human resources to make this possible.

XVII

A Canadian View

Mason L. Niblack

৹৹
৹৹

In response to a variety of warnings that student personnel services, including counseling, were in trouble on college campuses, efforts have been initiated not only in the United States but also in Canada to examine the situation. In Canada, a conference was convened using the title of an article by Emmett (1971), "Student Personnel Services—Who Needs Them?" Since this first conference, several other similar conferences have been held in Canada. The conclusions (or lack of conclusions) of these meetings have meaning both for student services and for college counseling.

However, a major issue not confronted by Emmet has been raised by Penney (1969): whether student personnel as a distinct discipline within the normal structures of higher education will survive the decade in its present form, if at all. Penney does not believe that the long-sought professional status of student personnel work will ever materialize. His belief is supported by other writers who contend that the disciplinary base of student personnel is too broad and lacks uniqueness, that its claim to eclecticism is simply an attempt to avoid being characterized as a garbage pail for unconnected service functions, and that Taylor's instrumentalism (1951) has so overwhelmed practitioners that narrow specialists have usurped roles formerly played by broad-based faculty members. A crucial concern of those now engaged in student personnel tasks, the survival problem, should be of particular significance to college counseling, one of the highly professionalized educational specialties not always contained within the student personnel structure in Canada.

Because of attempts by some leaders in the field to blend counseling and student personnel, the two are generally viewed on the American campus as tightly intertwined and inseparable. They often seem indistinguishable to the student, faculty member, administrator, and even to the neophyte counselor or student personnel administrator. The confusion is largely the result of the conceptualizations of student personnel people such as Williamson (1961), who maintained that counseling is the generic function of student personnel and proposed that all student personnel staff, regardless of specialty or functional responsibility, be considered counselors. This perspective has been echoed by Berdie (1966), Siegel (1968), and Tollefson (1969).

Mention of the difficulties experienced by student personnel in identifying a significant role and attaining status on the college campus is not intended as an argument for freeing counseling services from student personnel. Furthermore, I am not implying that student personnel services, broadly conceived, cannot be an integral part of the educational opportunities offered by a college to its students, faculty, and staff, nor that counseling is such a specialized student service that it requires a unique educational philosophy to ensure the effectiveness of its practitioners. Rather, I would suggest the need for new service models which assure complementary relationships between the service groups, particularly in Canadian colleges.

A conference jointly sponsored by the Canadian organizations of professional counselors and student personnel administrators provides one example of the internal difficulties faced by college student services. An observer could hardly suppress a feeling of dismay as participants became entangled in trying to describe the various ways in which their service was expected to function and how they perceived its relationship to other college services. Most seemed to have forgotten that any educational service, if it is to have significant impact in the college community, must derive its purpose and goals from the unique needs of that community. The conference participants had particular difficulty defining the role of the counselors whom they supervised or with whom they interacted. Perhaps because they were unable to agree on what they themselves should do as student personnel workers, they did not have the slightest idea what they wanted counseling staffs to do and, almost tragically, what constitutes a counseling staff in terms of training, orientation, and human potential. As a matter of fact, there was a perceptible reluctance, if not an outright refusal, to deal with the basic concepts of either counseling or student personnel administration and the differences or similarities between them.

Clearly, some further questions needed immediate discussion. Should professional counselors, as Warnath suggests (1971), assist student personnel in staff development at the risk of alienating the administrators of the parent organization by the mere offer of aid? Can counselors presume to offer assistance while engaged in reexamining their own role in the campus community? Should the counseling center attempt, as suggested by some such as the authors of the Canadian, then the American, *Guidelines for Counseling Services*, to break completely with the student personnel structure and seek alliances elsewhere on campus or to go it alone with responsibility directly to the president? In one Canadian institution, answers to these questions are of critical importance since it is obvious to almost everyone from the president to the entering freshman that the incompetence of the student personnel administrators is directly responsible for the ineffectiveness of the counseling service, which has been rigidly restricted to serving only those students with personal problems. One can only speculate on the impact which this center might make on its campus if its staff were free to relate their services to the potential needs of the campus community.

Professional counselors, regardless of training, have an ambiguous role on most Canadian campuses. The term *counseling* itself has a tremendously wide range of meanings in the academic community. Many faculty members in Canada perceive theirs as a counseling role when advising students on curricular choices. Almost any face-to-face contact between members of different campus constituencies has been labeled a counseling contact. But professional counselors have been unable to agree on how to define themselves for the public. One major eastern institution describes what is essentially its counseling service as a student advisory bureau.

Problems exist, however, beyond descriptive terminology or ambiguity of role. Some Canadian institutions follow the British pattern of student services described by Newsome in Chapter Sixteen—a pattern which includes the medical model for professional counseling. This model is supported by physicians who insist that only those who understand the whole man, including his biological functioning, can adequately counsel him. Whatever their motives, the result has been to restrict the special status of full counselors to medical practitioners.

The Canadian Union of Students (the student government organization) has, like its British counterpart, recommended change in existing counseling services to reflect its point of view. While not as strong as seems to be the case in Great Britain, there is a feeling among students that, as one of them stated, "Counseling is for students, right? Then, it should be a function of the Union of Students."

The counseling service in a few Canadian institutions is located in the department of psychology for what appears to be the somewhat obvious, but not necessarily sound reason, that psychology faculty are the people on campus who are supposed to be the most qualified to counsel. On a practical level, this arrangement relieves the institutional administration of confronting any problems which might be generated by establishing a separate counseling center with its own identity, administration, and budget.

And finally, the general feeling among the administrators of Canadian colleges is that professional counseling services should be made available only to registered students. Neither faculty, staff, nor other members of the campus community, such as spouses of students, are permitted to use the service. Although the rationale given relates to the expense involved, it is my opinion that this is simply a convenient excuse to avoid a serious examination of the role of the counseling services within the campus community as a whole.

Other structural models and operational styles exist in Canadian colleges, but those described seem most prevalent and problematical. However, no meaningful data are currently available by which one can accurately determine the similarities or differences in college counseling structures. Adequate data do not exist by which comparisons might be made of the status levels of counselors in relation to other college personnel or which might indicate the effectiveness of counselors with student clients. Moreover, we can only speculate from the general information available about the freedom which counseling staffs have in determining their own professional role. A study is currently in progress requesting data from two-year institutions (Miles, 1973), but only one short section requests information about the structural relationships or staffing patterns of student services.

The variety of structural bases for counseling in Canadian colleges has resulted in a frustrating ambivalence among professional counselors, particularly center directors, who serve both as administrators and as practitioners. They appear to me to be angry people without a tangible focus for their anger. They seem to be groping for a meaningful purpose for their activities, some objective to give their work significance. When asked whether counseling can make a difference on the Canadian campus, none seems to know what to use as a yardstick. This ignorance appears related to what Stubbins describes in Chapter One as a lack of freedom on the part of either individual counselors or the counseling staff to set their own goals, to operate outside the activity base established either deliberately or accidentally by the college administration.

Canadian counselors want to be part of the academic mainstream, to receive faculty status and other symbols which indicate full acceptance by their peers in academia, but they chafe at the institutionally imposed limitations placed on their professional efforts. They sense that the system diminishes their professional role. At the same time they tend to accept the fact that the system can be defended as administratively correct. They appear to have become lost in their effort to understand where, in this approach-avoidance conflict, they can find the most productive solution. They have begun to realize that, with increasing demands for accountability and evidence of effectiveness, the individual counseling contact is not enough to sustain them as a significant contributor to the goals of the college. They realize that, with the methods of evaluation to be used, they will have to exhibit something beyond their present work of improving the mental health of a restricted clientele. Their ambivalence seems also a part of their refusal to acknowledge the possibility that, as Halleck (1971) points out, counseling is part of the political forces within an institution. The reluctance of Canadian counselors to confront this issue directly may be due to the fact that they sense that it is this very issue which may determine whether professional counseling with its multitude of structural forms will be permitted to survive on the Canadian campus. The status quo, no matter how uncomfortable it may be for counselors, does at least allow them some place in the institution.

The same uncertainties which are besetting Canadian counselors are not limited to this one group of service personnel. Student personnel work in general appears to be in a state of disarray. What has happened to student personnel work in Canada is in large part exactly what has happened to student personnel work in the United States, except in greater degree. A state of administrative dysfunction exists. Aggravated by simple pressures from others in the institution, the inability of the various services to coordinate their efforts has left student personnel virtually impotent. If other administrators had deliberately designed a strategy to divide and minimize the effectiveness of this loosely connected professional group of service personnel, they could not have done better than they have done somewhat accidentally. When pressure is applied from either students or administrators, student personnel is often squeezed into helplessness. It has been unable to exert any resistance toward any other identifiable campus group with a unified force of its own. It has not been able to justify its existence or its internal relationships in terms which are acceptable to boards of governors or presidents. Unless the situation changes dramatically within the next year or two, student personnel services in Canada may not survive the seventies.

At this point, I feel the need to resurrect Alexander Pope's comment that only fools contest for forms of government and to refurbish the old cliché that, among men of goodwill, any organizational model will work. The whole issue can become tiresome; but it will not go away simply because those in student services refuse to deal with it or attempt to put the problem in a context different from structural difficulties. There is much more at stake for counselors and student personnel workers than a simple reduction of intergroup competition.

In my judgment, counselors, as members of the more currently legitimate profession, must clarify their procedures and goals and determine the institutional roles they will play in the educational process. Canadian counselors have not yet settled on a workable model or an acceptable administrative linkage system. Currently no model finds general argeement or favor among professional counselors in Canada. The one common thread which I find running through the counseling literature on this subject is the perceived need by counselors for the autonomy of counseling centers. *The Guidelines for Canadian University Counseling Services* emphasizes this point but, either recognizing the realism of campus politics or in an attempt to soften its impact, suggests that the counseling center administrator must report to the president or his representative. By including an unspecified representative of the president as the potential office to which the counseling center might report, the recommendation becomes no recommendation at all since the president of a college is free to name anyone as his representative. The role of the counseling center remains unspecified except as the president of any particular institution defines it through his choice of representative to supervise its activities and control its budget.

Hanfmann (1963) and Carruth (1965) argue for counseling center autonomy as a defense against the dangers for the center if it is placed under the control of either student personnel services or the health services. Identification with student personnel services, they believe, carries with it the possible loss of confidentiality in client communications and also association in the minds of students with disciplinary functions. They feel that identification with the medical health services will not only endanger confidentiality, but might lead to problems for the counselors within the medical elitist hierarchy.

The counselor in higher education, whether as a practitioner or director of a center, must clarify his role. He must be clear in his own mind about what he wants that role to be, and then he must determine what relationship he feels should exist between his service and other parts of the institution. His functions must be stated in terms that reflect significant professional service, not simply his public relations value to the institution. He must be especially confident about his goals and activities if he is reporting to a division head who has little understanding of the potential contributions which professional counselors can make to a college community.

Nothing can change for counselors in Canadian colleges until they can agree on a service model and a set of structural relationships within which they can build services clearly identifiable with institutional objectives. To ensure that significant change will occur in their role in higher education, further unified effort will be required of Canadian counselors beyond the hesitant first steps exemplified by the publishing of the *Guidelines*. Counselors will have to press for change across the country with a model which can be adapted to the needs of the full range of postsecondary institutions, yet one that shows unification of purpose and function within the profession of counseling itself. If counselors fail to determine themselves what they will do, how they will do it, to whom they should report, and how their services best fit the goals of the colleges, they may awake one day to find their positions have simply been defined out of higher education or modified to such an extent that their professional training is essentially irrelevant. In any case, if the present passivity of counselors continues, the counseling services in the college setting may be fragmented and dismembered even further, to the point where they may be unrecognizable as professional services.

Student personnel has a similar task before it. However, the terms of reference are much different. There is considerable ambiguity regarding exactly what student personnel services are. The definition of student personnel work has typically been presented as a simple listing of discrete functions, of which counseling often was one. Some authorities in student personnel attempted to define the field by identifying broad common features of the variety of activities engaged in by those identified with student personnel, again including counseling. Other writers such as Lloyd-Jones and Smith (1954) suggested that student personnel work was a type of teaching. However, examination of these points of view has left many in the field with the uneasy feeling that not a single characteristic has yet been identified which can be used as the foundation to support an integrated philosophy of student personnel services.

Those in the field must, it seems to me, search much deeper than they have so far, perhaps even questioning some of their basic terminology. Do student personnel and its appended term *services* reflect the fundamental role those in this operational arm of higher education want to play? If student personnel is an educational activity as many of us in the field believe it is, is the use of the term *student personnel worker* appropriate? Can professional counselors and student personnel workers who subscribe to a humanistic, developmental approach to students function in any significant way within those Canadian colleges oriented to the British and Germanic system of higher education, which places primary, if not total, emphasis on intellectual development?

In my opinion, one possibility exists for student personnel workers to develop significant roles for themselves in the campus community. It would require that they insist on their inclusion within the community of scholars and that they meet the standards of membership which demand that each individual in the academic community be a student in some sense and that all be scholars. Faculty members continue to exhibit their commitment to these standards through their scholarship and their role as learner within their disciplines. If student personnel workers would make this same commitment to scholarship and learning, they could shape a new role for themselves. Where before their tasks have been restricted to the classification, counting, and sorting of registered students, their new role would involve them as academics in an infinite variety of educational experiences for the entire campus community, learning experiences designed to humanize and individualize the learning processes. Regardless of their specialty, these student personnel workers would use their skills and knowledge to stimulate interest in the learning possibilities inherent in all life activities and, thus, to broaden perspectives toward learning for all those in the institution. In a sense, they would become the learning specialists of the college, a needed role which is now unfilled. Their areas of scholarship for such a role would grow out of the specific needs of those in the particular campus community of which they were members. With the growing pressure from students for learning experiences outside the classroom, with the increasing numbers of older students returning to college, with the special needs of ethnic minority and women students, and with similar demands being placed on institutions of higher education, the role I am proposing for student personnel workers is not unrealistic.

This new role for the student personnel educator would go beyond Hodgkinson's concept (1971) of a vice-president for human affairs whose function would be, in his words, "to humanize everyone and everything in the educational process." This approach would also go beyond Crookston's student development philosophy (Chapter Two) insofar as he concerns himself primarily with the developmental aspects and education of the typical registered undergraduate student, only one class of person within our college communities. With a common educational purpose, specialists in such areas as professional counseling or health services should find broad areas for cooperative efforts with those who are now in administrative roles.

Obviously there would be great difficulty in implementing such a philosophy. Many in higher education would view it as simply a return by those they perceive as members of an essentially non-academic splinter group to neohumanism in higher education. Some Canadian educators might see it as a threat to their rationalist positions. Others might see it as a threat to the sacred categories by which one's value to the institution is measured: classroom instruction, research, and extension (or public service). But those in student personnel cannot afford to be deterred by the possibility of ridicule or objection on the part of some of their academic colleagues. Their present situation is serious and will not improve unless a drastic step is taken to reformulate the entire field.

If student personnel educators would begin to implement this philosophy in their daily work and prove their credibility to some segment of the community of scholars, they might find many who would encourage their efforts. It is my hunch that the role I am proposing is one which is very much needed on almost every college campus. It would permit all segments of student personnel, including the professional counselors, to make a difference on Canadian campuses and to become the focus for the most important educational services in the colleges outside the classroom.

Epilogue

Can Counselors Make a Difference?

Charles F. Warnath

Just before sitting down to write this concluding chapter, I received a letter from a colleague in counselor education who indicated he was pessimistic about the future of student personnel and college counseling. On his campus, the student personnel structure is being dismantled and the counseling center staff reduced by 50 percent. This news was followed almost immediately by my learning from a graduate student in our student personnel program that at one of the universities with which he has been corresponding about a job possibility, the student personnel specialties have recently been decentralized and assigned to other administrative units with the dean of students transferred to a teaching department. I had previously decided to use a chapter title which would not commit me to viewing the future with either the assuring cliché of unmet challenges or the despair of inevitable decline. Prophesying about the future has always been a risky business at best and a certain method for alienating oneself from some colleagues. It is particularly hazardous in a period of flux when trends can be interpreted as going in several directions at the same time. However, the letter from my colleague and the information from the graduate student, since they confirmed other reports about college service personnel under siege, almost inspired me to use a title like: "Can College Counseling Survive?"

The temptation was great but I was repelled by the alternatives which such a title would imply. I am convinced that survival is not enough. Student services might indeed be permitted to exist on campus as an appendix in the collegiate body but with about as much use as the appendix in the human body. As for counseling services in particular, I do not feel that they can afford to fit Penney's (1972) description: "Most counseling centers in the past played a passive and reactive role on campus, were relatively isolated from the mainstream of student interests, provided a narrow range of adjustive and remedial services to a very small proportion of the student population, and were marginally involved in conducting research designed to evaluate their own activities." Student personnel services, professional counselors in particular, must, as President Bond (1972) of Sacramento State University points out, make a difference because they are part of the campus community. They must make a difference because, if enrolments continue to decline, as appears likely, funds will continue to decrease and administrative units not contributing to some central function of the college will have top priority for reduction or elimination. But perhaps even more importantly, professional counselors must make a difference if they are to regain some sense of usefulness. Bond (1972) feels that professional counselors have already lost their sense of usefulness and that the general society is not so sure that counselors are useful. The gloom which has pervaded meetings of directors and staff of college counseling centers over the past two years seems to confirm this.

A Pogo character once said, "We have met the enemy and they is us!" This motto might well be emblazoned on the shields of professional counselors. It sums up the greatest danger in our professional involvement on the college campus today and probably in other institutional settings as well. Those of us in an older generation have been heavily drugged with a client-centered or nondirective orientation not only toward clients but also toward our work settings, while the younger counselors are doing their own thing with counterculture existentialism or modish behaviorism. Few of us are willing to risk coming out from behind those shields and engaging the fundamental issues of our institutions. Hurst and his colleagues (1973) have confirmed the resistance of service personnel to modification of their roles while a student development model of service was in the planning stage at their university. Our colleges are facing a multitude of problems, many growing out of the inability of human beings to interact in mutually beneficial ways. Although counselors are broadly educated as social scientists, they have chosen to make use of only a fraction of their potential skills through the restricted medium of the counseling session. But a mental health service of this type is increasingly seen as a luxury. It is costly and does not relate to the central processes of the institution.

Counselors do not very often think about the relationship between their service and the expectations of their support sources. I have written earlier about the expectations of institutional administrators but the parents, governing boards, taxpayers, and legislators also serve to encourage or discourage programs or administrative services—some groups more than others, depending on the type of institution. Counseling and psychotherapy are understood by lay people to consist of certain processes: counseling tends to be identified most closely with academic advising and psychotherapy with psychiatric treatment. For those who themselves are unlikely to afford the services of a psychiatrist, the idea of psychotherapy available to college students simply because they are attending college seems unreasonable. The counselors who have locked themselves into a service model which can be explained only within therapy parameters run a higher risk of encountering institutional guidelines than counselors who are more closely identified with some central focus of the college. The counseling centers in the colleges and universities of the State of California are currently the prime example of this premise as they find themselves enjoined by legislative action from offering psychotherapy.

The point, however, is not whether counseling centers do, in fact, devote a substantial part of their time to psychotherapy but that the style of service delivery has encouraged laymen on and off the campus to interpret those services as basically psychotherapy—what the counselor does looks like psychotherapy and counselors have too often sounded like psychotherapists. Administrators, boards, and legislators are saying explicitly: "If you want to do long-term psychological counseling and psychotherapy, then you don't belong in a college or university. . . . There are other agencies where you can do that thing and get all the gratification and reward for it imaginable, and you can accept full responsibility and be held accountable for it. . . . Our resources are not used well when they get involved in those kinds of activities to the exclusion of others (Bond, 1972)."

Whether professional counselors in institutional settings should engage primarily or exclusively in one-to-one counseling is, in my judgment, an obsolete and meaningless question. The critical issue is the relationship of professional counselors to the central purposes and processes of the institution. In what core activities of the institution for which counselors have the knowledge and skills should they become involved? The first step in the evaluation of the services of professional counselors is to investigate the purpose of the services currently offered. If the answer is simply to help a few hundred late adolescents who happen to find the counseling center stay in college or make easier switches from one major to another, it is probable that counseling is about on par with the investment of the dean of students office in helping fraternities and sororities fill their quotas. If students want this service, then, perhaps, as I have suggested in *New Myths and Old Realities* (1971), they should pay for the service themselves through incidental fees as they do for physical health services. The evaluation can only be undertaken within the framework of institutional needs if the institution is paying the cost of the services. That will require that counseling staff know their institution thoroughly—its faculty and their relationships with students and each other; the administrative structure; the operation of the political forces within and on the institution; the special problems faced by identifiable groups within the college; the trends in student body composition; and the like. The effect of such an evaluation would be to force the counselors' attention away from the immediate inner workings of the minds of individual clients toward the surrounding environment and give the counselors a sense of their place within the institutional structure. They may be dismayed to discover the relatively insignificant role they have been playing within the institution or how that role has actually been counterproductive to the welfare of the very people they thought they were helping.

It is imperative that counselors develop a sense of belonging to the institution and a concern about the total range of its problems. I have pointed out earlier that without an understanding of the operations of the structure in which they work, they have been used for purposes that fit the needs of the institution which were not necessarily consistent with the needs of the student clientele. Institutions are faced with a variety of complex problems resulting from the rapid changes within society. For instance, new types of students are enrolling in increasing numbers and presenting colleges with unique demands. The counselors cannot ignore their responsibility to contribute to the solution of such problems.

In the context of making a difference on campus, counselors should be able to decide which knowledge and skills to use and which priorities to establish. Placing services within this framework may also circumvent two major blocks to changing the style of service delivery. First, the staff will better appreciate those skills and knowledge they possess which are unique within the college and help them recognize that traditional counseling uses only a fraction of their capabilities. As changes in service style are contemplated, those who are expected to implement the changes must be involved from the conceptual stage. This is particularly necessary for professional counselors whose rewards and satisfactions have been tied almost exclusively to one set of activities when they are faced with the possibility of reducing their investment in those activities. Professional counselors must be engaged in a planning process which will in a sense reintroduce themselves to their full professional potentials. If, for instance, a new service style is imposed only by directive, the variety of negative reactions described by Hurst and his colleagues (1973) in their experiment with a so-called student development model of service is highly predictable.

Second, as the staff discuss services in terms of campus needs —as differentiated from the needs of individual students who come to the counseling center—they will be forced to consider personalities, power structures, and relationships within the college. Reorganization of service styles to make a difference on campus cannot take place within a service agency without reference to the total institutional structure. The dean of students can unilaterally decide to abolish the positions of dean of men and dean of women and redistribute their responsibilities to newly created associate-dean positions but this internal reorganization has little effect on anyone in the campus community. Professional counselors, however, who decide to move into the campus community must understand the power structure and how it operates in order to determine which activities would be most effective and with whom planning for a particular activity needs to be carried out.

These procedures may seem superficially self-evident; however, the impression given by some professionals is that staff need simply decide internally to get involved in some outreach programs and begin to implement them. Penney (1972), for example, is not optimistic about what he calls the glorified counselor in a consulting role to decision-making staff members located in campus power centers; however, the context in which he places this new role is remarkably similar to that of the traditional counselor except that the counselor has moved his private practice out on campus. He decides on the focus and dimensions of his service and becomes the consultant-coordinator of its implementation. This approach is to be expected from professional counselors whose private practice orientation, discussed at length earlier, provides him with little or no awareness of the forces operating within the institution. Thus, not only is the probability high that a disjointed uncoordinated approach to outreach programming will result as each counselor does his own private-practice thing but also that the programs will meet resistance from recipient groups or the college managers.

Changes in the services of college counselors are mandatory but meaningful changes can only occur following a fundamental change in counselors' attitudes toward the focus of their services and toward their own capabilities. They will not be successful if they simply attempt to graft a new set of activities on an essentially traditional mental health service orientation. The most difficult attitude change will probably be shifting the primary focus from students to the institution. It will be necessary to perceive the welfare of students interwoven with the optimum functioning of the institution rather than to continue the current assumption that they must be primarily concerned with direct services to students in whatever form. It is evident that the needs of an institution in flux, beset by a multitude of new problems, are no longer being met by the aloof, uninvolved counseling center serving the usual selective clientele in the usual expensive ways. Nor will these needs be met by the uninformed counselor who takes his private practice out on campus as a self-designated consultant. What appears to have happened over the past decade is that as the needs of the institutions of higher education multiplied, college administrators found that the counseling center was carrying an ever smaller proportion of the responsibility for meeting those needs. Moving the same mental health services out on campus—putting a counselor in a residence-hall office, for instance—will not appreciably change the counselors' contributions. To help students, the counselors will have to concentrate on solving those problems which are central to the procedures and goals of the college. This will obviously be difficult for counselors, for their entire reward system since entering graduate school has been based on their skills in individual and group counseling.

As institutional needs increased without a parallel expansion of the services of the counselors, service vacuums developed and were filled by other personnel, sometimes considerably less qualified. In some cases, the human components of the problems were given a lower priority because of the type of personnel assigned to solve those problems. One example is the assignment of affirmative action programs to the business office where an accountant attempts to implement the programs from personnel data and budget sheets. Another example is the attempt to attract mature persons to enroll in college programs to offset declining enrolments among college-aged group. The job may be turned over to an administrator only dimly aware of the psychological problems facing this new population—how to overcome concerns about their abilities to compete, for instance. The result may be that other than running additional advertisements encouraging mature students to enroll, nothing is done to provide special preenrolment counseling, modify admission requirements, or establish special courses or programs for this group whose educational needs are different from those of the young adult.

The role which, in my opinion, professional counselors must adopt to become part of the central functioning of the college is that of applied educational specialist, not restricted to individual students or small groups, but concerned with critical problems within segments of the college. The mental health orientation will have to be dropped or at least given a low priority not only because the term mental health is so ambiguous that it cannot be defined in any system of evaluation of counseling effectiveness but also because, perhaps more importantly, the relationship of mental health, no matter how it is defined, to an educational institution is at best peripheral. Friendship as a professional service, which has become popular within the context of the existential movement, may be a saleable commodity when the client pays the fees, but it is not a service which a college can afford on scarce financial resources except, perhaps, through paraprofessionals, peer counselors, sympathetic faculty, and others who have been willing to learn the skills from professional counselors to implement their normal positive feelings toward the helping relationship.

Despite the fact that counselors may have ignored much of what they have learned in their counselor education programs, they do have the foundation for making significant contributions to their colleges. They do know about learning theory, motivation, attitude change, group processes, active listening, and the like. They simply have not been encouraged to apply their learning outside the traditional counseling process. They have not learned how to apply these skills broadly within an institutional setting and, not having been very much concerned about the operation of the institution, they do not have a sense of how or where to apply what they do know. Those on the job probably need to become involved in workshops and short courses in which they can participate in activities designed to give them experience in applying their knowledge in new ways. Counselor education programs should begin to emphasize courses, internships, and practicums which will prepare their graduates to work in a variety of ways and with a wide range of people in various settings. Not only should graduates have an appre-

ciation for the special problems of ethnic minorities, women, counterculture youth, and mature people, but they should also have
experience in working with administrators in coping with those
problems within an institutional setting. They also require opportunities to work with people from other disciplines and with a range
of paraprofessionals. Obviously, unless counselor education undergoes major changes, the task of refocussing the orientation of the
counselor will be extremely difficult since the graduate programs
sensitize the future professionals and give him the skills to solve the
problems it defines as the legitimate concern of his professional
group. Unlike Penney (1972), I am optimistic about changes in the
preparation of counselors if only because I do not believe that
counselor educators can much longer pretend that reality is as they
define it. Too many of their graduates are in trouble in the institutions which have hired them. The message of momentous changes
affecting those whom they have ill-prepared to cope with those
changes will, I think, reach the ivory tower. Professional counselors,
perhaps with some completely new title, should emerge whose
ability to make significant inputs to institutions of higher education
will be greatly expanded.

College administrators require a steady flow of accurate feedback from within the system if the institution is to survive and,
incidentally, if they are to protect their own positions. Few people
within the college setting have as great potential for observation,
evaluation, and communicating about conditions within the institution as professional counselors, despite the fact that they have not
been specifically trained for using those skills in other than the
counseling situation. To carry out this function, however, the
counselors will first have to develop a sense of being a part of the
institution and having some responsibility for its welfare. It is
imperative that they learn how to use their knowledge and skills in
ways which have broader application than to the narrow confines
of the counseling room. Nor can they simply move their private
practice to some other location on campus. The colleges badly need
the types of inputs which professional counselors can make at all
levels of institutional life. As President Bond (1972) says: "If you
are truly concerned about the total learning environment, you'll get
out from behind that desk and those one-to-one relationships and

use all of your knowledge and skill to try to impact that institution. The university ought to be different because there is a counseling center there. Ask yourself whether it is different because you're there; or whether if you stopped existing you would only be missed by those few students who use your services. I think that's the question you've got to ask yourself, and by God, if I were you, I'd make damn sure the university was different because I am there."

I am optimistic enough to believe that Bond reflects the feelings of significant numbers of college administrators in this country who will give professional counseling staffs an opportunity to experiment with new role models. Recognizing that most counseling centers have been staffed only to levels which would permit their exploitation for public relations purposes, I believe, nevertheless, that counselors can argue effectively with administrators to be permitted to increase their total effectiveness in solving institutional problems and at the same time train enough paraprofessionals (older students, interested faculty, wives of students and other housewives, campus ministers, and the like) to cover, for a minimal wage or course credit, the friendship and vocational guidance counseling. I remain convinced that most counseling services should be supported by (hence, supervised by) students through their student government or other appropriate organization. Vocational guidance, as one part of the overall placement activities of the college, might continue as an institutional service, but integrated with the alumni office, placement office, computer center, audiovisual center, and other information retrieval and dissemination units. Its purpose essentially would be assistance in the selection of relatively short-range job possibilities, stripped of the current charade of long-range career planning based on two or three interviews and the results of a few indecisive tests.

The services which can be lumped under the general heading of mental health, such as growth groups and counseling with problems of identity, self-esteem, interpersonal relations, and the like, should be student-supported and administered. The recipients of the service should decide which services they want and who they want to offer them. They should decide on the types of services and the makeup of the staff: the proportion of females and ethnic minority staff, for example. This implies that the control and responsibility for hiring, firing and dispensing funds allocated for student services be assumed by student government. Adequate job security can be assured service personnel as they face successive turnovers of those in student government through limited-term, renewable contracts between these personnel and appropriate student organizations. It makes no sense to me, for instance, why students should continue to support a physician in the health center who has the reputation of serving as a fundamentalist preacher and praying over a woman student who has come in for a pregnancy test. It is equally absurd for a counselor to be continued in a service role for students when students have strong negative feelings about him. Student services should belong to the students and used by the students for their purposes. If they wish a professional counselor or student personnel worker to serve as ombudsman, as Penney (1972) suggests, that would be their decision, but the institution should get out of the business of deciding the services students need and the personnel to offer those services.

As for the service personnel which the institution does support, they would, then, be absolutely clear that their major responsibility was to direct their knowledge and skills to achieving the goals and purposes of the college. This would mean that as the problems changed or if the institution itself underwent major modifications, those trained as professional counselors could adapt their inputs to the new organizational forms. Greater flexibility of services in professional counselors employed by the college would, I believe, avoid what appears to some as an insoluble problem: What happens to the counseling center if the college itself is decentralized as it offers more field programs, enrolls a predominantly transient and parttime clientele, and becomes largely an administrative hub for a variety of fluid educational experiences, such as geographically separated satellites and independent study arrangements with individual students? Obviously, there is no good rationale for a college of this type to support resident mental health specialists; however, the need for educational and organizational specialists to help solve the multitude of personnel and educational problems inevitable in the new arrangements will increase—not diminish.

Will the colleges accept professional counselors in new roles? The answer, in my judgment, is no, unless the counselors move to identify themselves with the central processes and goals of the colleges and their subunits. The counselors cannot and will not be permitted to suddenly burst out of their center offering a menu of outreach programs. It is imperative that they first begin an active campaign of showing interest in what is going on throughout the campus community. They are, after all, not barred from talking to faculty and administrators about the problems those people are facing; they are not denied access to faculty senate and student government meetings; they are not rejected as observers at most faculty and student organization meetings. Student personnel and counseling staff have failed in the past to impact the campus because they have shown almost no interest until they suddenly burst on the scene to offer their expertise to some student or faculty group. Most faculty and students have absolutely no idea about counselors other than that they apparently solve problems by talking to people individually or in small groups. When counselors held joint appointments in departments, it has been my experience that few showed the slightest interest in doing some of the drudge work for the department and, in fact, few have bothered to regularly attend departmental or school meetings. It has also been my experience that when a counselor or director does show an interest, he will ordinarily find a welcome from the faculty. Counselors have never learned that in the generally informal politics of academia, interest and effort are prime requisites to involvement. Most meetings are open and regular attendance is often the only qualification for slipping into a contributor's role. But first, counselors have to want to make the effort.

College counselors are in a position where they will have to do something to shore up their sagging fortunes. Whether they can move fast enough to establish their role as essential to the college is problematic, but they do not have an alternative. Either they become active or they will be eliminated. If they continue to restrict themselves to private practice, their days on the college campus are likely numbered. If they attempt to move out on campus without prior acceptance by faculty, students, and administrators as professionals who are knowledgeable about the college and its operations, they will most likely be rejected. In my judgment, it is critical that they plan their actions to take advantage of their acceptance as potential contributors to the campus community. The initial step is giving concrete evidence of an interest and concern beyond that expected of ancillary staff. They have few choices. Hopefully, counselors can survive long enough to establish themselves as knowledgeable participating members of the campus community. College counselors do possess the potential for becoming valuable assets to their institutions. It is up to them to show others that they can make a difference.

References

ACKER, D. C., DANSKIN, D. G., AND KENNEDY, C. E., JR. "Student Characteristics in Curriculum Planning." *Journal of College Student Personnel,* 1967, *8,* 381–384.

ADELSON, D., AND KALIS, B. L. *Community Psychology and Mental Health—Perspectives and Challenges.* San Francisco: Chandler, 1970.

ALBEE, G. W. "The Uncertain Future of Clinical Psychology." *American Psychologist,* 1970, *25,* 1071–1080.

AMERICAN PERSONNEL AND GUIDANCE ASSOCIATION. "Ethical Standards." *Personnel and Guidance Journal,* 1961, *40,* 206–209.

ARGYRIS, C. "Conditions for Competence Acquisition in Therapy." *Journal of Applied Behavioral Science,* 1968, *4* (2), 147–177.

ARGYRIS, C. *Intervention Theory and Method: A Behavioral Science View.* Reading, Mass.: Addison–Wesley, 1970.

ASTIN, A. W. "The Functional Autonomy of Psychotherapy." *American Psychologist,* 1961, *16,* 75–78.

AUBREY, R. F. "Misapplication of Therapy Models to School Counseling." *Personnel and Guidance Journal,* 1969, *48,* 273–278.

BANDURA, A. "Behavioral Psychotherapy." *Scientific American,* 1967, *216* (3), 78–86.

BANDURA, A. *Principles of Behavior Modification.* New York: Holt, Rinehart and Winston, 1969.

BANNING, J. H. "Campus Community Mental Health: A Model and Status Report on Western Campuses." Paper presented at the American Psychological Association Convention. Washington, D.C., 1971.

BANNING, J. H. "Continuing Education Activities at Campus Mental Health Facilities in the West." *Monograph No. 4.* Boulder, Colo., March 1972a.

BANNING, J. H. "The Ecological Perspective: Its Implications for the Training of Campus Mental Health Personnel." Paper presented at the sixth Annual Workshop Concerning Emotional Problems of College Students. Greeley, Colo.: July 1972b.

BANNING, J. H., AND THE MENTAL HEALTH CONSULTATION ON THE CAMPUS TASK FORCE. "Consultation: A Process for Continuous Institutional Renewal." Report on the mental health services program of the Western Interstate Commission for Higher Education. Boulder, Colo., Sept. 1972c.

BANNING, J. H., AND THE PREVENTIVE INTERVENTION TASK FORCE. "New Designs: Prevent Educational Casualties, Promote Educational Growth." Report on the mental health services program of the Western Interstate Commission for Higher Education. Boulder, Colo., Sept. 1972d.

BANNING, J. H. "Today's Realities Yesterday's Training." *Newsletter— Improving Mental Health Services on Western Campuses.* Boulder, Colo., Nov. 1972e.

BARCLAY, J. R. *Foundations of Counseling Strategies.* New York: Wiley, 1971.

BEHAR, V. "A Study of Those Personality Characteristics Which Distinguish Between College Continuers and Noncontinuers." Unpublished master's thesis. West Virginia University, Morgantown, 1971.

BENDIX, R. *Embattled Reason.* New York: Oxford University Press, 1970.

BENNETT, C. C. "Community Psychology: Impressions of the Boston Conference on the Education of Psychologists for Community

Mental Health." *American Psychologists,* 1965, *20* (10), 832–835.

BENNIS, W. G. "The Sociology of Institutions or Who Sank the Yellow Submarine?" *Psychology Today,* 1972, *6,* 112–120.

BENNIS, W. G. *The Leaning Ivory Tower.* San Francisco: Jossey-Bass, 1973.

BENNIS, W. G., BENNE, K. D., AND CHIN, R. (Eds.) *The Planning of Change.* (2nd ed.) New York: Holt, Rinehart and Winston, 1969.

BERDIE, R. F. "Student Personnel Work: Definition and Redefinition." *Journal of College Student Personnel,* 1966, *7,* 131–136.

BERDIE, R. F. "The Study of University Students: Analyses and Recommendations." *Journal of College Student Personnel,* 1972, *13,* 4–11.

BERNARD, J. *Academic Women.* University Park: Pennsylvania State University Press. Reprint. New York: Meridian Press, 1966.

BERNSTEIN, B. "Social Class, Speech Systems and Psychotherapy." *British Journal of Sociology,* 1964, *16,* 54–64.

BERRY, J. B. "The New Womanhood: Counselor Alert." *The Personnel and Guidance Journal,* 1972, *51,* 105–108.

BETTELHEIM, B. Statement to the House Special Subcommittee on Education. March 20, 1969.

BEVAN, W. "Higher Education in the 1970s: A Once and Future Thing." *American Psychologist,* 1971, *26,* 537–545.

BLACK, J. D. "Responsibility of the Counselor for Influencing the College Climate of Learning." Paper presented at American College Personnel Association. Boston, Mass., April 10, 1963.

BLACKMAN, H. J. *Humanism.* Baltimore: Penguin Books, 1968.

BLOOM, B. L. "Training the Psychologist for a Role in Community Change." *Division of Community Psychology Newsletter,* Nov. 1969.

BLOOM, B. L. "Problems of Ecology on the College Campus: the Socio-Cultural Environment." *The Journal of the American College Health Association,* 1971a, *20* (2), 128–131.

BLOOM, B. L. "A University Freshman Preventive Intervention Program: Report of a Pilot Program." *Journal of Consulting and Clinical Psychology,* 1971b, *37* (2), 235–242.

BOND, J. Address to the National Counseling Centers Directors Conference at Vail, Colorado. Mimeographed. Colorado State University, 1972.

BORDIN, E. S., SR. *Psychological Counseling.* New York: Appleton–Century–Crofts, 1955.

The Boston Women's Health Book Collective. *Our Bodies, Ourselves.* New York: Simon and Schuster, 1971.

BOWER, E. M. "K.I.S.S. and Kids: A Mandate for Prevention." *American Journal of Orthopsychiatry,* 1972, *42,* 556–565.

BOWERS, D. G., AND FRANKLIN, J. L. "Survey–guided Development: Using Human Resources Measurement in Organizational Change." *Journal of Contemporary Business,* in press.

BRAYFIELD, A. H. "Community Mental Health Center Programs." *American Psychologist,* 1967, *22,* 670–673.

BRAYFIELD, A. H. "Developmental Planning for a Graduate Program in Psychology." *American Psychologist,* 1969, *24,* 669–674.

BRONOWSKI, J. *The Common Sense of Science.* New York: Random House, 1955.

BROVERMAN, I. K., BROVERMAN, D. M., CLARKSON, F. E., ROSENKRANTZ, P. S., AND VOGEL, S. R. "Sex-Role Stereotypes and Clinical Judgments of Mental Health." *Journal of Consulting and Clinical Psychology,* 1970, *34,* 1–7.

BROWN, L. D. "Research Action: Organizational Feedback, Understanding, and Change." *Journal Applied Behavioral Science,* 1972, *8,* 697–711.

BROWN, R. D. *Student Development in Tomorrow's Higher Education—A Return to the Academy, Monograph 16.* Washington, D.C.: American Personnel and Guidance Association, 1972.

Canadian University Counseling Association. *Newsletter,* Fall, 1972.

CAPLAN, G. *Principles of Preventive Psychiatry.* New York: Basic Books, 1964.

CAPLOW, T., AND MC GEE, R. J. *The Academic Marketplace.* New York: Basic Books, 1958.

CARKHUFF, R. R. *Art of Helping.* Amherst, Mass.: Human Resource Development Press, 1972.

CARKHUFF, R. R. "Differential Functioning of Lay and Professional Helpers." *Journal of Counseling Psychology,* 1968, *15,* 117–126.

CARKHUFF, R. R. *Helping and Human Relations: A Primer for Lay and Professional Helpers.* Vol. 1. *Selection and Training.* New York: Holt, Rinehart and Winston, 1969a.

CARKHUFF, R. R. *Helping and Human Relations: A Primer for Lay and Professional Helpers.* Vol. 2. *Practice and Research.* New York: Holt, Rinehart and Winston, 1969b.

Carnegie Commission of Higher Education. *New Students and New*

Places: Policies for Future Growth and Development of American Higher Education. New York: McGraw-Hill, 1971.

CARRUTH, J. F. "The Student Counseling Service: A Model." Paper presented to the American Psychological Association, Sept. 1965.

CARTTER, A. "Scientific Manpower for 1970–1985." *Science,* 1971, *172,* 132–140.

CHESLER, P. *Women and Madness.* Garden City, New York: Doubleday, 1972.

CHU, F. D., AND TROTTER, S. "The Mental Health Complex, Part I: Community Mental Health Centers." *Nader Report on Community Mental Health Centers,* 1972, *1,* Chap. II, p. 21.

CLARK, A. W. "Sanction: A Critical Element in Action Research." *Journal Applied Behavioral Science,* 1972, *8,* 713–731.

CLEMENT, P. W., AND SARTORIS, P. C. "Clinical Students Evaluate Present APA-approved Training Programs and Make Suggestions for Changes." *Journal of Clinical Psychology,* 1967, *23,* 57–62.

CLOTHIER, R. C., AND OTHERS. "College Personnel Principles and Functions." *The Personnel Journal,* 1931, *10,* 11.

COFFEY, H. S. "The School of Psychology Model." *American Psychologist,* 1970, *25,* 434–436.

COLADARCI, A. "Dean's Message." *The Educator,* Autumn 1972. School of Education, Stanford University.

COLE, H. "Process Curriculum and Creativity." *Journal of Creative Behavior,* 1970, *4,* 243–259.

COLE, N. S. *On Measuring the Vocational Interests of Women.* ACT Research Report No. 49, March 1972. Research and Development Division, American College Testing Program, Iowa City, Iowa.

CORZIER, M. *The Bureaucratic Phenomenon.* Chicago: University of Chicago Press, 1964.

COWEN, E. L. "Social and Community Interventions." *Annual Review of Psychology,* 24, 1973 in press.

CROOKSTON, B. B. "Coping with Campus Disruption." *Student Development Staff Papers,* Colorado State University, 1969, *1,* 1–24.

CROOKSTON, B. B. "An Organizational Model for Student Development." Paper delivered at the annual meeting of the Northwest College Personnel Association, Oct. 1970.

CROOKSTON, B. B. "A Developmental View of Academic Advising as Teaching." *Journal of College Student Personnel,* 1972a, *13,* 12–17.

CROOKSTON, B. B. "An Organizational Model for Student Development." *NASPA Journal,* 1972, *10,* 3–13.

CROOKSTON, B. B., AND BLAESSER, W. W. "An approach to planned change in a college setting." *Personnel and Guidance Journal,* March 1962, 610–616.

CROSS, K. P. "New Roles for Deans and Counselors." *Journal of the National Association of Women Deans and Counselors,* 1972, *36* (1), 19–26.

DAWES, R., ENGLAND, G., AND LOFQUIST, L. H. "A Theory of Work Adjustment." *Minnesota Studies in Vocational Rehabilitation,* 1964, *15,* No. 38.

DOHERTY, M. A. "Sexual Bias in Personality Theory." *The Counseling Psychologist,* 1973, *4,* in press.

DRESSEL, P. L. "Whence and Whither General Education." *Current Issues in Higher Education.* Washington, D.C.: American Council on Education, 1961.

DREYFUS, E. A., AND KREMENLIEV, E. "Innovative Group Techniques: Handle with Care." *The Personnel and Guidance Journal.* 1970, *49,* 279–283.

DYER, W. "Congruence and Control." *Journal of Applied Behavioral Science,* 1969, *5,* 161–173.

ELTON, C. F., AND ROSE, H. A. "Students Who Leave Engineering." *Engineering Education,* 1971, *62,* 30–32.

EMMETT, T. A. "Student Personnel Services—Who Needs Them?" *College and University Business,* 1971, *51* (5), 47–49.

ERIKSON, E. H. *Childhood and Society.* (2nd ed.) New York: W. W. Norton, 1963.

FELDMAN, K. A., AND NEWCOMB, T. N. *The Impact of College on Students.* San Francisco: Jossey-Bass, 1969.

FERGUSON, C. K. "Concerning the Nature of Human Systems and the Consultant's Role." *Journal Applied Behavioral Science,* 1968, *4,* 179–193.

FORD, D. H., AND URBAN, H. B. "College Dropouts: Successes or Failures?" In L. A. Pervin, L. E. Reik, and W. Dalrymple (Eds.), *The College Dropout and the Utilization of Talent.* Princeton: Princeton University Press, 1966.

FRAZIER, E. F. *Black Bourgeoise.* New York: Collier Books, 1962.

FREEDMAN, M. B. *The College Experience.* San Francisco: Jossey-Bass, 1967.

FRIEDERSDORF, N. W. *A Comparative Study of Counselor Attitudes Toward the Further Education and Vocational Plans of High*

School Girls. Unpublished dissertation. Lafayette, Indiana: Purdue University, 1969.

GAGNE, R. M. "Instruction and the Conditions of Learning." In L. Siegel (Ed.), *Contemporary Theories of Instruction.* San Francisco: Chandler, 1967.

GARDNER, J. W. *Self-renewal: The Individual and the Innovative Society.* New York: Harper and Row, 1963.

GIORGI, A. P. *Psychology as a Human Science: A Phenomenologically Based Approach.* New York: Harper and Row, 1970.

GOLANN, S. E. "Community Psychology and Mental Health: An Analysis of Strategies and a Survey of Training." In I. Iscoe and C. Spielberger (Eds.), *Community Psychology: Perspectives in Training and Research.* New York: Appleton–Century–Crofts, 1970.

GOLDBERG, P. A. "Are Women Prejudiced Against Women?" *Transaction,* April 1968, 28–30.

GOLDIAMOND, I., AND DRYUD, J. "Some Applications for Implications of Behavior Analysis for Psychotherapy." In J. M. Shlien (Ed.), *Research in Psychotherapy.* Washington, D.C.: American Psychological Association, 1966.

GOLDMAN, L. "Tests and Counseling: The Marriage That Failed." *Measurement and Evaluation in Guidance,* 1972, *4,* 213–220.

GOLDSTEIN, A P., HELLER, K., AND SECHREST, L. B. *Psychotherapy and the Psychology of Behavior Change.* New York: Wiley, 1966.

GORDON, J. E. "Project Cause, the Federal Anti-Poverty Program, and Some Implications of Sub-Doctoral Training." *American Psychologist,* 1965, *20,* 334–339.

GORDON, T. *Parent Effectiveness Training.* New York: Wyden, 1970.

GRAZIANO, A. M. "Clinical Innovation and the Mental Health Power Structure: A Social Case History." *American Psychologist,* 1969, *24* (1), 10–18.

GREENLEAF, E. A. "How Others See Us." *Journal of College Student Personnel,* 1968, *9,* 225–231.

GRUENBERG, E. M., AND HUXLEY, J. "Mental Health Services Can Be Organized to Prevent Chronic Disability." *Community Mental Health Journal,* 1970, *6,* 431–436.

GUERNEY, B. G., STOLLAK, G. E., AND GUERNEY, L. "A Format for a New Mode of Psychological Practice: Or How to Escape a Zombie." *The Counseling Psychologist,* 1970, *2* (2), 97–104.

HAETTENSCHWILLER, D. L. "Counseling Black College Students in

Special Programs." *The Personnel and Guidance Journal,* 1971, *50,* 29–35.

HALLECK, S. L. *The Politics of Therapy.* New York: Science House, 1971.

HALMOS, P. *The Faith of the Counselors.* New York: Schocken Books, 1966.

HANFMANN, E., JONES, R. M., BAKER, E., AND KOVAR, L. *Psychological Counseling In A Small College.* Cambridge, Mass.: Schenkman, 1963.

HANSEN, L. S. "A Model for Career Development Through Curriculum." *Personnel and Guidance Journal,* 1972, *51,* 243–250.

HARMON, L. W. "Sexual Bias in Interest Measurement." *Measurement and Evaluation in Guidance,* 1973, *6,* in press.

HARVEY, J. "Administration by Objectives in Student Personnel Programs." *Journal of College Student Personnel,* 1972, July, *13* (4), 293–296.

HECKLINGER, F. "Let's Do Away With The Dean." *NASPA Journal,* 1972, *9* (4), 317–320.

HEDLUND, D. E. "Preparation for Student Personnel: Implication for Humanistic Education." *Journal of College Student Personnel,* 1971, *12,* 324–328.

HEIDEGGER, M. *Being and Time.* New York: Harper and Row, 1962.

HINKLE, J. E., AND MOORE, M. "A student couples program." *The Family Coordinator,* 1971, *20* (2), 153–158.

HODGKINSON, H. L. "How Deans of Students Are Seen by Others—And Why." *NASPA Journal,* Summer, 1970.

HOFSTADTER, R. *Social Darwinism in American Thought.* Boston: Beacon Press, 1955.

HOLDER, H. D. "Mental Health and the Search for New Organizational Strategies." *Archives of General Psychology,* 1969, *20,* 709–717.

HORNER, M. "Fail: Bright Women." *Psychology Today,* 1969, *3.*

HORNER, M. S. "The motive to avoid success and changing aspirations of college women." Unpublished manuscript. Harvard University, 1970.

HORNEY, K. *The Neurotic Personality of Our Time.* New York: W. W. Norton, 1937.

HUDSON, R. I. (Chmn) *Guidelines for Canadian University Counseling Services.* Canadian University Counseling Association, N. D.

HURST, J. C., AND IVEY, A. E. "Toward a Radicalization of Student Personnel." *Journal of College Student Personnel,* 1971, *12,* 165–168.

HURST, J. C., WEIGEL, R. G., MORRILL, W. H., AND RICHARDSON, F. C. "Reorganizing for Human Development in Higher Education: Obstacles to Change." *Journal of College Student Personnel,* 1973, *14,* 10–15.

HUXLEY, A. *Brave New World.* New York: Random House, 1932.

ISCOE, I., AND SPIELBERGER, C. D. "The Emerging Field of Community Psychology." In I. Iscoe and C. Spielberger (Eds.), *Community Psychology: Perspectives in Training and Research.* New York: Appleton–Century–Crofts, 1970.

IVEY, A. E. "The Association for Human Development: A Revitalization for APGA." *Personnel and Guidance Journal,* 1970, *48,* 527–532.

IVEY, A. E., AND MORRILL, W. H. "Confrontation, Communication, and Encounter: A Conceptual Framework for Student Development." *NASPA Journal,* 1970, *7,* 226–234.

IVEY, A. E. *Microcounseling: Innovations in Interviewing Training.* Springfield, Ill.: C. C. Thomas, 1971.

JACKSON, G. R. "Black Youth as Peer Counselors." *The Personnel and Guidance Journal,* 1972, *51,* 280–285.

JOHNSON, D. *Reaching Out.* Englewood Cliffs, N.J.: Prentice–Hall, 1972.

JOURARD, S. M. "I–Thou Relationship Versus Manipulation in Counseling and Psychotherapy." *Journal of Individual Psychology,* 1959, *15,* 174–179.

JOURARD, S. M. "On the Problem of Reinforcement by the Psychotherapist of Healthy Behavior in the Patient." In F. J. Shaw (Ed.), *Behavioristic Approaches to Counseling and Psychotherapy: A Southeastern Psychological Association Symposium.* University: University of Alabama Press, 1961.

JOURARD, S. M. *Personal Adjustment.* New York: MacMillan, 1963.

KAEL, P. "The Current Cinema." *The New Yorker,* Oct. 28, 1972, 130–138.

KAISER, L. R. "Campus Ecology: Implications for Environmental Design." Unpublished manuscript. University of Colorado Medical School, 1971.

KATZ, D., AND KAHN, R. L. *The Social Psychology of Organization.* New York: Wiley, 1966.

KATZ, J. "Climate in Which Goals are Evolving." Address at the Directions in Higher Education Conference. Salem College, 1972.

KATZ, J. (Ed.) *No Time for Youth.* San Francisco: Jossey-Bass, 1968.

KAUFFMAN, J. F. "New Challenges to Student Personnel Work." *NASPA Journal*, 1970, *8*, 12–16.

KELL, B. L., AND MUELLER, W. J. *Impact and Change.* New York: Appleton–Century–Crofts, 1966.

KELLY, J. G. "Antidotes for Arrogance: Training for Community Psychology." *American Psychologist*, 1970, *25*, 524–531.

KELLY, J. G. "The Quest for Valid Preventive Interventions." In J. C. Glidewell (Ed.), *Issues in Community Psychology and Preventive Mental Health.* New York: Behavioral Publications, 1971.

KEYNES, J. M. *The General Theory of Employment, Interest, and Money.* New York: Harcourt Brace Jovanovich, 1936.

KIRK, B. A. "The Challenges Ahead in Counseling and Testing." *College Student Personnel Work in the Years Ahead.* Student Personnel Series No. 7, American Personnel and Guidance Association, Washington, D.C.

KIRK, B. A. "Women in Counseling Psychology." In C. B. Nelson and J. S. Sexton (Eds.), *Women in Psychology.* Monterey, Calif.: Brooks/Cole (in press).

KIRK, B. A., FREE, J. E., JOHNSON, A. P., MICHEL, H., REDFIELD, J. E., ROSTON, R. A., AND WARMAN, R. E. "Guidelines for University and College Counseling Services." *American Psychologist*, 1971, *26*, 585–589.

KOILE, E. A. "Student Affairs: Forever the Bridesmaid." *NASPA Journal*, 1966, *4*, 65–72.

KOILE, E. A., HARREN, V. A., AND DRAEGER, C. "Higher Education Programs." *Review of Educational Research*, 1966, *36*, 233–255.

KORN, H. A. "Counseling and Teaching: an Integrated View." *Journal of College Student Personnel*, 1966, *7*, 137–140.

KORN, H. A. "Higher Education Programs and Student Development." *Review of Educational Research*, 1969, *39*, 155–171.

KRAMER, H. C., BERGER, F., AND MILLER, G. "Student Concerns and Sources of Assistance." Unpublished manuscript. Cornell University, 1972.

KRASNER, L. "The Therapist as a Social Reinforcement Machine." Paper presented at the Second Conference on Research in Psychotherapy. Chapel Hill, University of North Carolina, May 1961.

KRASNER, L. "Behavior Control and Social Responsibility." *American Psychologist*, 1962, *17*, 199–203.

KUHN, T. S. *The Structure of Scientific Revolutions.* Chicago: University of Chicago Press, 1962.

KUNCE, J. T. "The Effectiveness of Poverty Programs: A Review." In J. T. Kunce, and C. S. Cope (Eds.), *Rehabilitation and the Culturally Disadvantaged*. Columbia: University of Missouri Press, 1969.

LAFRANCE, R. C. "Room to Move." Proposal submitted to Office of Health, Education and Welfare, 1971.

LAFRANCE, R. C. "Room to Move, a Redefinition." Unpublished manuscript, 1972.

LAYTON, W. L., SANDEEN, C. A., AND BAKER, R. D. "Student Development and Counseling." *Annual Review of Psychology*, 1971, *22*, 533–564.

LERNER, M. "The Human Potentials Movement, a Pattern of Meaning Needed." *The Los Angeles Times*. Oct. 19, 1972, Part II, p. 7.

LEVI, A. W. "Existentialism and the Alienation of Man." In E. N. Lee and M. Mandelbaum (Eds.), *Phenomenology and Existentialism*. Baltimore: Johns Hopkins Press, 1967.

LEVINSON, H. "The Clinical Psychologist as Organizational Diagnostician." *Professional Psychology*, 1972, *3*, 34–40.

LEWIS, J. A. "Counselors and Women: Finding Each Other." *The Personnel and Guidance Journal*, 1972, *51* (2), 147–150.

LIKERT, R. *The Human Organization*. New York: McGraw-Hill, 1967.

LIPPITT, R. O., WATSON, J., AND WESTLEY, B. H. *The Dynamics of Planned Change*. New York: Harcourt Brace Jovanovich, 1958.

LLOYD-JONES, E. M., AND SMITH, M. R. *A Student Personnel Program for Higher Education*. New York: McGraw-Hill, 1938.

LLOYD-JONES, E., AND SMITH, M. R. *Student Personnel Work as Deeper Teaching*. New York: Harper and Row, 1954.

LOUCH, A. R. *Explanation and Human Action*. Berkeley: University of California Press, 1969.

MAGER, R. F. *Goal Analysis*. Belmont, Calif.: Fearon, 1972.

MAGOON, T. M. *1971–72 Counseling Centers Data Bank*. University of Maryland Counseling Center, College Park, Md., 1972.

MAGOON, T. M., AND GOLANN, S. E. "Nontraditionally Trained Women as Mental Health Counselors/Psychotherapists." *Personnel and Guidance Journal*, 1966, *44*, 788–793.

MANN, P. A. "Accessibility and Organizational Power in the Entry Phase of Mental Health Consultation." *Journal of Consulting and Clinical Psychology*, 1972, *38*, 215–218.

MARCUSE, H. *One-dimensional Man*. Boston: Beacon Press, 1968.

MARX, M. H., AND HILLIX, W. A. *Systems and Theories in Psychology*. New York: McGraw-Hill, 1963.

MASLOW, A. H. *Motivation and Personality.* New York: Harper and Row, 1970. (2nd ed.)

MATHENEY, K. B. "Counselors As Environmental Engineers." *Personnel and Guidance Journal,* 1971, *49,* 439–444.

MAYER, R. R. *Social Planning and Social Change.* Englewood Cliffs, N.J.: Prentice-Hall, 1972.

MC CARTHY, B., AND MICHAUD, P. "Companions: An Adjunct to Counseling." *The Personnel and Guidance Journal,* 1971, *49,* 839–841.

MC CULLY, C. H. "The School Counselor: Strategy for Professionalization." *Personnel and Guidance Journal,* 1962, *40,* 681–689.   .

MC GOWAN, J. F. (Chmn.) "Counseling Psychology: Its Quest for Professional Identity." *Proceedings of the 78th Annual Convention of the American Psychological Association,* 1970, *5,* 919–920.

MC GRATH, E. J. "Bring Back General Education!" *Change,* 1972, *4* (7), 8–9, 64.

MEAD, M. *Culture and Commitment: A Study of the Generation Gap.* Garden City, New York: Natural History Press, 1970.

MEEHL, P. E. "Second-Order Relevance." *American Psychologist,* 1972, *27,* 932–940.

MICHAEL, D. N. "On the Social Psychology of Organizational Resistances to Long-Range Social Planning." Speech presented at the 25th Anniversary Symposium on Technology in Organizations of the Future. Ithaca, New York, 1970.

MILES, F. A. "A Study of Counseling Services in Canadian Community Colleges." 1973.

MILES, M. B. "Planned Changed and Organizational Health: Figure and Ground." In R. O. Carlson, A. Gallaher, M. B. Miles, R. J. Pellegrin, and E. M. Rogers (Eds.), *Change Processes in the Public Schools.* Eugene, Ore.: Center for the Advanced Study of Educational Administration, 1965.

MILLER, F. T., AND APONTE, J. F. "A Monitoring System for Community Stress." Unpublished manuscript. University of North Carolina, Chapel Hill, N.C.

MILLER, G. A. "On Turning Psychology Over to the Unwashed." *Psychology Today,* 1969, *3* (7), 53–54 and 66–74.

MILLER, G. A. "Psychology as a Means of Promoting Human Welfare." *American Psychologist,* 1969, *24,* 1063–1074.

MILLS, D. H. "Counseling and the Culture Cycle: Feeling or Reason?" *Personnel and Guidance Journal,* 1971, *49,* 515–522.

MILTON, O. *Alternatives to the Traditional.* San Francisco: Jossey-Bass, 1972.

MOGAR, R. E. Toward a Psychological Theory of Education. *Journal of Humanistic Psychology.* 1969, *9,* 12–52.

MOORE, M., AND DELWORTH, U. "Initiation and Implementation of Outreach Programs." Technical Report No. 2 (unpublished manuscript). Fort Collins, Colo., 1972.

MORRILL, R. G. "The New Health Services Model for the Comprehensive Neighborhood Health Center." *American Journal of Public Health,* 1972, *62,* 1108–1111.

MORRILL, W. H., AND FORREST, D. J. "Dimensions of Counseling for Career Development." *The Personnel and Guidance Journal,* 1970, *49,* 299–305.

MORRILL, W. H., AND HOYT, D. P. "The Training of Counseling Psychologists for Outreach Activities." *Colorado State University Student Development Series, 8,* 1971.

MORRILL, W. H., AND HURST, J. C. "A Preventative and Developmental Role for the College Counselor." *The Counseling Psychologist,* 1971, *2* (4), 90–95.

MORRILL, W. H., IVEY, A. E., AND OETTING, E. R. "The College counseling center: A center for student development." In J. C. Heston and W. B. Frick (Eds.), *Counseling for the Liberal Arts Campus.* Yellow Springs, Ohio: Antioch Press, 1968.

MORRILL, W. H., AND OETTING, E. R. "Outreach programs in college counseling: A survey of practices." *Journal of College Student Personnel,* 1970, *11,* 50–53.

MOSES, J. L. "Utilization of the Behavioral Scientist in Industry." *Professional Psychology,* 1970, *1,* 367–370.

MYERS, I. B. "The Myers-Briggs Type Indicator." Educational Testing Service, Princeton, N.J., 1962.

NIBLETT, R. "The Quest for Authority." *The Times Higher Education Supplement.* Jan. 19, 1973, p. 13.

NYGREEN, G. T. "The College Counseling Center of the Future." *Journal of College Student Personnel,* 1962, *4,* 32–34.

OETTING, E. R. "A Developmental Definition of Counseling Psychology." *Journal of Counseling Psychology,* 1967, *14,* 382–385.

OETTING, E. R., IVEY, A. E., AND WEIGEL, R. G. *The College and University Counseling Center.* Washington, D.C.: American College Personnel Association, 1970.

ORWELL, G. *1984.* New York: Harcourt Brace Jovanovich, 1949.

PARKER, C. A. "Institutional Self-Renewal in Higher Education." *Journal of College Student Personnel,* 1971, *12,* 405–409.

PARSONS, F. *Choosing a Vocation.* Boston: Houghton Mifflin, 1909.

PATERSON, D. G. "The Genesis of Modern Guidance." *The Educational Record,* 1938, *19,* 36–46.

PATERSON, D. G., SCHNEIDLER, G. G., AND WILLIAMSON, E. G. *Student Guidance Techniques.* New York: McGraw–Hill, 1938.

PATTERSON, C. H. *Counseling and Psychotherapy: Theory and Practice.* New York: Harper and Row, 1959.

PENNEY, J. F. "Student Personnel Work: A Professional Stillborn." *Personnel Guidance Journal,* 1969, *47,* 958–962.

PENNEY, J. F. *Perspective and Challenge in College Personnel Work.* Springfield, Ill.: Charles C. Thomas, 1972.

PFAFFMAN, C. "The Behavioral Science Model." *American Psychologist,* 1970, *25,* 437–441.

PIETROFESA, J. J., AND SCHLOSSBERG, N. K. *Counselor Bias and the Female Occupational Role.* Detroit: Wayne State University. ERIC Document, CG 006 056, 1970.

POOLE, P. H. "The Pattern of Counselors as Part-time Teaching Faculty in the California State Colleges and the University of California." Mimeographed. California State University, Fresno, Calif., 1971.

POTTHARST, K. W. "To Renew Vitality and Provide a Challenge in Training—The California School of Professional Psychology." *Professional Psychology,* 1970, *1,* 123–130.

Proceedings: Annual Conference of University and College Counseling Center Directors. Hosted by Colorado State University, Fort Collins, and University of Colorado, Boulder, at Manor Vail Lodge, Vail, Colo., Oct. 10–13, 1972.

PYLE, R., AND SNYDER, F. "Students as Paraprofessional Counselors at Community Colleges." *Journal of College Student Personnel.* 1971, *12,* 259–262.

RATNER, R. A. "Drugs and despair in Vietnam." *The University of Chicago Magazine,* May/June 1972, 15–23.

REICH, C. A. *The Greening of America.* New York: Random House, 1970.

REISMAN, D., AND OTHERS. *The Lonely Crowd.* Garden City, New York: Doubleday, 1950.

Report of the President's Commission on Higher Education. *Higher Education for American Democracy.* Vol. 1. *Establishing the Goals.* Washington, D.C.: Government Printing Office, 1947.

RIMMER, R. H. *The Harrad Experiment.* Los Angeles: Sherbourne Press, 1966.

RIOCH, M. J. "National Institute of Mental Health Pilot Study in Training Mental Health Counselors." *American Journal of Orthopsychiatry,* 1963, *33,* 678–689.

RIOCH, M. J. "Changing Concepts in the Training of Therapists." *Journal of Consulting Psychology,* 1966, *30,* 290–292.

ROCHE REPORTS. "Reflections from Harvard on One Million Dropouts." *Frontiers of Psychiatry,* 1972, *2,* 1–2.

ROGERS, C. R. *Freedom to Learn.* Columbus: Charles Merrill, 1969.

ROGERS, C. R. *Counseling and Psychotherapy.* Boston: Houghton Mifflin, 1942.

ROGERS, C. R. *Client Centered Therapy.* Boston: Houghton Mifflin, 1951.

ROGERS, C. R. "Persons or Science? A Philosophical Question." *American Psychologist,* 1955, *10,* 267–278.

ROSE, H. A. "The Effect of the Preadmission Interview on Students of Doubtful Academic Ability." *College and University,* Fall, 1965, 80–83.

ROSE, H. A., AND ELTON, C. F. "Testing, on the Bias." *Journal of College Student Personnel,* 1971, *12,* 362–364.

ROSE, H. A., AND ELTON, C. F. "Identification of Potential Personal-Problem Clients." *Journal of Counseling Psychology,* 1972, *19,* 8–10.

ROSZAK, T. *The Making of a Counter Culture.* New York: Doubleday, 1969.

SANFORD, R. N. (Ed.) *The American College.* New York: Wiley, 1962.

SANFORD, R. N. *Self and Society.* New York: Atherton Press, 1966.

SANFORD, R. N. *Where Colleges Fail.* San Francisco: Jossey-Bass, 1967.

SARASON, S. B. *The Creation of Settings and the Future Societies.* San Francisco: Jossey-Bass, 1972.

SCHLOSSBERG, N. K. "A Framework for Counseling Women." *The Personnel and Guidance Journal,* 1972, *51* (2), 137–143.

SCHMUCK, R. A., RUNKEL, P. J., AND LANGMEYER, D. "Improving Organizational Problem Solving in a School Faculty." *Journal of Applied Behavioral Science,* 1969, *5,* 455–482.

SCHULBERG, H. C., AND BAKER, F. "The Caregiving System in Community Mental Health Programs: An Application of Open-Systems Theory." *Community Mental Health Journal,* 1970, *6,* 437–446.

SEARS, R. R. "The Multiple Department Concept." *American Psychologist*, 1970, *25*, 482–483.

SEGAL, S. J. "Student Development and Counseling." *Annual Review of Psychology*, 1968, *19*, 497–508.

SHERMAN, J. *On the Psychology of Women: A Survey of Empirical Studies*. Springfield, Ill.: Charles C. Thomas, 1971.

SIEGEL, M. (Ed.) *The Counseling of College Students*. New York: Free Press, 1968.

SIKES, W., SCHLESINGER, L., AND SEASHORE, C. "Concepts and Practices for Campus Innovation Teams." Unpublished manuscript. National Training Laboratories, Washington, D.C.: 1972.

SILBERMAN, C. E. *Crisis in the Classroom*. New York: Random House, 1970.

SKINNER, B. F. *Walden II*. New York: Macmillan, 1948.

SLOVIN, T. "The Undergraduate Internship in Student Development." Unpublished manuscript. University of Massachusetts, Amherst, 1972.

SMITH, W. G. "Critical Life-Events and Prevention Strategies in Mental Health." *Archives of General Psychiatry*, 1971, *25*, 103–109.

SOUTHWORTH, J. A. "Report of the Task Force on Training and Supervision." *Proceedings from 21st Annual Conference of University and College Counseling Center Directors*, Vail, Colo., 1972.

STEWART, L. H., AND WARNATH, C. F. *The Counselor and Society: A Cultural Approach*. Boston: Houghton Mifflin, 1965.

STUBBINS, J. "The Politics of Counseling." *Personnel and Guidance Journal*, 1970, *48*, 611–618.

STUBBINS, J. *The Counselor in His Institutional Web*. Mimeographed. California State University, Los Angeles, 1971.

SZASZ, T. S. *The Myth of Mental Illness*. New York: Harper and Row, 1961.

SZASZ, T. S. *The Manufacture of Madness*. New York: Harper and Row, 1970.

TAUBE, I., AND VREELAND, R. "The Prediction of Ego Functioning in College." *Archives of General Psychiatry*, 1972, *27*, 224–229.

TAYLOR, H. "The Philosophical Foundation of General Education." In *General Education*. Fifty-first yearbook, Part I. University of Chicago: National Society for the Study of Education, 1952.

TERMIN, L. M. *The Measurement of Intelligence*. Boston: Houghton Mifflin, 1916.

THELEN, M. H., AND EWING, D. R. "Roles, Functions, and Training in Clinical Psychology: A Survey of Academic Clinicians." *American Psychologist,* 1970, *25,* 550–554.

THOMAS, A. H., AND STEWART, N. R. "Counselor Response to Female Clients with Deviate and Conforming Career Goals." *Journal of Counseling Psychology,* 1971, *18,* 352–357.

THOMPSON, A. S., AND SUPER, D. E. *The Professional Preparation of Counseling Psychologists: Report of the 1964 Greyston Conference.* New York: Teachers College, Columbia University, 1964.

THORESEN, C. E. "On Developing Personally Competent Individuals: A Behavioral Perspective." Paper presented at the Annual Meeting of the American Psychological Association, September, 1970.

THORESON, R. W., AND HAUGEN, J. L. "Counseling Practices: The Challenge of Change to the Rehabilitation Counselor." In J. T. Kunce and C. S. Cope (Eds.), *Rehabilitation and the Culturally Disadvantaged.* Columbia: University of Missouri Press, 1969.

TOFFLER, A. *Future Shock.* New York: Random House, 1970.

TOLLEFSON, A. L. "The Counseling Basis of Student Personnel Services." Mimeographed, 1969.

TOLLEFSON, A. L., AND BRISTOW, R. M. "A Philosophy of College Student Personnel Services: An Integralist Point of View and Functional Relations Concept." Paper presented to the Student Personnel Association of California Colleges, Oct. 1964.

TOYNBEE, A. In A. C. Eurich (Ed.), *Campus 1980: The Shape of the Future in Higher Education.* New York: Dell, 1968.

TRUAX, C. B., AND CARKHUFF, R. R. *Toward Effective Counseling and Psychotherapy: Training and Practice.* Chicago: Aldine, 1967.

TYLER, F. B., AND SPEISMAN, J. C. "An Emerging Scientist Professional Role in Psychology." *American Psychologist,* 1967, *22,* 839–847.

TYLER, L. E. *The Work of the Counselor.* New York: Appleton–Century–Crofts, 1953.

TYLER, L. E. "Reflections on Counseling Psychology." *The Counseling Psychologist,* 1972, *3* (4), 6–11.

VONTRESS, C. E. *Counseling Negroes.* Boston: Houghton Mifflin, 1971.

WAGENFELD, M. O. "The Primary Prevention of Mental Illness: A Sociological Perspective." *Journal of Health and Social Behavior,* 1972, *13,* 195–203.

WALZ, G. R., SPROULE, G., PRINGLE, M., AND SKINNER, J. "Integrated Model of Counselor Behavior." In R. G. Havelock (Ed.), *Training for Change Agents.* Ann Arbor, Michigan: Center for Research on the Utilization of Scientific Knowledge, 1972.

WARNATH, C. F. "Ethics, Training, Research: Some Problems for the Counseling Psychologist in an Institutional Setting." *Journal of Counseling Psychology,* 1956, *3,* 280–285.

WARNATH, C. F. "Counseling Psychology or Adjunct Psychology?" *Counseling News and Views,* 1968, *20,* 2–6.

WARNATH, C. F. "The Service Agency Consumer Views the Internship in Counseling Psychology." *The Counseling Psychologist,* 1969, *1,* 37–39.

WARNATH, C. F. *New Myths and Old Realities: College Counseling in Transition.* San Francisco: Jossey-Bass, 1971.

WARNATH, C. F. "College Counseling: Between the Rock and the Hard Place." *The Personnel and Guidance Journal,* 1972, *51* (4), 229–234.

WARNATH, C. F. *College Counseling Center Survey.* Mimeographed. Oregon State University, 1972.

WARNATH, C. F. "The School Counselor As Institutional Agent." *The School Counselor,* 1973, *20,* 202–208.

WATSON, D. L., AND THARP, R. G. *Self-Directed Behavior.* Belmont, Calif.: Brooks/Cole, 1972.

WEBB, W. B. "The University-wide Department of Psychology Model." *American Psychologist,* 1970, *25,* 424–427.

WEBER, M. *The Theory of Social and Economic Organization.* New York: Free Press, 1947.

Webster's New Dictionary of Synonyms. Springfield: G. and C. Merriam, 1968.

Webster's Third New International Dictionary. Springfield: G. and C. Merriam, 1969.

WEINBERG, C. *Social Foundations of Educational Guidance.* New York: Free Press, 1969.

Western Interstate Commission for Higher Education. *Newsletter— Improving Mental Health Services on Western Campuses.* March 1972.

WESTERVELT, E. M. "A Tide in the Affairs of Women: The Psychological Impact of Feminism on Educated Women." *Journal of Counseling Psychology,* in press.

WILLIAMSON, E. G. *How to Counsel Students.* New York: McGraw-Hill, 1939.

WILLIAMSON, E. G. *Student Personnel Services in Colleges and Universities.* New York: McGraw-Hill, 1961.

WILLIAMSON, E. G., AND DARLEY, J. G. *Student Personnel Work.* New York: McGraw-Hill, 1937.

WRIGHT, J. J. "Environmental Stress Evaluation in a Student Community." *Journal of the American College Health Association,* 1964, *12,* 325–336.

YERKES, R. M. *A Point Scale for Measuring Mental Ability.* Baltimore: Warwick and York, 1913.

ZAPKA, J. "Student Involvement in University Health Programs." *Journal of the American College Health Association,* 1972, *20* (4), 252–256.

ZUSMAN, J., AND ROSS, E. R. "Evaluation of the Quality of Mental Health Services." *Archives of General Psychiatry,* 1969, *20,* 352–357.

Author Index

Subject Index

324

D

Darwinism, social, in counseling, 37-38
Data collection for consultation, 222
Development. *See* Human development; Student development
Developmental task in human development, 57-58
Diagnosis as counseling function, 27-28
Directors of counseling centers. *See* Counseling Center directors
Disadvantaged, the, psychology for, 111-112
Douglass College, women's studies at, 180
Dropouts: in Great Britain, 261-262; reduction of, 197-198
Drugs, counseling center for, 149-151

E

outreach programs, 159-160
Education as model for outreach program, 160-162
Encounter groups: as innovation, 206; for women, 188
Ecological/transactional approach to
Equal Employment Opportunities Commission, 182-183
Evaluation: in community mental health, 126-131; in human development, 58, 60-61
Everywomen's Center as outreach program, 153-154
Existentialism: in counseling, 31; in developmental teaching, 53-54

F

Freshmen: orientation of, 139; preventive intervention program for, 154-156
Futurists, counselors viewed by, 16-17

G

General education: decline of, 49-57;

the department and, 51; humanism in, 54; methodology of, 50-51; philosophical conflict in, 49-50; role of in higher education, 47-49; terminology of, 52-53
Graduate education. *See* Counselor education
Great Britain: educational changes in, 260-264; student services in, 259-274

H

Higher education: and general education, 47-49; student-centered, 48-49
Higher Education Act of 1965, 163
Hospital, counseling center in, 236
Human development: defined, 57; education for, 47-65; institutional organization of, 63-65; model of, 52-53; need for, 61-63; teacher functions in, 59-61
Humanism: and college counselors 23-24, 26-27, 29, 36; in general education, 54

I

Indiana University, inhouse research of, 195
Institution: changing environment of, 1-5; as client, 120-126, 208, 291-292; as a community, 118-119; and counseling, 32-36; counselor impact on, 18, 286-298; mental health needs of, 126-128; as parent, 238-242; and student, 89-90
Instrumentalism in general education, 49-51, 56, 65
Interns in counseling center, 146-149
Intervention: by counselors, 31, 82-84, 122-123; preventive, for freshmen, 154-156; strategies of, 141, 146, 149, 151, 153, 154, 156, 162